Literacy and Bilingualism:
A Handbook for ALL Teachers

Literacy and Bilingualism: A Handbook for ALL Teachers

Second Edition

by

María Estela Brisk
Boston College

and

Margaret M. Harrington
Providence Public Schools

LEA LAWRENCE ERLBAUM ASSOCIATES, PUBLISHERS
2007 Mahwah, New Jersey   London

Senior Acquisitions Editor: Naomi Silverman
Editorial Assistant: Joy Tatusko
Cover Design: Tomai Maridou
Full-Service Compositor: MidAtlantic Books & Journals, Inc.

This book was typeset in 10/12 pt. Book Antiqua, Italic, Bold, and Bold Italic with Bauer Bodoni and Windsor.

Lawrence Erlbaum Associates, Inc., Publishers
10 Industrial Avenue
Mahwah, New Jersey 07430
www.erlbaum.com

CIP information for this volume can be obtained by contacting the Library of Congress.

ISBN: 0-8058-5506-8 (paper)

Books published by Lawrence Erlbaum Associates are printed on acid-free paper, and their bindings are chosen for strength and durability.

Printed in the United States of America

10 9 8 7 6 5 4 3 2 1

To my students and their students   M.E.B
To my husband Gene   M.M.H

Contents

Preface .... *ix*

1 Literacy and Bilingualism 1
    Literacy Development 2
    Bilingual, Biliterate, Bicultural 4
    Interaction between the Languages 7
    Knowledge Needed to Read and Write 8
    Factors Affecting Literacy Development 11
    Conclusion 13

2 Working Effectively with Bilingual Students 15
    Learning about Students 16
    Languages in the Classroom 20
    Development of Language, Literacy, and
        Content Knowledge 25
    Cultures in the Classroom 27
    High Expectations and Appropriate Support 33
    First Day, First Month, First Year in a Second
        Language Environment 42
    Homes and Communities as Partners of
        Literacy Development 45
    Embedding Strategies into District Mandated
        Approaches to Literacy 46
    Conclusion 47

3 Approaches with Focus on Writing 48
    Drawing as Prewriting 52
    Mailbox Game 56
    Dialogue Journals 62
    Rhetorical Approach 66
    Process Writing: Computers 70

4 Approaches with Focus on Reading 82
    Word Cards 86
    Shared Reading 92
    Response to Literature 96
    Reader-Generated Questions 102
    Cross-Age Project 107

5   Approaches with Focus on Oral Discourse 114
        Student-Directed Sharing Time and Group Discussion 117
        Anticipation Guide 122
        Talk-Write Approach 125

6   Approaches with Focus on Language 130
        Dictogloss 137
        Vocabulary Connections 140
        Language Experience Approach 145
        Show Not Tell 149

7   Approaches with Focus on Teaching Literacy in
    the Content Areas 153
        Graphic Organizers: Semantic Mapping 159
        Cooperative Learning Strategies: Jigsaw 163
        Situational Context (SC) Lessons 169

8   Individualized and Small Group Instruction
    with Support of Tutors 173
        Reformulation Strategy 177
        Read Aloud Intervention 183

9   Learning from Students' Performance 187
        Assessment 187
        Teacher Research 198
        Conclusion 208

Appendix A: Protocol to Gather Information about Learners 211
Appendix B: Books with Multicultural Themes 214
Appendix C: Popular Books Taught in American English
    and Language Arts Classes 221
Appendix D: Books to Supplement Content Area Instruction
    for ELL Students 227
Appendix E: Assessment Practices 239

References 241
Student Book References 251

Author Index 257
Subject Index 263

Preface

GOALS AND APPROACH

The rise of immigrant students in the United States and, indeed, in most countries, along with the concern for foreign language education throughout the world, requires appropriate tools for teaching literacy. The demands of modern society require high proficiency in literacy. Research and practice have advanced understanding of the reading and writing process. Numerous exciting approaches for teaching reading and writing have emerged from such work. Careful research has proven their effectiveness.

Most of this research has been done with English-speaking students learning to read and write in English as their native language. There are, however, numerous classroom situations where students learn to read and write in a second language. There are students who are native speakers of other languages in more than 50 percent of the classrooms in the United States where the instruction is in English. For the deaf, English is a second language. Some schools promote English as a second language (ESL) programs where literacy is taught in English. With the advent of bilingual education, literacy is introduced in the students' native languages. English-speaking students learn to read and write in a second language in foreign language classrooms or in bilingual education programs.

We wrote this handbook to apply proven techniques, derived from working with bilingual learners,[1] to teaching literacy in the 21st century. Complete and straightforward instructions are accompanied by accounts of teachers experimenting with a variety of approaches[2] to enliven instruction in reading and writing native as well as second languages.

---

[1]A bilingual learner is a student who knows more than one language to varying degree of ability or is in the process of acquiring a second language.

[2]We chose the word approaches or "the method used or steps taken in setting about a task" (Random House dictionary) rather than methods or strategies. Approaches better defines the range from very detailed to broader procedures for teaching literacy illustrated in this book.

"The pendulum of approaches to literacy instruction continues to swing as educators debate the merits of skill-based and meaning-based approaches."[3] Those presented in this handbook do not embrace any of these extreme beliefs.[4] Literacy uses need to make sense in order for students to acquire and develop them. In turn, students need skills to make use of literacy. Literacy programs "should be designed to provide optimal support for cognitive, language, and social development, within this broad focus, however, ample attention should be paid to skills that are known to predict future reading achievement."[5]

These approaches share a number of characteristics that help motivate students of varying language abilities to develop literacy. They:

- Encourage students' creativity.
- Tap on students' knowledge as the basis for learning.
- Allow for students to regulate the degree of difficulty.
- Encourage functional uses of languages.
- Reinforce all language skills (listening, speaking, reading, and writing).
- Include engaging activities.
- Encourage student interaction and active participation.
- Practice skills in meaningful contexts.

All approaches recommended in this handbook encourage the integration of all language skills in teaching literacy. However, some emphasize writing, others emphasize reading, yet others work on all language skills, including oral proficiency.[6]

These literacy approaches can be effectively used in classrooms where literacy instruction takes place in a second language. But teachers must modify and adapt these approaches by incorporating students' language and culture and taking into consideration factors affecting bilingual – bicultural individuals. Thus, this handbook analyzes first the characteristics of bilingual–bicultural students and then explains reading and writing acquisition and development for such students.

---

[3]Perez (1998) p. 261.

[4]See Gee (1992) for a discussion on the circularity of this debate.

[5]Snow, Burns, and Griffin (1998), p. 9.

[6]Speaking or signing a story, explaining an event, or discussing a topic are part of students' literacy knowledge. This concept is particularly important for teaching the deaf, whose natural language, American Sign Language (ASL), is not written. For more information on teaching deaf students see Paul (1998).

FIELD-TESTED APPROACHES

The approaches presented in this handbook have been modified and tested with bilingual populations of different ages and language backgrounds in bilingual, ESL, mainstream, special education, and deaf education classes. Even teachers in special subject classes have tried them. Pauline, a middle school music teacher, used process writing (see chapter 3) to have her students learn and write about modern American composers. Half of her 40 students were Chinese bilinguals with varying ability in English. These approaches have also been tested in foreign language classrooms in the United States and abroad.

The students ranged from preschool through high school. The students' languages included English, Spanish, Portuguese, Haitian Creole, Hebrew, Cape Verde Creole, Chinese, Greek, French, Japanese, Arabic, Russian, Khmer, Korean, Armenian, Polish, and others.

In all of these languages, as well as in all of these contexts, the authors related linguistic-based strategies to sound educational principles. Stepping back from what they and the numerous teachers they have prepared have learned about how to motivate students to acquire literacy in either their native or second languages, they describe techniques that are readily available to teachers entrusted to develop the basic educational skill, literacy.

This handbook makes the most successful approaches available to other university classes, to professionals leading workshops, and to teachers themselves who wish to experiment on their own. Each approach has been utilized in a variety of settings. At first, teachers were skeptical about whether specific approaches would work in their classrooms. Some secondary school teachers initially considered some approaches too childish for their students. Conversely, elementary teachers were concerned that some of the techniques were too advanced for their pupils. Both groups were, in most cases, pleasantly surprised by how easily they could adapt approaches for their particular needs.

OVERVIEW AND CHANGES IN THE SECOND EDITION

After carefully evaluating the most promising approaches, we wrote this handbook for a broad audience, teachers in any type of classroom where bilingualism plays a role. The new edition includes five new approaches with their corresponding classroom implementation. The material has been reorganized into nine chapters. The introduction to each chapter includes additional theoretical material addressing the theme of the chapter. The description of the new organization follows.

Chapter 1 outlines current notions of literacy and explains the com-
plexities of bilingualism and the process of literacy development for students who function in more than one language or who are learning a
second language. Students vary significantly in the way they become
bilingual, how they use their languages, what they need to know to be
able to read and write, and how their learning is influenced by social and
personal factors. Students, then, differ in how they acquire and develop
literacy. In tailoring approaches to meet their students' needs, teachers
must have the knowledge of and understand the process involved in
learning to read and write in more than one language, and their students'
unique developmental characteristics.

Chapter 2 highlights the essential elements of instruction for bilingual or second-language learners. This chapter includes some of the material of the first edition as well as new material on issues of language,
culture, and literacy development of students completely new to the English language.

Chapters 3, 4, 5, 6, 7, and 8 contain 22 different approaches that were
successfully employed in elementary and secondary level classes. Rhetorical Approach, Anticipation Guides, Dictogloss, Reformulation, and Read
Aloud are new. Process Writing and Process Writing with Computers
from the first edition were folded into one. Situational Context (SC) Lessons
replaced Critical Autobiographies. SC lessons represent a more developed version than the original Critical Autobiographies. For each approach, we state the steps for implementation, provide references for further reading, and conclude with an account of how the approach fared in
an actual classroom. Case studies illustrate experiences in mainstream,
bilingual, ESL, deaf education, and special education classrooms with students of different ages and linguistic and cultural backgrounds. Chapter 3
includes five approaches that focus on writing, chapter 4 describes approaches helpful for reading development, chapter 5 presents approaches
that support oral language development, chapter 6 focuses on language
development, chapter 7 includes approaches helpful for literacy in content area instruction, and chapter 8 illustrates how tutors can support
teachers using approaches suitable for individual or small group work.

The concluding chapter explains how teachers can improve their instruction by reflecting on students' performance. The chapter explores assessment strategies and action research.[7] This chapter illustrates strategies
for assessing students, collecting data, analysis, and reflection. These tasks
are deeply embedded in instruction and assessment, making research a

---

[7]See Donahue, Van Tassell, and Patterson (1996); Freeman (1998); and Myers (1985) for
information on teacher research.

natural outcome of good teaching and assessment. The new version includes annotated bibliographies with sample books to support literacy within language and content area classes.

This handbook provides teachers valuable tools to increase their understanding of bilingual learners in order to maximize instruction. Straightforward explanations of the procedures, which are further illustrated by case studies, allow teachers to use the content of this handbook on their own or in teacher-led study groups. Because of the variety of approaches, teachers can select what best matches their students' needs and their own teaching style.

USING THIS HANDBOOK

Teachers can use this handbook to expand their understanding of literacy and bilingualism, implement literacy approaches and assess student development, and learn through reflection. To build knowledge about literacy, bilingualism, and the development of literacy, we recommend that teachers, in addition to reading the first and second chapters, read some of the additional sources cited. Teachers should establish students' needs (see section on assessment in chap. 9), choose one or two approaches according to these needs, do additional readings recommended for each approach, and set goals for literacy development. In planning implementation, teachers should also establish assessment strategies to go along with teaching.

The classroom is ripe with opportunities to learn about literacy development of bilingual learners. Given the idiosyncratic nature of learners, especially when more than one language and culture are involved, observation of student behavior can provide much needed clues as to how to best teach such students. By implementing recommendations in this book, teachers can investigate how bilinguals learn, the effect of instruction on their literacy development, or any more specific concerns that emerge from the daily experience of working with students (see chap. 9). Reflection over time is the best way to assess student development. Thus implementation, assessment, and research are deeply connected. Together they can improve teaching and learning.

Teachers can test additional approaches that develop in the future, using the bilingual–bicultural perspective recommended in this handbook. They should also follow the research steps (see chap. 9) in order to explore the effectiveness of the new approach to teach bilingual learners.

Research is an essential component of teacher preparation. To learn how to work with bilingual learners, preservice and in-service teachers must experiment with and reflect on practices recommended in teacher education courses. Direct connection between course content and implementation of practices in a classroom makes for lasting learning and accurate views of how to teach students who are becoming literate in their first and/or second language.

LANGUAGE OF LITERACY INSTRUCTION

Literacy instruction of immigrant and language-minority students is often entangled in political battles of language choice.[8] This book is not about in which language to teach literacy, but about how to teach literacy to bilinguals and second-language learners given the language of instruction, be it English only, English and Spanish, French, Japanese, Vietnamese, or others as well as foreign language instruction for native English speakers.

There is no question that in U.S. schools the ability to read in English is fundamental to master content area materials. Although some believe that literacy in English is achieved by teaching it directly in English regardless of literacy skills of students, bilingual education programs promote introduction to literacy in the native language of students. Research on literacy of bilinguals has shown that there is high correlation between native language and second-language literacy ability even with languages of dissimilar writing system. There is higher correlation with reading than with writing.[9]

Choice of language for literacy development is closely related to curricular policies, which go beyond the scope of this book. We believe that there are approaches to instruction and assessment that allow bilingual students to develop literacy in their first or second language or both. The classroom context must value and take advantage of the students' linguistic and cultural knowledge. Students must be encouraged to have a positive attitude toward their bilingualism because they perform better when they consider that their bilingual abilities help rather than hinder development of their individual languages.[10] Teachers need to understand the interaction between literacy and bilingualism and apply appropriate instructional and assessment practices to enhance the opportunity for successful outcomes.

---

[8]See Brisk (2006, chap. 2) for a summary of the debate around language and bilingual education.

[9]See Cummins (1991) for a complete review of the literature.

[10]Hakuta and D'Andrea (1992) and Jimenez, García, and Pearson (1995) observed this phenomenon in their research.

ACKNOWLEDGMENTS

We have learned much about the recommendations in this handbook from our own students in both teacher education programs and classrooms. We would like to especially thank those teachers who allowed us to use their classroom research and practice to illustrate the teaching approaches included in this handbook, specifically (listed alphabetically): Angela Burgos, Judy Casulli, Caroline Clark, Meredith Dadigan, Katherine Darlington, Susan Drake, Nicole Gregorio, Nicole Gunderson, Afra Ahmed Hersi, Anthony Jacobs, Mary Jacques, Alice Kanel, Musetta Leung, Andrew Mahoney, Antolin Medina, Elizabeth E. Morse, Ivelisse Nelson, Ciara O'Connel, Renate Weber Riggs, Charles Skidmore, Mary Eileen Skovholt, Milissa Tilton, Laurie Whitten, and Peggy Yeh.

We would also like to recognize María's graduate students who contributed to the theoretical research and annotated bibliographies added to the second edition: Julian Jefferies, Swati Mehta, Caroline Potter, and Margarita Zisselsberger.

Literacy and Bilingualism:
A Handbook for ALL Teachers

1

Literacy and Bilingualism

Teaching literacy to bilingual students requires an understanding of such individuals and the many variables that will affect their performance. Bilinguals function with two or more languages and negotiate more than one culture. Regardless of the language they are using at any time and how well they know it, bilinguals are still influenced by the knowledge of other language(s) as well as by their cross-cultural experience. Bilingual students perfectly fluent in English are different from native speakers of English who do not know another language or have not experienced another culture. The additional and different knowledge they bring to schools must be considered in the teachers' perspective of the students, teaching strategies, and curricular considerations.

The circumstances of literacy acquisition for bilingual students are, in many ways, uniquely individual. Some students are already bilingual when they first encounter the written word and others are literate in their mother tongue when they first learn a second language. The age of the onset of literacy may also vary. Some children start at home before attending school, others develop literacy in kindergarten or first grade, yet others may not start literacy until later due to interruptions in their education.

Becoming biliterate involves learning the linguistic and cultural characteristics of literacy in each language and it requires coping with language and cultural differences. Additionally numerous personal, family, and situational factors affect the performance of bilingual learners. Awareness of what students must learn and the factors affecting them assists teachers working with bilinguals regardless of the curricular content and the language of instruction in their particular classroom.

To prepare themselves to work effectively with bilingual learners teachers must understand the following:

- Literacy development.
- Significance of being bilingual, biliterate, and bicultural.
- Interaction between languages in a bilingual learner.
- Knowledge needed to read and write.
- Factors affecting literacy development.

LITERACY DEVELOPMENT

Literacy has been defined from different viewpoints, all of which contribute to understanding literacy development among bilinguals. Literacy has been defined in relation to context and process. "Literacy is control of secondary uses of language (i.e., uses of language in secondary discourses)."[1] Primary discourses serve for communication among intimates who share a great deal of knowledge such as family, friends, and neighbors. Secondary discourses are those used in institutions such as schools, stores, workplaces, government offices, churches, and businesses. Literacy's functions differ according to institutional contexts. Schools require academic papers, logical discussion of issues, and comprehension of academic texts of various disciplines. In stores, literacy serves mainly for labeling and pricing. Interpreting memoranda and regulations is required in many government offices.

For some bilingual learners, these two discourses are also distinguished by language. The native language often is used only in primary discourses, and secondary discourses occur mostly in the second language. Consequently, bilingual students may not be exposed to the full range of literacy experiences in either language nor have the benefits of smooth transition from familiar to school literacy given that the discourses as well as the languages may be different.

Literacy is also defined as a psycholinguistic process including letter recognition, encoding, decoding, word recognition, sentence comprehension, and so on. Students developing literacy in two languages can learn the psycholinguistic process through one language, but must learn the specific symbol system, words, grammar, and text structure of each language.

---

[1]Gee (1989), p. 23.

Others believe literacy is a social practice that "assumes participation in a community that uses literacy communicatively."[2] The function of literacy may be culturally defined. Differences in schools' uses of literacy may be disconcerting to students who come from a different country. In many schools in the United States, students are expected to participate in discussions of topics incorporating their own ideas, whereas in many Latin American schools, students are expected to recite what they memorized from texts.

Bilingual learners becoming literate must learn how to use literacy in different contexts and for different purposes and how to encode and decode language. They must master these skills for each language and each cultural context.

Literacy is developmental (i.e., children get better at it with time and experience). The language for secondary discourse may start developing at home through conscious efforts of parents or family members. Literacy development at school is then a continuation and enhancement of efforts started at home. Sometimes parents inculcate their children to literacy practices familiar to them from when they went to school, which may no longer be advocated by the school.[3] Mutual adjustment and understanding between home and school practices greatly enhances and facilitates literacy acquisition.[4]

Learners acquire literacy from exposure to authentic text in authentic situations. Home and public places contain much written language that becomes familiar to children. However, for some children, words they see in the environment may not be in the language they know and therefore, this written language does not assist in the natural process of literacy acquisition. An English-speaking parent can seize opportunities to teach reading while pouring juice from a bottle with the label *apple juice*, while crossing streets attending to the *walk/don't walk* signs, or while reading with the child the name of the animals listed on the cages at the zoo. Parents who speak other languages usually lack such literacy support for their languages in their natural environment.

Students also acquire literacy through instruction in the specific psycholinguistic subprocesses. To be able to read or write, students must learn and develop automaticity in such skills as letter and word recogni-

---

[2]August and Hakuta (1997, p. 54.) See also Daiute (1985) and Faltis and Hudelson (1998) for additional definitions of literacy.

[3]Goldenberg, Reese, and Gallimore (1992) illustrated how parents focused on teaching children phonics, whereas the school advocated a whole language approach to literacy.

[4]Saravia-Shore and Arvizu (1992) contains many studies illustrating literacy in the home and school.

tion, encoding, and decoding. Bilinguals may learn such skills in both languages. Although they may be able to apply the process and strategies learned in one language to their new language, a process called transfer, they still need to learn specific characteristics in each language.

BILINGUAL, BILITERATE, BICULTURAL

There are many reasons why students become bilingual. Many children are raised speaking a language different from the one used in school. Immigrant children need to learn the new country's language. Deaf children learn English as a second language when they start to read and write. English-speakers learn other languages in school or as sojourners[5] in foreign countries. Some children are raised speaking more than one language. Thus, bilingual students are defined by their experience with more than one language and culture and not by attendance in a bilingual education program.[6]

"Bilinguals know more than one language to different degrees and use these languages for a variety of purposes."[7] They may understand, speak, read, and write their languages very well, or they might be in the process of developing any of the language skills in either of the languages. The use of each language can vary from casual daily conversation to academic uses. Proficiency and use are closely interrelated because proficiency facilitates use and use promotes proficiency. Levels of proficiency and amount of use change for each language throughout the life of a bilingual. Intensive exposure to a second language, as in the case of immigrant children or sojourners (children who live temporarily in another country), disrupts development of the native language, which may become their weaker language. Some students study this language when they reach high school, regaining fluency.

Biliteracy is "the acquisition and learning of the decoding and encoding of and around print using two linguistic and cultural systems in order to convey messages in a variety of contexts."[8] Bilinguals can have different degrees of biliteracy. When evaluating literacy of bilingual students it is important to distinguish between literacy (i.e., being able to function as

---

[5]Sojourners are children of businessmen or professionals who stay temporarily in the country.

[6]For more extensive readings on bilingualism see Bialystok (2001), Grosjean (1982, 1989), Lyon (1996), McLaughlin (1984), and Romaine (1995).

[7]Brisk (2006, p. 2).

[8]Pérez and Torres-Guzmán (2002, p. 60).

a literate person in either language), and specific proficiency to read and write in a particular language. A group of first graders are at grade level in literacy, as well as in proficiency, in both languages if they read at grade level in both languages. On the other hand, if eighth graders can only read first-grade level books in English, while they can read eighth-grade content-area books in Chinese, they have an eighth-grade level of literacy, but only a beginner level reading proficiency in English.

Literacy skills are acquired only once through one language and then applied to the new language. Thus, literacy ability in one language supports the acquisition of literacy in another.[9] Learners who recognize the benefits of knowing one language in acquiring literacy skills in the other become more proficient in literacy skills in the second language.[10]

Because languages are not alike, learners need to acquire the idiosyncrasies of the new language. Literate students have the concept of decoding, know that different genres require different text structures, and so on. They do not have to learn everything, just the subtleties that distinguish the languages. Different languages have different rules. Although business letters written in Spanish and in English will have a heading, body, and salutation, the organization of the body greatly differs. A letter written by a Latin American will start with something personal to establish a relationship before going to the business matter. When composing a letter, an American will go straight to the purpose of the letter.

Students acquiring literacy in two languages simultaneously may learn literacy skills through either and then apply them to the opposite language. For example, Arabic students in Israel learning to write in both Arabic and Hebrew learned the process approach to writing in their Hebrew as a second language class and then applied these skills to writing in Arabic.

Bilinguals' knowledge of the cultures and ability to function in the cultural contexts of these languages greatly vary. Contact with a new culture challenges once firmly held beliefs and behaviors. Some bilinguals flow naturally between the cultures, whereas others may reject one of the cultures.

Culture influences literacy uses and values, prior knowledge, text organization, and connotation of words. Students learn the uses and values of literacy from their experiences in their culture. When confronted with another culture, they need to learn and understand new values and solve

---

[9]See Cummins (1991) for an extensive review of the literature.

[10]Jimenez, Garcia, and Pearson (1995) illustrated the difference in literacy achievement between a student who believed both her languages helped and one who did not.

possible conflicts.[11] For example, Christina, an English as a Second Language (ESL) teacher, was always amazed at her Vietnamese students' concern for their penmanship. Penmanship is a highly valued component of literacy within the Vietnamese education.

Bilingual students bring to the class all the knowledge acquired through their cultural experiences. These relate both to the parents' ancestral culture and the students' own life experiences. When the content of texts or the topics of writings are familiar and interesting to learners, they are more successful in reading and writing. When students are working in their second language, choosing familiar topics can have a dramatic effect on their performance. For example, a group of sixth-grade immigrant students who had been characterized by their mainstream teacher as timid and with limited English proficiency, surprised their teacher and English-speaking colleagues when they read and discussed the book *Guests* and wrote about their own experiences as immigrants. With experience and increased language knowledge, students can then venture into writing about new and less familiar topics.

Culture dictates the organization of text.[12] When asked to provide a written description of their students, a Mexican teacher wrote an essay containing factual information as well as her feelings toward the children; a Korean teacher provided a succinct, numbered list of characteristics; and an American teacher wrote a factual description. Biliterate writers need to understand the cultural context of their audience to determine the text structure they need to use. Biliterate readers need to understand the cultural context of the writer to set their expectations for text organization.

Word connotations are defined by the cultural context. Students who do not know the culture miss the full meaning of words. When asked to give associations to the word *creature*, a group of Japanese students gave the word *being*. In the reading, the author's intended meaning was of a *monster*. The Japanese students lost the sense of the sentence by not knowing this added meaning often used in the American culture.

Being bilingual, biliterate, and bicultural is a balancing act that needs support from teachers and families. Often students feel that one language is competing with the other rather than assisting it. Obtaining fluency and accuracy in two languages is hard work, but it can be highly beneficial in a world of increasing multilingual encounters. For students who live a bilingual reality it is best to nurture both languages and cultures.

---

[11]Pérez (1998) illustrated the differences in sociocultural contexts for a variety of cultural groups.

[12]Connor (2002), Connor and Kaplan (1987), and Hinkel (2002) contain rich information on structure of text and cultures.

INTERACTION BETWEEN THE LANGUAGES

Language choice, codeswitching, and the use of both languages when performing literacy activities, regardless of the language of the text, are natural phenomena among bilinguals. The fact that bilinguals use both languages is not evidence of confusion, but just the tapping of their linguistic resources. Bilinguals choose a particular language to speak, read, or write for a variety of reasons: level of proficiency, specific topic, characteristics of their audience, setting, motivation to practice a language, and so on. Diego,[13] a high school student, wrote dialogue journals in his computer class. Because the teacher only spoke English, he would start his journal entries in English, saying as much as he could. Then he would switch to Spanish to expand on the topic and say all those things he could not express as well in English. Given the introduction in English and the teacher's rudimentary knowledge of Spanish, she was able to read and respond to Diego.

Codeswitching is the alternate use of two languages.[14] These switches can occur within the discourse, where the person starts in one language and then switches to the other, between sentences, or even within sentences when only a phrase or word is in the other language. Language switching, which is more common in the oral than in the written language, is not random, but rather, governed by functional and grammatical rules. Bilinguals usually codeswitch when interacting with other bilinguals. The reasons for this switching are many and well documented. It can simply be that a word comes more readily in one language, a topic is easier to discuss in one language, there is a desire to express an added meaning by changing language, or the student has no equivalent expression in the other language. Eva wrote a paper in Spanish using an occasional word in English: "Algunos viernes tenemos *girl scouse, música, ciencia . . .*" (Fridays we have Girl Scouts, music, science . . .). Her experience with Girl Scouts has been only in the United States, so she does not have an equivalent in Spanish.

Formal texts may switch languages to establish the cultural identity of a character. The children's book *Sing, Little Sack* is a story written in English about a Puerto Rican girl. Spanish is used occasionally to highlight the child's culture. For example, the lullaby her mother sang to her as a child, as well as expressions such as *mi niña* (my child) and *mamá* (mother), appear in Spanish.

---

[13]The names of all students mentioned in this handbook have been changed for confidentiality.

[14]Romaine (1995) explained extensively the phenomenon of codeswitching.

Literacy ability in a second language flourishes in environments where the use of the native language is supported. Bilingual students can often explain better in their native language the contents of a reading done in their second language. They may also find it helpful to discuss and plan writing in their stronger language, although the product is in their second language. When writing in a second language, students may switch to their native language to avoid interrupting the flow of what they want to say for lack of language proficiency. For example, Allison wrote dialogue journals with her high school French teacher. She wrote as much as she could in French, but when missing a word or structure she would switch to English: "*Last night,* nous avons aller a *Spooky World.* Il est tres *scary, and fun.*" As students develop their weaker language, they use it more for reading and writing.

Topic, personality, and attitude toward mixing languages dictate whether bilinguals choose to use their native language or not during literacy activities in the second language. A Ukrainian student used Ukrainian to write about his early childhood experiences, but English to write about his school in the United States. Mabel was very timid and insecure about using English unless she was sure it was correct. Her initial writings included a lot of Spanish. Her brother, on the other hand, showed no fear of using English. His writings were all in English peppered with mistakes.

Even when encouraged to use the native language as a resource, students may refuse to do it. Yuki refused the opportunity to write in Japanese when she got stuck in her English writing. Her teacher was literate in both Japanese and English and could have helped her put into English what she wrote in Japanese. But, Yuki believed that using Japanese was not appropriate in an English lesson.

Learning a new language, like all learning, requires accommodation of new structures into existing ones. Thus, bilinguals do not function as two monolinguals shutting off one language while using the other, but as an integrated individual with two active languages affecting each other and serving as efficient resources for communication.

KNOWLEDGE NEEDED TO READ AND WRITE

Bilinguals need three types of knowledge to become literate in a particular language. They need to know the language, especially the written form of the language; they need to know literacy; and they need to know the content of what they are reading or are going to write about. This content knowledge is connected with the culture of the author. They also need to put all of this knowledge together when reading and writing.[15]

Knowing a language means mastering the structure of text given the genre (i.e., letters, stories, essays, and so on); using words and idiomatic expressions to convey the intended meaning or interpreting words correctly; applying the rules of grammar to long text, sentences, and words; and using appropriate sound — letter correspondence and orthography. Learners must be aware that written and oral languages differ. Level of formality, distance, and cultural norms define the specific characteristics of the written version of the language. In the case of students who use American Sign Language (ASL), the difference is more pronounced because it involves difference in modality, sign versus script, and language, ASL versus English.

Knowledge of literacy from the point of view of a writer includes determining purpose for writing, identifying an audience, establishing the genre and voice, as well as mastering directionality, formatting, mechanics, and punctuation. A reader must master similar skills, but from the opposite perspective, establishing the purpose and organization of the text, the intention of the writer, and understanding the mechanics to be able to decode the text.

Some aspects of language and literacy knowledge are language-specific, whereas others can be applied to both languages. For example, each language has its own vocabulary. Certain words can be very similar in two languages, allowing a bilingual to understand words in the other language. Speakers of Italian, French, Spanish, and Portuguese would have little trouble understanding the English word *language*. Literate Spanish speakers know punctuation symbols, but they need to learn that the exclamation and question marks are only used at the end of a sentence in English and not at the beginning and end as in Spanish. However, literate Japanese speakers need to learn the whole concept, because punctuation is not a characteristic of Japanese written script.

Knowledge of content refers to the concepts and associations (schema) the readers and writers have. Such knowledge includes what they know in general and what their particular cultural knowledge is on a subject. Students may have general knowledge about herbs, but Mexican students may have greater knowledge of their medicinal power. In their culture, herbs are widely used for healing.

---

[15]Hulstijn and Matter (1991) and Birch (2002) address in depth reading in a second language.

Concepts may overlap in the different languages, may be somewhat similar, or be totally different. When the reader and writer come from different cultures, the interpretation of themes may cause difficulties regardless of language proficiency. A third-grade Chinese student was quite capable of reading and understanding a third-grade level story in English about family members who sat down for a lunch of steamed rice. He was quite confused and unable to read when presented with a first-grade level story about children making *rock* stew. His prior knowledge facilitated the comprehension of the former story and not of the latter, even though the language as such was easier in the rock stew story.

In order to read or write, students must bring together simultaneously their knowledge of language, literacy, and concepts. Difficulties in one aspect may affect the performance in the others. Knowledge of content can affect reading comprehension and the ability to compose, regardless of language proficiency. Vicki's high school advanced ESL class voted to write about superstition. Mae, a Chinese student very familiar with this topic, wrote a very well-organized and complete first draft. The writing was interesting and devoid of many language errors. Gennadi, on the other hand, unable to understand the concept, wrote a few sentences that made little sense. Gennadi's lack of prior knowledge affected his language and literacy performance.

Limited knowledge of language can limit students' writing regardless of depth of prior knowledge. Amal's Arabic students had demonstrated ability to write in English in previous lessons, but had great difficulty writing about Ramadan in English. Although they were familiar with the topic, they were not familiar enough with the English vocabulary related to Ramadan to express their ideas in English. Their lack of language affected their written products.

Limited knowledge of vocabulary and lack of cultural knowledge make the reading of social studies texts difficult for literate bilingual students. It is not uncommon for the authors of such texts to use various words and phrases to mean the same thing. Choua, a sixth-grade Hmong student, was quite confused and exasperated while studying about the American Revolution. She explained to her teacher that she understood that the British were fighting the Colonists, but could not figure out who those "Red Coats" were, and for whom they were fighting. Knowledge of the complex language of texts is essential to understand its content. For example, this sentence from a history text includes a confusing structure "The British did not import only raw materials and ideas from other countries" (p. 407).[16] Unless the students understand the structure *not only*

---

[16]Garcia, J., Gelo, D., Greenow, L., Kratch, J., and White, D. (1997).

they may interpret that the British did not import raw materials or that they only imported raw materials. Success in literacy activities not only depends on literacy skills, but also on the development of language as well as cultural knowledge needed to cope with the variety of texts to which students are exposed in schools.

FACTORS AFFECTING
LITERACY DEVELOPMENT

Contextual and personal variables affect the process of literacy development and the level of achievement of bilingual students. For this reason, bilingual students develop literacy skills at different rates, including different rates for each language. Therefore, teachers need to know and understand each student individually and be aware of their literacy level in each language.

Contexts of literacy development include factors in the society at large, the school, and the home of the students. Bilinguals may become literate in an environment where they are exposed to two or more languages, or in a monolingual environment where everything is mostly in one language, but through instruction they acquire another language.

Sara, María, and Angélica were exposed to English and Spanish literacy since childhood. Sara is equally proficient in both languages, whereas Angélica's English far surpasses her Spanish. María, although fully proficient in English still makes occasional errors in writing typical of second-language learners. Differences in external factors contributed to their difference in abilities. Sara was raised in Florida and was exposed equally to both languages at and outside school; Angélica grew up in New England where she attended schools where the instruction was only in English. She was exposed to literacy in Spanish at home and during her occasional visits to Latin America. María lived in Latin America until she was an adult, where she studied English from preschool through college.

The amount of environmental literacy in each language, both at home and outside the home, as well as the status and economic viability of the languages support or hinder motivation to learn to read and write in specific languages. The type of writing system, status of the languages, and whether they have been standardized, shape attitudes about difficulty or worth of learning specific languages.[17] Both Sara and María lived in envi-

---

[17]See Brisk (2006) and Brisk, Burgos, and Hamerla (2004) for a complete account of factors influencing bilingual students.

ronments where knowledge of both languages was highly desirable for social and economic reasons. Usefulness and status of Spanish in New England is not comparable to English. Angélica's motivation came from within the family, not the society.

Language characteristics influence and restrict educational decisions with respect to developing literacy in home languages. Spanish is an efficient language to teach children to read. With appropriate instruction and materials, students can master reading within the first couple of grades. The writing system is similar enough to English to establish a strong foundation to acquisition of written English. In an educational environment that pressures bilingual programs to transfer students as quickly as possible, Spanish allows programs to have students reading in Spanish before switching completely to English. Other languages present different challenges. For example, Chinese is not only a very different writing system than English, but it takes much longer to learn it. In China, not until sixth-grade do students master enough written Chinese to read a newspaper.[18] Teaching reading to Chinese bilinguals and its implications on bilingual education policies have to be seen in a different light than those for Spanish speakers.

Home literacy habits, attitudes toward literacy and languages, perceptions of the function of literacy, and uses of literacy in specific languages influence the children's attitude, motivation, and proficiency. A survey that Lisa, a mainstream teacher, carried out with the families of her Asian and Spanish-speaking students revealed similarities and differences between ethnic groups as well as between families. Asian children tended to be read to by older siblings, whereas Spanish speakers were read to by their parents. Religious topics were common reading material among Spanish-speakers. Both groups had some families that were more invested than others in their literacy practices at home.

Families' concept of literacy and their practices may be congruent with the school, may be very different from the school's,[19] or may be a combination of beliefs.[20] Level and quality of communication and understanding between home and school influences students' acquisition of literacy.

---

[18]See Leong (1978) for teaching reading in Chinese.

[19]Heath (1983) described families that carried out literacy practices congruent with the school's and those whose practice greatly differed from those of the school.

[20]Duranti and Ochs (1995) described a bicultural approach to literacy development in the home of Samoan children.

Schools influence students' achievement by the effectiveness of approaches used to teach literacy, teacher expectations, and specific languages promoted.[21] Students will experience more favorable learning conditions in contexts where the languages they are learning are used and the attitudes toward them are positive. Respect for the students' own language, even if it is not used for instruction, favors learning because it reflects respect for the students themselves and their families.

Personal variables include age, when the languages were learned, level of proficiency in the languages, cultural norms for language use, when literacy in each language was introduced, level of literacy ability, educational background, and attitudes toward the languages.[22]

Personal variables affect the individuals directly and interact with the social variables to make the learning conditions more or less favorable for general literacy development and for proficiency in particular languages. Gabriel is a high school student born in the United States of Puerto Rican parents. He can speak Spanish well enough to get along in his community, but is unable to read or write in it and unwilling to learn. He speaks, reads, and writes English fluently, although his academic achievement in school does not reflect superior levels of literacy. Educational background and attitudes shaped Gabriel's Spanish proficiency and unwillingness to improve his Spanish. Lack of formal schooling in Spanish prevented him from learning to read and write in Spanish. Gabriel also has a confused attitude toward Spanish. Although he claims it is useful to be bilingual, he quietly refuses to cooperate in his Spanish-language class. The society at large and school pressure Gabriel to embrace English and not value his Spanish heritage. On the other hand, his family tells him he is Puerto Rican. Thus, the root of Gabriel's inability to decode in Spanish cannot be found in literacy, but in Gabriel's life story.

CONCLUSION

Becoming bilingual, biliterate, and bicultural is desirable for students who have the opportunity or the need to experience more than one language and culture. It is not, however, an easy accomplishment. The students' individual characteristics in interaction with the environment help

---

[21]For full explanation of these variables, see Brisk (2006) and Mackey (1968).

[22]Brisk (2006); Lightbown and Spada (2003); and Lyon (1996) contain more detailed explanations of these variables.

or hinder the process. Teachers who want their students to succeed in literacy learning must accept the students' bilingualism and understand the complexity of biliteracy. They need to assist these students' literacy development by building literacy, language, cultural knowledge, and a positive attitude toward their bilingualism. The advantages of high levels of bilingualism justify fomenting it in schools. Schools that are not equipped to instruct students in two languages can still encourage students to continue development of their other languages.

2

Working Effectively
with Bilingual Students

Good literacy practices are not enough to develop literacy when students function in more than one language and culture. Teachers must know their students as bilingual/bicultural learners even if they themselves know only one language and are charged with teaching in one language. Teachers must consider language and culture within the approaches they use, whether the program is bilingual, ESL, mainstream, or foreign language. Students' level of language proficiency should not deter teachers from having high expectations, but it should alert them to provide assistance to reach those expectations. In this chapter we explicitly illustrate how teaching bilingual learners is not just simply good teaching. Addressing the needs of these students in ways that work is paramount. These practices can be beneficial for all students. For bilingual learners, however, they are not an option; they are essential.

Implementation of the approaches recommended in this book requires teachers to consider the following issues:

- Learning about students
- Languages in the classroom
- Development of language, literacy, and content knowledge
- Cultures in the classroom
- Expectations and Support
- First day, first month, first year in a second language environment
- Grouping for instruction
- Homes and communities as partners
- Embedding strategies into district mandated approaches to literacy

LEARNING ABOUT STUDENTS

Bilingual students' learning is influenced by personal, home, and situational factors. Knowledge of students is key to good literacy instruction. Teachers are better able to teach, motivate, and evaluate students when they know about them, their families, and their environments. They also need to know them specifically as readers and writers. Teachers, when possible, should use both languages to learn about their students because people tend to reveal different things when using one or the other language.

Students are individuals very different from each other. No assumptions should be made from their last name or physical characteristics. Linda, a bilingual ASL/English teacher, works with four severely handicapped children who also are deaf or hard of hearing. Although in a program for deaf children, they all have completely different language backgrounds. Haitian Creole is the home language for one child and English for another. English is spoken in the home of one of the Spanish-background children and Spanish is the home language of the other. Similarly, families show complete difference in ASL ability, from none, to some signs, to fluency by at least one member of the family.

Demographic information clusters ethnic groups as Hispanic, Asian, and so forth. Within those clusters, however, there are very different cultural groups. Bilingual learners should be known not as Hispanic but as Puerto Rican, Colombian, or Salvadoran. Among Asians, Korean, Japanese, and Chinese represent very different cultural groups. Students themselves do not appreciate this confusion. "Most of my friends think I'm Chinese, because I look like a Chinese person. Some think I'm Japanese. I like being Korean . . ." expressed Rose with annoyance.

Bilingual students differ in terms of how they identify with their different cultures. Environmental factors such as the attitudes of friends and family members greatly influence the way in which bilingual students choose to see themselves, and the way in which they would like others to see them. Even students who feel close ties to their family's culture and ethnicity may still experience some ambivalence about their bicultural identities. Bilingual children and teenagers face powerful pressures, specific to youth, to assimilate with images of American culture. In forging their personal identities, they take cues from their peers, from popular music, and from magazines, TV shows, and movies. But bilingual students face another, common challenge of reconciling the images of American youth culture with the images, traditions, and beliefs of their family's cultural heritage. Some bilingual students may respond to these conflicting pressures by developing distinct public and private identities.

Such students recognize that what is "normal" at home may mark them as "strange" or "foreign" in public. Other bilingual students may feel compelled to conceal or suppress their ethnic and cultural identities, and may refuse to speak their native language in public. Within these students' families and larger cultural communities, such deliberate, acute American assimilation can sometimes be considered "ethnic betrayal"; as a consequence, bilingual youth may be branded with disparaging nicknames such as "Oreo" ("Brown or Black on the outside, White on the inside") or "Twinkie" ("Yellow on the outside, White on the inside")[1]

Bilingual students may receive different language input in the various contexts in which they function. The amount of language use and support they receive in these various contexts will influence development of each language. Teachers need to know which language bilinguals use, for what, and with whom. They need to show students their awareness and interest in their bilingualism. Melissa went to help Herman, a kindergarten child in a mainstream class. Although five, he was characterized as working at the level of a three-year-old. Melissa found out that although English was his strongest language, he used ASL with his deaf mother, and Spanish with his grandparents, with whom he spent every weekend. Melissa, bilingual in English and ASL, started to use both languages in her work with Herman. This child's literacy, as well as classroom behavior, dramatically changed for the better in the four months that Melissa worked with him.

Learning about students' general interests and concerns helps teachers initiate students to literacy or new skills through topics of interest to them and related to their background experience. Seeing Maria writing repeatedly "mamaamaapapa" (mother loves father), the teacher asked her "Y que hay de tu perra?" (What about your dog?). Maria's eyes lit up and she quickly wrote "Yo tenyo una pera negra que se llama Rinse" (I have a black dog called Rinse). Familiarity with the students' experiences also helps teachers find appropriate reading materials, interpret and revise writing, and understand their interpretation of text. Melissa brought a pile of books when using the Reading Aloud approach with kindergarten students. By letting the students choose the books, she learned the books they liked and their favorite topics. This led her to bring books of authors the students enjoyed and on topics that sparked their interest.

Bilinguals make use of all their resources in both languages when confronted with a new and difficult task. Familiarity with the students'

---

[1]Suarez-Orozco and Suarez-Orozco, (2001), p. 104.

languages helps teachers to understand their performance. For example, bilingual students interpret the second-language writing system using both their knowledge of the native and second languages. A combination of how they pronounce the word in English with their knowledge of sound—letter correspondence either in English or in their first language play a role in their invented spelling. A Vietnamese child spelled the word *shoe* as *xu*, which is the way that those sounds would be spelled in Vietnamese. A Spanish-speaking child wrote *DN* for The End. He pronounced *the* as *de* and *end* as *en*. Many Spanish speakers have difficulty with the *th* sound and with final consonant clusters. Understanding why these children spell words the way they do helps us realize that they have good decoding skills. All they need to learn are the specific rules of English and how to pronounce English. It is a language and not a literacy issue. The lesson needs to be focused on language and not on literacy skills.[2]

Students use their cultural knowledge to interpret text and create text. This can lead to misinterpretations and inappropriate text organization and use of words when reading and writing in a second language. Knowing the students' culture and how it influences language allows teachers to help students bridge these cultural gaps to reach full literacy proficiency in the new language.

Language attitudes influence learning. Bilinguals and their families benefit from positive attitudes toward both languages. Teachers can help bilinguals achieve this goal. Andrés, a seventh-grade Puerto Rican student, refused to participate in his ESL class. The first entry in his dialogue journal was in Spanish. Assisted by a bilingual colleague, the ESL teacher found out that Andrés felt that Americans did not like him or care about him. He wanted to go back to Puerto Rico. The ESL teacher wrote a short sentence explaining that she did care about him. Andrés' attitude changed radically. He switched to writing his journals in English and slowly began to participate in class.

Teachers who work with many linguistic groups cannot be expected to know about all of the languages and cultures of the students. An awareness of these differences and careful observations of their students can begin to teach them what to expect and why. It is not an easy task to know all students thoroughly in a class. It is even worse in the case of middle and secondary schools, where teachers work with large numbers of stu-

---

[2]See Pérez (1998); Swan and Smith (2001) for information on common language and literacy characteristics and problems when learning English of students of specific language backgrounds.

dents in one discipline. The task is complicated even more when students' cultural experiences are varied and different from the teacher's own life experience, values, and assumptions.

Teachers do not need to learn all at once the rather lengthy list of important factors affecting bilingual students (see Appendix A). Instead, they can find out systematically about them while engaging students in activities that will help their literacy development.

The approaches recommended in this book allow exploration into the students' minds and lives, because while implementing the approaches, students constantly contribute with their ideas. For example, students may reveal students' cultural views on a topic while discussing their opinions using the Anticipation Guide (chap. 5). Students reveal feelings, family situations, difficulties in school, language needs, and even difficulties they may be having in math through dialogue journals. Caroline learned a great deal about her adolescent students through dialogue journals. Vinh, a Vietnamese student, frequently commented on his difficulties in adjusting to life in the United States: "When I come to the United States I really sad because I don't have any friend . . ." Beatriz revealed a difficult family situation. Vicki discussed her tendency to get angry easily.

Drawing as Prewriting projects (chap. 3), as well as other writing activities, provide a wealth of information about students' lives, families, and their cultures. A Vietnamese kindergarten teacher adapted Drawing as Prewriting to find out more about her students' families and home literacy activities. She asked the students to do their drawings about home activities. The children took their projects home and asked parents or caretakers to write additional comments further explaining their drawings. The teacher found out a lot about family literacy and homework activities, language use, and family life in general. Some parents even stopped by to provide additional information.

Prereading activities that elicit background knowledge and response activities following reading are rich in associations with students' own knowledge and experiences. Sylvia, a fifth-grade bilingual teacher, rolled down the world map to stimulate brainstorming about explorers in preparation for reading about the topic. Timid one-word responses popped here and there until Eduardo, a recent arrival from Guatemala, stood up, walked to the map and gave the class a lesson on Magellan. Eduardo's previous schooling had provided him with knowledge of this aspect of history that most of the other students lacked. Eduardo was ready to read, whereas the rest of the class needed to do a lot more preparation.

Situational Context (SC) lessons (chap. 7) inform teachers most about their students, especially as bilingual learners. SC lessons help students analyze objectively something in their social context. They study the facts, relate them to themselves, and seek solutions. For example, a political lesson analyzed how foreign relations affect the treatment of immigrants in the United States. Students studied foreign relations with various countries and read newspapers articles on the topic. They read *Baseball Saved Us* and discussed why Japanese Americans were interned in camps during World War II. They reflected on this story and their own immigrant experiences.

Students form their own notions about reading and writing while developing literacy. Conferences held during process writing reveal a great deal about learners. Hank, an ASL/English student, explained his belief that paragraphs were ruled by size while discussing his paper with the teacher. Through discussions and showing Hank examples of paragraphs in books, Lisa helped him realize that paragraphs were tied to meaning.

Another way to learn about students as readers and writers is to interview them and ask them direct questions about these two processes. Terri asked the students in his seventh-grade science class such questions as: What do they read/write at home? At school? Who helps them and how? What do they like to read/write? In which language do they prefer to read/write? What is easy, what is hard to read/write? How do they choose a reading/a topic to write? What do they do before reading the book/writing a piece? What do they do when they find a word they don't know? and so on.

Through these interviews, Terri found out about these students' and families' literacy habits, their preferences, and strategies. Some students get help from parents, others from siblings, yet others get no help at home. Some glance through the book before starting to read, others start right away, others check the table of contents. Some write what they are told by the teacher, others prefer to write when they are not ordered to do it.

LANGUAGES IN THE CLASSROOM

Choice of language and purpose for using the language are ever present in classrooms with bilingual students. Choice of language for the teacher depends on the type of program and language proficiency of the teacher. Students should always have choice of language situated in a functional context. Certain situations call for one language rather than the other regardless of what the student prefers. This section addresses:

- Use of languages for literacy instruction.
- Functional use of the languages.

Use of Both Languages for Literacy Instruction

Literacy instruction takes place in the students' native language, in their second language, or in both.[3] Bilingual learners can benefit from the use of both languages, regardless of the language being used for literacy instruction. Bilingual programs, by definition, provide literacy instruction in both languages. Development of native language literacy insures bilingualism and establishes literacy knowledge that serves as the foundation of literacy in other languages. Second-language or monolingual programs do not include teaching in the native language in their curriculum. Nevertheless, teachers who use a bilingual—bicultural approach take advantage of the native language in the process of literacy development of the second language, even if they themselves do not know the language of their students. Teachers should never forbid the use of the home language because "The mother tongue does not take over but is a necessary conversation lubricant. Even if it was possible to banish it from the classroom, it could never be banished from the pupils' minds."[4] Use of the heritage language will not get in the way of learning English. It is only natural for the learner to want to return to the mother tongue when learning a new language, especially if the content matter being learned is particularly difficult.

There are pedagogical and psychological reasons for using the native language. Students' native languages provide access to academic content, allow more effective interaction, and are part of the students' overall language and literacy knowledge. Valuing the native languages shows respect for the students and families and gives the languages status in the school. It even helps develop proficiency in the second language.[5] High school teachers are concerned that use of L1 leads to discipline problems. Kara, however, found the reverse to be true. When she stopped forbidding the use of L1 within the context of certain rules, the behavior of her class dramatically improved. A positive attitude toward the native language of students is particularly important when it is not the language of the larger society. Minority languages are vulnerable to losing status and respect.

Allowing students to function in both languages and in an environment that accepts both cultures is a necessary tool to learn in greater

---

[3]For a review of the research on the various choices see Lombardo (1979).

[4]Butzkamm, 1998, p. 95.

[5]Lucas and Katz (1994) describe uses of native languages in high schools with multicultural populations.

depth about the students. In the case of beginners, they may only label pictures in the second language, whereas they write more extended and informative text in the native language. More advanced students may associate topics with one or the other language and prefer to write about or discuss them in a particular language. Using both languages gives them opportunities to include more topics.

Sometimes students do not take advantage of the knowledge they have in one language to acquire the other. Often they think that their native language is getting in the way of learning the second language and they should repress it. Teachers need to show students how their knowledge of one language can help the development of the other. For example, a bilingual science teacher had written on the board *carnivorous, herbivorous,* and so on. She asked the students to guess what kind of animals they were. Her Spanish-speaking students remained silent. She then pointed at the root of the words and asked them if there were similar words in Spanish. After they realized that *carni* was close to *carne,* the Spanish word for meat, and *herbi* to *hierba,* the Spanish word for hay, herbs, and grass, they reached the correct meaning. Even when languages are totally different, knowledge of concepts supports reading and writing about those concepts in the second language.

The native language, for students who are just developing English, is a better tool for thinking. For example, the Drawing as Prewriting approach (see chap. 3) is very useful for students new to English because they can express themselves through drawing. Older students may find this approach too childish. The teacher can suggest to these students to write in their heritage language and then illustrate the ideas through drawings so that the teacher can understand. From that the teacher or peers can help the author write a sentence or two in English. Eventually the student may start directly with the drawing.

Teachers who know the language of their students can help them while composing in the second language. Alma's students had read a story in English and were now discussing it in Bosnian. They were assigned to write a summary in English. While her students were discussing, Alma listened to their conversation and noted key words that she felt would be needed for the summary. She then taught the students how to say and write those words in English while they put together a story map. The students not only used those words when writing the summary, but also used them appropriately in other writings later on. In the past, students were frustrated because they could discuss the story in Bosnian, but did not have the words to then write about it in English.

Teachers who instruct in English can still take advantage of the students' native language to promote literacy and learning. They

- Encourage discussion in the native language while planning or revising or when discussing readings.
- Allow bilingual students to write in their L1 and English, and perhaps a combination of the two.
- Carry out Cross-Age Projects (see chap. 4) with students who share their native languages.
- Do paired writing activities, and place bilingual students with native English speakers. Allow the pair to present the story to the class both in English, and in the bilingual students' L1. Perhaps the writing pair's finished story could be a dual-language text.
- Teach the whole class simple greetings and phrases in various languages. Perhaps post these phrases on a bulletin board or various places around the classroom.
- Allow bilingual students to create comic strips in their L1, or write and illustrate stories and non-fictional pieces in their L1, just as their English-speaking classmates are doing in English. When bilingual students share their stories with the class, they may present in their L1, as well as with an English translation.
- Display different alphabets and writing systems. Bilingual students could share and discuss their L1 writing system with the class, and all students could try out different writing systems.
- Allow bilingual students to respond in the primary languages to demonstrate comprehension of content taught in English.
- Seek assistance from tutors, aides, teachers, parents, or other students who speak their L1.
- Make materials in other languages easily accessible and readily available for students in the classroom; this could include books, magazines, posters, videos, bilingual dictionaries, and others.
- Encourage the school library to have materials in every language represented by the school's student body.[6]

Functional Use of the Languages

Language serves to communicate ideas. Therefore, the choice of language in the classroom should help in the communication of ideas. Mayra left

---

[6]Freeman and Freeman (1998); Gravelle (2000).

it up to the student leader in her bilingual classroom to set the choice of language when discussing science topics during Student-Directed Group Discussion. The rest of the students tended to follow the leader using English, Spanish, or codeswitching. The purpose of the activity was to learn science, and to learn to research, present, and write ideas. Either language would serve that purpose.

Language use enhances language proficiency. To motivate students to use a particular language, the teacher must create the circumstances for students to have to use the language. In the Mailbox Game approach (see chap. 3), used in a Two-way bilingual program, English-speakers were motivated to write in Spanish when communicating with native Spanish-speakers and vice versa. Cheryl used the Jigsaw approach (see chap. 7) for readings in her ESL class to encourage quiet students to talk. Each expert group studied one third of the story well. Then groups were formed with students who had each read part of the story in order to piece it together. A Japanese student admitted that it was so much harder to make herself understood to other students than to the teacher. Her group needed her to be thorough and clear because her piece was important for understanding the whole reading. She was stressed but grateful for the opportunity to have to use the language for real communication.

Children have a very pragmatic view of the choice of languages. Basically they will use the language that the interlocutor knows. It is hard to induce children to use a particular language in order to learn it. Therefore, if the goal is to develop a particular language, students need to be provided with authentic opportunities where they must use that language, and preferably in a friendly and relaxed context. Some students in Peggy's bilingual class choose to function mostly in Spanish, their stronger language. They can, however, use English when dealing with monolingual people. For example, Peggy's sister, who only speaks English, assisted these third graders with their science fair projects. All students participated actively. Yadira wrote a thank-you letter to the visitor. It was her first attempt at writing in English. She wrote:

Dear Ms. Eileen:

You are a good helper. Thank you for the candys an the pencils
I am glad of you. Becuase you are so good for the pizza
Thank you you are a good helper

Sincerely,

Yadira

DEVELOPMENT OF LANGUAGE, LITERACY, AND CONTENT KNOWLEDGE

Language, literacy, and content knowledge are needed to develop literacy in a second language or language variety. Instruction must reflect this connection. For students in bilingual programs, even when the literacy instruction is in the heritage language, students still need the academic language and the content knowledge demanded in schools. Students who are being instructed through their second language have the same needs. For them knowledge of the second language, regardless of age and level of schooling, may mean starting from the basics. These areas of knowledge integrate in different ways. Teachers should:

- Develop reading and writing simultaneously with speaking and listening skills in the second language.
- Teach the English language in the context of literacy development.
- Develop literacy while developing content knowledge.

Holistic Approach to Second Language and Literacy Development

In acquiring a second language, students learn to listen, speak, read, and write in the language. Oral and written language development are best done together to reinforce each other. There is no need to wait for advanced oral language proficiency to start literacy in the second language.[7] Students can be introduced to books and be encouraged to do some writing. Word Cards, Reading Aloud, Shared Reading (see chap. 4), and Drawing as Prewriting (see chap. 3) are some approaches that can be used from the very beginning with the second language. They develop both the written and the oral skills.

There are some students who will be more daring in the written language than the oral because the written language allows time for reflection, correction, and preparation. For example, a seventh-grade Japanese student read a 10-chapter mystery book and wrote summaries in his ESL class with great confidence. He did not dare speak English initially. Oral communication with his teacher, who knew Japanese, was in Japanese. Eventually his success in literacy gave him courage to try English orally.

---

[7]Hudelson (1984) studies the development of literacy in the second language of students with limited oral proficiency.

Teaching the Second Language in the Context of Literacy Instruction

As teachers develop their students' ability to use the oral and written language, they also must develop the language itself. Being able to understand or convey the intended meaning depends a lot on the accuracy of language use. Students need to expand their vocabulary, learn text-, sentence-, and word-level grammar, develop comprehensible pronunciation and sound-symbol correspondences, and acquire accurate spelling. Close observation of students while speaking and reading gives a teacher a sense of students' language needs. Writing is perhaps the best medium to gauge language needs. When teaching writing it is important not only to focus on students' ability to develop topic, organize a piece, follow the text structure required by the genre, and reflect voice, but also to analyze vocabulary and grammatical structures. Often what appears as problems with writing are really limited language knowledge. Writing "bed to bed" stories, i.e., stories that recount chronologically what happened during a day, is a safe way to construct a piece of writing with limited vocabulary and grammatical structures. For example, a first grader of Lithuanian background started his story with: "*last niht I got a spider bite but I didit now what bet me. My eye was swolen.*" He quickly reverted to:

> *I went to the Doctor. Then I went to scooll*
> *I went to sleep*
> *then my mom wake me up*

The switch to the chronological account allowed him to write a longer piece with no language demands. The first sentence has voice but needs language development, the second part of the story is uninteresting but his language is accurate. In order to encourage the first type of writing, teachers need to support second language development of the students. Exposure and practice as well as explicit teaching of the language helps both the development of oral and written discourse as well as of the second language. Chapter 6 outlines students' language needs and approaches to address them.

Teaching Language and Literacy to Support Content Learning

In order for students to acquire content they need the language used in the academic context and literacy knowledge to read and produce the type of text found in this context. Most teachers are aware of the demands of vocabulary knowledge for the various content areas. Teaching content area, at minimum, requires teaching vocabulary. In addition, Schleppegrell (2004) proposes that academic discourse include personal, factual, and analytic genres. In order for students to function in these various genres, they need to understand the purpose of the text, the grammar and vocabulary needed. The natural tendency of children is to write personal recounts or narratives (personal genres). Literacy instruction must include introduction to other genres expected in content classes. For example, science classes require explanations of procedures, the ability to tell and write about what happened in the course of an experiment (procedural recounts). Social studies classes require historical accounts as well as the more advanced historical arguments, where points of view need to be supported.

The development of this academic language needs to be done with an *additive* perspective. The language students use daily to communicate among themselves is appropriate for that purpose; the academic language is taught, not as a better language, but as an additional language that they need to perform in academic contexts.

Literature can also support content knowledge acquisition. There are many books that contain teaching narratives, where content is introduced through the familiar and easier style of stories. Teachers should collect such stories to read during reading and writing time as students are covering the topics during content area time. For example, the book *Math Appeal* contains a number of math riddles that are good to reinforce math concepts but it can also be used for phonics practice because the riddles are written in rhyme. Appendix D includes examples for science, social studies, and mathematics.

CULTURES IN THE CLASSROOM

Culture consists of the values, traditions, social and political relationships, and worldview created, shared, and transformed by a group of people bound together by a common history, geographic location, language, social class and/or religion.[8]

Culture influences the students' and teachers' performance in the classroom. The body of knowledge about the world and about language the students bring was shaped by their culture. Teachers should use it at

---

[8]Nieto (2000), p. 139.

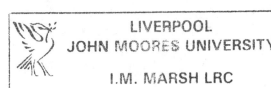

the foundation for new learning. In addition, students need to become familiar with the culture of the new society, if they are going to success-fully function in it. This section discusses the following:

- Use students' cultural background as a tool for learning.
- Use culturally relevant instruction.
- Use materials that support heritage culture and introduce American culture.
- Become cultural brokers.

Cultural Background as a Tool for Learning

"Knowledge is built incrementally through the recursive expansion of children's prior understandings in meaningful dialogue and socially significant interactions."[9] Cultural background shapes students' prior knowledge. Prior knowledge, together with language proficiency and lit-eracy ability, holds the key to reading comprehension and development of topic for writing. Teachers can take advantage of prior knowledge to motivate students to read and write and facilitate the process when stu-dents are developing language and literacy ability. Giving students choice of topic for their writings stimulates prior knowledge.

When initiating students to second-language reading, teachers can use books in the second language that have culturally familiar themes (see Appendix B). For example, the book *Paper Crane* that Peggy used for Shared Reading (chap. 4) contains a theme very familiar to Chinese stu-dents. The book *Everybody Cooks Rice* illustrates how different cultures use rice in their diet. The book *My First American* addresses the theme of making friends in a new environment, an extremely relevant topic for im-migrant students. *The Magic Shell* by Nicholasa Mohr accounts the con-flicts a Dominican boy has with adapting to a completely different way of life in New York City. There's also a series of books written in English, with lots of Spanish words intertwined about a girl named Gabby and how she deals with being bilingual/bicultural.

Using students' prior knowledge enhances motivation to read and write. Students are excited to read books that raise familiar topics and they write endlessly about topics close to them. Education is also about expanding this knowledge. Teachers need to introduce students to reading and writing about topics related to their new host culture (see Appendix C)

---

[9]McCarty and Watahomigie (1998), p. 81.

and other unknown topics that further their education. To enhance reading comprehension and the quality of composing, teachers must develop students' knowledge in preparation to read or write something. For example, in preparation for writing in his seventh-grade bilingual science class, Terry always had students do a hands-on activity, discuss pictures, or go on a field trip related to the topic, followed by creating a semantic map to discuss the topic, organize the subthemes, and develop vocabulary. Only then did the students write.

Even more effective is to relate newly learned concepts to the students' experience. For example, Peggy asked a group of American-born students of Dominican background about their feelings toward the Dominican Republic, whether they felt they were American or Dominican, and whether their relatives in the Dominican Republic truly understood their lives in the United States. Following a lively discussion, Peggy introduced the parallel situation of the American colonists, their feelings toward England, as well as King George III's apparent lack of understanding of the colonists' point of view.

Culturally Relevant Instruction

A pedagogy that is culturally relevant ensures that all students achieve to high standards. It provides opportunities for students to build on previous knowledge and experiences when learning new content. It is more than an acknowledgement of special holidays and cultural celebrations. Teachers use culture to enhance learning. Students from all backgrounds benefit when their cultures and home experiences are an integral part of the learning process. Besides affecting how students communicate in the classroom, cultural practices help shape students' thinking processes.[10]

Students learning in a culturally relevant environment know they are held to high standards. They are taught to believe in themselves and their peers and are highly motivated to succeed. All those involved in the students' learning clearly communicate their expectations for learning and success. They nurture mutual respect for all students and foster a genuine belief that all students can be successful learners.

Learning is an active process in culturally relevant instruction. Teachers act as facilitators. They assist students in making connections between home experiences and school experiences. In a program for Navajo children "students identified as nonverbal and nonanalytic, when presented with familiar cultural-linguistic curricular content, became highly verbal,

---

[10]Hollins (1995).

ventured opinions and spoke up in class, and easily made inductive generalizations, a form of analytic thinking."[11] Additionally, teachers provide opportunities for students to work on projects that are both culturally and socially meaningful. For example, as the culminating activity for their unit on recycling, Lucy's 3rd bilingual class decided that they would clean up the playground across the street from school. The glass bottles and aluminum cans that littered the playground were recycled. The students then wrote a letter to the mayor asking permission to hang posters at the park encouraging people to recycle. Students wrote the posters in the predominant languages of the community: English, Spanish, and Hmong.

Culturally relevant instruction centers on the student. That is, learning is based on cooperation and collaboration. Students direct their learning by teaming up with other students on research projects and assignments. They share responsibility in their learning by initiating group projects, taking part in student-led discussion groups, and creating activities that extend to their communities.

Teachers can look to their students' families and neighborhoods for resources that will assist in providing culturally relevant instruction. Many parents and family members are more than willing to assist in the classroom, but may not know how they can help. As they get to know students better, teachers find out more about family members also. Instead of seeing the students and their families as needy and helpless, teachers who adopt a culturally relevant pedagogy look to their students' families and communities as resources with myriad "funds of knowledge."[12] When Diane was teaching her students a unit on electricity, Francina mentioned to her that her father was an electrician in the Dominican Republic. Diane asked him to come in to the class and help teach a few lessons with her. He eagerly accepted and brought an expertise to the lessons that Diane did not have.

Cross-Cultural Materials

Teachers can collect a variety of culturally relevant materials for their classrooms (see Appendix B). Literature-based lessons and activities can give students opportunities to think critically about different cultures compare and contrast different cultures, and draw comparisons to their own.

---

[11]McCarty and Watahomigie (1998) p. 81.
[12]Moll et al. (1992).

In addition to books, artwork, photographs, music recordings, flags and other decorations are some examples of supplementary materials that help bring culture to life in the classroom. Teachers should openly encourage students and their families to bring in books and other cultural artifacts of their own, to share with the rest of the class. This can lead to opportunities for students, family members and other guests to teach the class about some of the things that make their culture unique.

Teachers should be especially attentive to the cultures and nationalities represented by their students; they will demonstrate interest in students' backgrounds, and model attitudes of acceptance for all cultures by choosing culturally relevant books and other thematic instruction to incorporate into their curricula. Regardless of a classroom's demographics, however, students should be exposed to books that depict major themes of America's multiculturalism: immigration stories, various cultural traditions, and different ways that bicultural individuals reconcile their disparate identities are all rich topics for study. As students encounter culturally relevant stories, they are made to reflect on their own background, lifestyle and family heritage; moreover, they develop a greater appreciation of the many different traditions and cultures of people both in America and abroad.

In addition, teachers should introduce typical American texts and themes to their bilingual students (see Appendix C). These should be analyzed and cultural contrast brought to the surface. It is particularly important for teachers who themselves come from the American culture to be aware that the knowledge and values reflected in those text are not the norm but just representations of a different culture. One way to address the different cultural perspectives is to read the various cultural perspectives of universal themes, for example weddings. As the different cultural perspectives are raised students and teachers begin to understand that there are different ways of viewing the world.

Teachers as Cultural Brokers

Regardless of the linguistic and cultural background and the specific assignment, teachers working with bilingual students must help them and their families understand and function within the school and the larger society. Prior knowledge may be contradictory to America understandings. Teachers need to act as brokers. For example, a teacher wondered why Nestor, a Portuguese student, did not make the association between *Thanksgiving* and *turkey* on a worksheet. Portuguese people serve turkey for Christmas. They have no associations with the traditional American Thanksgiving because it is a totally new concept for them.

Teachers' role as literacy instructors extends to helping students adjust to the new culture and teaching them how to use the language and literacy skills they are developing effectively in the new society. Teachers need to teach the function of literacy in the American context, the cultural knowledge needed to comprehend text, the specific meaning of words beyond the literal definitions contained in dictionaries, and the structure of text particular to the new culture.

Different cultures use printed text for different purposes. For example, in many countries newspapers are rather thin and contain mostly news, whereas in the United States they serve multiple purposes. People read the newspapers not only for news but to decide on entertainment, sales, car shopping, and much more. In the United States information is frequently disseminated through printed text. Everywhere we go there is a brochure to read about a particular institution. Directions are always given in writing. This extended use of print can be overwhelming for learners from cultures where oral communication is the norm. When presenting an authentic text, teachers should do it in a complete cultural context. A mainstream teacher regularly wrote the two lunch selections on the board for the benefit of her bilingual students. This way they could learn the vocabulary. Students checked under their choice as they came in. Miguel, a recent arrival from Mexico, not only needed to be taught the menu choices but the whole concept of schools serving lunch and having a choice. In his country students do not eat lunch at school but go home in the early afternoon to have the main meal of the day.[13]

Different cultures view the use of reading and writing in school differently. In the American context we emphasize proficiency. We want students to be proficient readers and writers. Other cultures are more guarded. For example, Dien[14] reports that Vietnamese families do not encourage adolescents to read fiction because they want control over ideas they may draw from such readings. In addition in the Vietnamese culture writing is highly valued. Students may be reluctant to write personal narratives because they consider the topic and their own skills unworthy. Content-area reading and writing can help such students bridge the cultural discontinuities in literacy.

World knowledge and the meaning of words in the cultural context are essential to comprehend text. Students reading text written by an author of a different culture may have difficulty understanding unless

---

[13]Heath (1986) discusses the need to focus on context when teaching literacy to students who experience a new language and culture.

[14]Dien (1998) and other chapters in the volume by Perez (1998) contain rich examples of how different cultures approach literacy.

teachers give students the background they need. As illustrated in the Vocabulary Connections approach (see chap. 6), seventh graders from Latin America interpreted the word *plantation* as a piece of agricultural land. They were reading about the Civil War in the United States. The teacher had to explain the social and historical meaning of plantations in the South. Students quickly understood and related it to comparable situations in Latin America.

Teachers must also explain the organization and content of text depending on the genre. For example, a persuasive essay is a foreign concept to American Indians[15] who believe in presenting both sides of the argument for a reader to decide.[16] Even grammar can be culturally defined. Eskimos use the modal *would* to soften an assertion. ". . . the stories are going down generations of natives to the younger generations so the customs *wouldn't* be forgotten."[17] Using *would* is preferable to *will* because there is no certainty that it will happen. This is consistent with Eskimo talk that requires circumspection.

Teachers as cultural brokers build a bridge between the students and the intended meaning of the author when reading, and between students and their audience when writing. Comparing, contrasting, and finding similar circumstances in the students' culture help.

Often immigrant students are accused of plagiarism. Using sources verbatim is not uncommon in other cultures, particularly those that foster memorization of text. Teachers need to teach students how to paraphrase information that they find in text and how to quote when they want to write verbatim. They also need to explain that copying is not considered appropriate in American writing.

HIGH EXPECTATIONS AND APPROPRIATE SUPPORT

Language development, educational experience, and difficult life circumstances make the task of teaching many bilingual students challenging, but should not act as a deterrent to having high expectations for such students. These expectations must be backed by support provided to the students so that they can reach these goals.

Approaches recommended in this book allow students to control the level of difficulty. Regardless of ability, all students should be required to

---

[15]We followed the recommendation of McCarty and Watahomigie (1998) in our choice of the term "American Indian" to refer to indigenous groups in the United States.

[16]Conklin and Lourie (1983), chapter 11 and Connor and Kaplan (1987) address the cultural differences among languages.

[17]Basham and Kwachka (1991) p. 41.

participate to the extent that they can. For example, Chiet, a recent arrival from China in a mainstream kindergarten, was able to participate alongside her classmates in the Word Card activity because all she needed to bring was a new word every day. Serious personal circumstances had delayed Nestor's cognitive development, yet he could participate as well as the other students by using the Drawing as Prewriting approach. He drew elaborate pictures and then dictated the story to his teacher. It took several months before Nestor started writing his own short sentences. Some students in the class could write on their own after drawing, yet others were beyond needing to compose first through drawings and could write directly, illustrating later. All the students in the class produced books, yet each worked to his or her own individual potential.

Sometimes the demands of the curriculum are difficult because of language, cultural content, or limited education. Teachers should not waiver in their expectations, but they should find ways to provide the appropriate support. A major source of support can be tutors (see chap. 8). Strategies that help students reach curriculum goals are helpful to all students. They are, however, essential for bilingual learners, especially when instruction is in their second language. For example, José, a high school student with fluency in English, found the social studies book difficult. Lisa used the KWL approach to help him cope with the content. Lisa drew three columns on the board with the letters K, W, and L. They filled the column "K" with all he knew or thought he knew about the subject and "W" with all he wanted to learn about the topic. He read the selection and then filled the "L" column with all he had learned after reading. During the discussion that accompanied filling out the first two columns Lisa was able to clarify vocabulary, concepts, misconceptions, and most important, the lack of prior knowledge that José had on the subject.

Other helpful strategies are:

- Providing explicit instruction.
- Modeling tasks.
- Facilitating transitions.
- Providing practice opportunities.
- Providing corrective feedback.
- Becoming a partner in the reading and writing process.
- Organizing the classroom into flexible groups.
- Using homework as a preparation to function in class.
- Allowing extra time to complete tasks.

- Teaching vocabulary before reading or writing.
- Using the computer.

Explicit Instruction

Teachers show students exactly the process they need to go through to achieve what they want. They practice with the students and continue giving support until they can do it independently. For example, Tricia, working with a group of ESL high school students, carefully taught them how to write summaries. She used Graphic Organizers, KWL, predicting, and looking for the main idea to enhance reading comprehension of passages. Then she taught students to look for things they did not understand, for the main idea, and for important and unimportant details. She insisted that students use their own words. The focus on the main idea and modeling the process helped students improve their summary writing and eliminated the practice of copying from the original text.[18]

Explicit instruction avoids frustration, especially when students are in the early stages of developing a second language. When Peggy teaches social studies units to her students, she has them formulate factual questions about what they are learning. She gives them a graphic organizer with the words: who, what, when, where, why, and how. Upon reviewing their questions, she found that many students were writing questions such as: *Where did the Pilgrims landed?* or *When did Thomas Jefferson wrote the Declaration of Independence.* Peggy used the opportunity to explicitly teach the proper verb form for this type of question.

Modeling

Teachers demonstrate to students what they are requested to do by carrying out the activity while thinking aloud. Often students may not follow instructions either because they are given in their weaker language or because they are unfamiliar with what the teacher wants them to do. School tasks that may seem routine to teachers are often very strange to children because they were neither part of their previous schooling nor used at home. One high school student told about his frustration of seeing the completed products after an assignment that he failed to understand, "As soon as I saw the final product, I realized what the teacher wanted. I could have done it. I wanted the assignment to start all over again."

---

[18]Prinz (1998) contains a full account of this project.

Modeling or showing samples helps students understand what they are expected to do. Linda introduced Drawing as Prewriting to her deaf students by drawing pictures while signing her thoughts. She pondered what to draw, what crayons to choose, what to add in the picture, and what to write down. The children watched her carefully and soon started to imitate. Some, of course, even copied her picture but eventually would draw their own.

Facilitating Transition

Teachers need to allow time and support students when they are not used to a particular approach. Sarah used Process Writing with her high school ESL students. Horacio refused to plan before writing. He was an intelligent and well-read young man who could write on complex topics. When it was time for writing he would start right away and produce several pages. His writings looked disorganized to his teacher, often going off on tangents. After three weeks of working with him, Sarah finally succeeded in having him brainstorm on a topic of interest. He then chose one aspect of it and together they created a semantic map while they discussed the topic in more depth. The resulting essay was clear, organized, and well developed. Both teacher and student were pleased with the results. Sarah's perseverance, patience, and flexibility paid off.

Some approaches require students to do something totally different from the expected classroom behavior. Students appear confused either because of the innovative nature of the approaches, or the fact that they were not used in the country where they initiated their schooling. Elena decided to use Reader-Generated Questions in her sixth-grade social studies class. When she asked students to formulate questions prior to reading, the students refused, claiming that only teachers asked questions. It took Elena the whole 45-minute period to eradicate a belief that had been established after several years of traditional schooling where teachers lecture and ask questions while students listen and respond.

Practice

Rehearsing and repetition help retain language skills. This practice does not have to be tedious and boring. Poems, songs, and games are helpful ways to work with language. For example, Yoko used a game to practice vocabulary and sound—letter correspondence with her ESL students. She said the first word and then the students took turns saying words that started with the last letter of the previous word. For example: *kangaroo—October—rabbit—Tuesday*, and so on. To assist her learners, she wrote the words on the board so that they could clearly see the last letter of the word.

After collecting a number of words through the Word Card activity, Kim developed a board game for her second-grade Vietnamese students who were learning English. She drew a start to finish winding trail. In some boxes she wrote words, and in others she drew the equivalent pictures. Groups of students took turns, putting their pieces in the start box. The student who won the first turn moved his piece to the first square with the word *squirrel*. Without hesitation, he jumped to the square with the picture of the squirrel. When students could not guess which was the corresponding picture or word, or they guessed wrong, they just moved to the next square. Thus, the more words they knew, the faster they could move.

Corrective Feedback

There is a delicate balance between promoting language accuracy and discouraging students with correction. Constant correction interrupts the thinking process and overtaxes short-term memory. On the other hand, students developing a language need feedback to approach accuracy. In the case of bilingual learners with varied input in each language, teachers cannot be sure that the natural environment is going to provide appropriate models for the students to learn naturally. Therefore, some measure of corrective feedback is necessary. Jin was doing Drawing as Prewriting in English with her second-grade Chinese students. Brandon insisted on doing the writing himself. Jin encouraged him to sound out words every time he requested spelling assistance. In addition, she would help with selected words. For example, after sounding out *caught*, he wrote *caut*. Jin told him to add a *g* after *au*. He added *gh*, arriving at the correct spelling. He only needed some encouragement to help him remember how to spell the word. Reformulation (chap. 8) and Dictogloss (chap. 6) include feedback in the approach itself.

Teacher as a Partner in the Reading and Writing Process

Teachers can facilitate the reading and writing process by intervening where the students are having difficulty. Reading aloud with expression, writing down what the students try to compose, sounding out words for spelling, and reading aloud to revise a piece are among the types of intervention that efficiently assist students.

Reading aloud with expression while students listen greatly enhances reading comprehension and the development of knowledge of text structure. When students can follow along with the text, it enhances the acquisition of sound—letter correspondence. Even students fluent in oral language profit from listening to a good reader. June, a mainstream social studies teacher, read aloud test items for the benefit of her bilingual students.

Writing down what students dictate takes the stress off beginning writers in their second language. Reiko's student dictated the sentences for her initial drawings during the Drawing as Prewriting approach. After the first few sessions, the student ventured to write by herself such sentences as "This is Boston Common," "Fish is many." A first-grade teacher sat at a computer with a student who refused to write. The student dictated the first sentence; the teacher encouraged him to write the next. Together they wrote a whole page story alternating typing the sentences. When the page was printed the student took full credit for the story. He also continued to write on his own after that session.

Sounding out words to the students can help them spell. For example, Brandon wanted to write the word *gigantic*, but he couldn't spell it and couldn't sound it out. Jin sounded it out for him and he was able to spell it correctly. Leo, a Spanish as a second language teacher, used Semantic Maps and Process Writing with his high school students. During revision he would read aloud a student's piece. Students themselves found incongruencies and mistakes while Leo read.

Flexible Grouping[19]

All students' needs can be best met when the class is organized in various types of grouping from whole class, to small groups, to pairs or individuals working by themselves. Students can be grouped in teams of comparable abilities, similar interests, specific language or literacy needs, or heterogeneously. Group variation allows for development of different strengths and needs. No student should be kept in the same group all the time. Students, especially at the secondary level, may resist working in groups because they come from a schooling experience where there was no such practice. Teachers need to be sensitive to these cultural differences and develop strategies to help students work together and see the value of this cooperation. Pauline, an English-speaking music teacher, had a number of Chinese bilingual students in her class, including two new arrivals that spoke only Chinese. She divided her 40 students into groups of five. Each group included English speakers, Chinese students fluent in both languages, and those with more limited proficiency in English. Using both languages, students communicated and created final drafts in English of American composers for inclusion in the class anthol-

---

[19]See Radencich and McKay (Eds.) (1995) and Caldwell and Ford (2002) for explanation and examples of the use of flexible grouping in a variety of classroom contexts.

ogy. All students, regardless of language ability, contributed to the group's product. Close work with English speakers in the small groups helped Chinese students gain confidence to later actively participate in the oral presentation of their projects in front of the whole class.

Groups should be created to facilitate bilingual learners' participation. Daniel, a high school Portuguese-speaking student, showed different levels of participation during group work. When in groups that included some of his friends, both English-speakers and bilinguals, he participated in discussions, wrote his own notes down, and resorted to his bilingual classmates when unable to express himself or to understand. However, in groups with only English-speakers who were not his friends, he did not speak at all and mostly copied from other students' papers.

Homework

Teachers should assign homework to prepare students to function in class the following day rather than only assigning what they did not do in class. For the Vocabulary Connections approach, homework can be looking up the assigned words in the dictionary and writing down the definitions, so that the following day the teacher can concentrate on the discussion about the words. For writing approaches, it can be thinking about the topic they want to write about, doing a Semantic Map, and reading about it, so that when they come to class they can start working on the draft or discussing what they will write. For reading approaches it can be watching a video or reading an easier text, either in L1 or L2. For Word Cards, students can think of the word or words they will bring for the activity and drawing a picture that represents the word, so when they come to class they can tell the word and show their picture. For Jigsaw, the expert group can do research on their piece of the puzzle. ESL and mainstream teachers can have students read in the native language or ask adults at home about topics that they will read or write in class in English. When parents are bilingual and the teacher is not, homework can be a key element to prepare students for what will be covered in class. Parents can discuss the topic in their L1, provide English vocabulary, and so on. But, even if parents speak only L1, if they knew what the subject was, they could help prepare the students in their L1 for what they would be learning the next day in L2.

When homework is to prepare students for class as suggested here, then any help that they get at home is useful. When homework is just worksheet or workbook tasks, having adults do them for the children defeats the purpose of the assignment.

Extra Time

Students who are working in the second language or have difficulty with
their native language, can profit from extra time to get their task accom-
plished. Unlike fluent speakers of the language, students functioning in a
second language not only have to think of the content but also of the language they need to express or understand the content. Steve, a seventh-
grade Russian student, never wanted to revise his work. He felt under
pressure to hand in the work. He expected the teacher to make the corrections. When the teacher implemented process writing to help him produce his science papers and allowed him extra time before handing in the
papers, he was more willing to make revisions.

Vocabulary Development

Vocabulary can be a challenge in reading comprehension and expression
in writing. Besides the sheer number of words that bilingual learners need
to acquire, there are characteristics of the words in the second language
that may cause difficulty. Among them are: acoustic similarity ("on the
contract" for "on the contrary"), homophones (I, eye), homonyms (tear,
tear), clipping (prof for professor), acronyms (MCAS), and so on.[20] There
are a number of ways to assist students in understanding the meaning of a
word when reading a passage. Among the most common are finding clues
in pictures, tapping background knowledge, and using context clues.
Sometimes these strategies work and sometimes they do not. Nicole assisted a teacher by working individually with a student who had arrived
from Greece. She soon discovered how these strategies some times worked
but other times contributed to confusion. For example, when reading an
early-second grade leveled book about a Native American boy, Lila came
across the word *tepee* that appeared in the sentence, "The boy ran away
from the tepee." To figure out the meaning, she looked at the picture on
the page that showed a boy running into the woods with a Native American village behind him and his little sister standing on the edge of the village watching him. When Nicole asked Lila for the meaning of *tepee*, she
said it meant *sister* based on the picture that featured the sister more than
the tepee. Readers often use their general knowledge to guess comprehension. These attempts are not always successful. For example, Lila read a
paragraph about farmers and the tools that they use. One of the questions
following the paragraph was a multiple-choice question that asked, "What

---

[20]See Birch (2002) for a thorough analysis.

is a tool?" Lila picked the answer that said, "A tool is a crop that farmers grow." Using context to guess meaning is not always successful. When Nicole asked Lila what the word *fossil* meant, she said it meant "a painting or picture because the characters in the book saw fossils at the museum." Nicole's experience with Lila demonstrates that these types of confusions can only be spotted when students work individually with an adult or more experienced learner. Teachers need to take advantage of tutors to support their students' learning and comprehension of new vocabulary.

Second language learners have so much vocabulary to develop that it should be done throughout the content areas. There are number of approaches mentioned in this book that support vocabulary development, such as the Vocabulary Connections and other approaches (chap. 6), Word Cards (chap. 4), Semantic Mapping (chap. 7), providing words when doing Drawing as Prewriting (chap. 3), Dialogue Journal (chap. 3) and Read Aloud (chap. 8).[21]

Use of the Computer

Word processing, spell checkers, E-reader, reading and content area programs, language practice exercises, and Internet access provide support for literacy development. The word processor motivates students because it takes away the drudgery of using paper and pencil and revising drafts. The final product is a lot neater. "I feel writing on the computer is easier and faster. Another thing is that it is easier to make neat because you don't have to worry about eraser marks" (sixth grader).

Good quality software can provide meaningful opportunities to read and write. There are stories with interactive features, and in some cases, in a variety of languages that provide good reading and language practice. The E-reader can be very helpful to second language readers because they can select text that the program sounds out for them, since sometimes L2 learners know the oral but not the written version of words. Other software programs as well as the Internet motivate students to read in order to do research. It is important to be flexible. Debbie, a Spanish as a second language high school teacher, allowed her students to choose the type of program in which they wanted to work. Some students chose word processing, database, and other creative programs, whereas others preferred drill and practice programs that allowed them to build confidence in the language. Eventually, these students used word processing to do creative writing.

---

[21]See also Allen (1999) and Nagy (1988) for extensive treatment of vocabulary teaching.

E-mail has been widely used to connect one group of students with students in other places allowing them to practice reading and writing skills in different languages. This type of interaction makes students truly aware of the need to use appropriate and comprehensible language because they need to be understood and it is very public. It also motivates students to use both their languages through a real need to communicate.[22] Debbie registered Spanish as a second language classes with the global satellite telecommunications project *Orilla a Orilla*.[23] Debbie's class was paired with a class in Chile. Her students wrote letters in Spanish introducing themselves and e-mailed them to Chile. They also prepared a box of gifts to send to Chile. Students brought gifts and wrote why these objects were important to them. Next they carried out a project about Chile. They e-mailed questions to their Chilean partners to seek assistance with their research project. Other cooperatively developed projects followed. According to Debbie, the students were highly motivated to use the language and greatly improved their Spanish.[24]

FIRST DAY, FIRST MONTH, FIRST YEAR IN A SECOND LANGUAGE ENVIRONMENT

Students with no knowledge of English who are entering school in the United States for the very first time face many new experiences and challenges. It is likely that the schools in the United States look very different from the schools in their native countries. The routines and procedures are often in sharp contrast to what they are accustomed. Many teachers working with English Language Learners find that the first few months are a difficult time for both them and their new charges. If the teacher does not speak the native language of the student, little to no communication is possible between them. A teacher can become frustrated and the student may feel alone and isolated. Even teachers who speak the native language of the students may find that adjustment is still difficult. In her experience, Peggy finds that even though her newcomer Latino students are entering a classroom in which everyone speaks Spanish, some still have problems adapting to the classroom environment and the way that classes are conducted and assignments completed. Additionally, although

---

[22]Cummins and Sayers (1995) write about the power of computers and internet communication.

[23]The program's Web page address is http://www.orillas.org. The e-mail address is orillas-support@igc.org

[24]Isom (1995).

all students speak the same language, since they come from various countries with diverse cultures, misunderstandings and misinterpretations still arise.

At the beginning of each chapter on the approaches, we have provided suggestions for how to adapt lessons for beginning English learners. However, even some of these suggestions assume a rudimentary knowledge of English. Questions still remain about what and how to teach newly arrived, non-English-speaking students. There are steps that teachers can take during the first few weeks to help newcomers adjust to the U.S. educational system. It is extremely helpful for teachers to find out as much as they can about the language and culture of the newcomers. Signs in the students' first language can be placed around the room along with the English equivalent. Multilingual posters illustrating different alphabets or names of children in their own language, as well as phrases in other languages can be displayed in the room.[25] Teachers and students can learn a few key phrases in the students' language.[26] Books in the students' native languages can be placed in the school and classroom libraries.

On that first day new students can be overwhelmed with the sights and sounds of their new environment. The first days should be a time of orientation for them. If there are students who speak the same language as the new students, teachers should assign them as buddies or partners who will guide them through those first days. They can also seek out people in the community who might volunteer to work with the students for the first month or so. If there are no students or members of the community who share a common language with the newcomers, teachers should ask for volunteers who will be responsible for assisting the new students. Providing the newcomers with an identification card listing important personal information (name, class assignment, teacher's name, home address and telephone number, list of other children in the school who are fluent in the same language) may relieve any anxiety the student may have about getting lost. Giving the newcomers a picture of the students in their class along with their names can be a foundation for socializing.[27] Likewise, students can be given a booklet of important phrases along with appropriate pictures or drawings that depict activities or needs (e.g., bathroom, nurse, water, telephone, playground, cafeteria, gymnasium, recreation center, fire drill).

---

[25]Schwarzer (2003).
[26]Cary (2000).
[27]Einhorn (2002).

During the first few months, since students have unique personalities and learning styles, teachers should take their cues from them in regards to teaching in and learning English. Some students may eagerly begin to speak, read and write English from the first day, while others are more reticent. Newly arrived students should not be forced to participate in English-speaking activities during this time, although they should not be excluded from them either. Rather they should be encouraged to listen and observe and participate actively only when they are ready.

Teachers should be flexible in their assignments and requirements of newcomer students. Students should be allowed to communicate both orally and in written form in their first language. Some students may even have brought schoolbooks from their native countries that correlate with the units of study being implemented in their new school. They should be encouraged to utilize these resources. Further, students can obtain valuable information on the Internet, since sources there are provided in multiple languages.

Other ways that teachers can help newly arrived students in their learning include:

- Teach students key phrases that will help in learning, such as: Can you help me? I have a question. I don't understand. Can you repeat that?[28]
- Concentrate on the message or intent of the response and not on formation or grammar, when students do respond in English.
- Dedicate a portion of each lesson to language-related objectives.[29]
- Meet with newly arrived students before a lesson to orient them on key words and ideas pertaining to the lesson using sheltered instruction.
- Have learners match pictures/photos with simple sentences or labels.
- Try to include visuals, gestures, hands-on activities, graphs, and realia in the lessons.
- When reading aloud sit the newcomers right next to you or provide them with a copy of the text so that they can follow along.
- When reading aloud, stop more frequently during the reading to check for comprehension, but mindful of not disrupting the flow too much.

---

[28]Einhorn (2002).

[29]Gersten et al. (1998); Echevarria et al (2004).

- Have high expectations but support them and be sensitive of their situation.

HOMES AND COMMUNITIES AS PARTNERS OF LITERACY DEVELOPMENT

Teachers and parents contribute to the literacy experience of students, complementing and reinforcing each other. In the case of bilingual students, they also collectively contribute to the students' full linguistic development. Neither can do it alone, but together they can build a strong foundation. Bilingual learners need development of both languages, of social as well as academic literacy skills, and of knowledge to support literacy in English. Language proficiency, educational background, and views of literacy learning determine what teachers and parents can offer to the students. For example, the school may not be able to provide instruction in the native language, but the family can. Teachers should then encourage the family to strengthen the native language including literacy rather than, as often happens, press them to switch to English. It is better to let the school take care of the English, but both can support the work that the other is doing.

Schools that offer bilingual literacy still benefit from any help the parents give their children. Homes have many opportunities to provide rich literacy experiences in either language. The key is maintaining a proper balance and reinforcing the notion that both languages are important. Constant and trusting communication between parents and teachers can help establish what each can offer and how each can reinforce the work of the other. Melissa had been using Reading Aloud in English with Herman, a trilingual English, Spanish, and ASL hearing child of a deaf mother. Three months into the project, Melissa invited Herman's mother to join them. Herman was embarrassed and hesitant to sign the stories to his mother. With his mother's encouragement he gained confidence and read her several books, signing the text in ASL. After he was finished, the mother taught him signs he did not know for animals and pictures in the books. This activity changed the mother's negative perceptions of her son's interest in books and general behavior. She decided to start reading with him at home, using the books that she had kept on the top shelf of a closet out of his reach.

When neither parents nor teachers can provide skills, community resources should be tapped. Often a teacher does not know the students' native languages and the parents are not literate in it. Parents can enroll their children in after school programs offered by community organiza-tions where the children's native languages are developed. Bilingual col-lege students can also be tapped (see chap. 8). A fourth grade mainstream teacher was delighted when a Greek pre-service teacher was assigned to do field work in her class. The pre-service student not only helped a Greek recent arrival but developed helpful language lessons for all the other second language learners.

EMBEDDING STRATEGIES INTO DISTRICT MANDATED APPROACHES TO LITERACY

Often teachers are under the pressure to implement district-mandated approaches and feel at a loss as to how to include innovations. The ap-proaches included in this book can easily be adapted. Adaptation is often necessary because the district mandates rarely include concern for bilin-gual learners in mainstream classes.

For example, the Writer's Workshop model has been adopted by many districts. This model can be substantially improved for second language learners by following the steps of the Rhetorical Approach. Figure 2–1 shows how one school embedded the Rhetorical Approach into Writers' Workshop.

The first five steps of the Rhetorical Approach scaffold the planning process thereby helping bilingual students produce richer pieces. Mary's students demonstrate the impact of Rhetorical Approach on their writing (see chap. 3).

One school uses the Anticipation Guide (chap. 5) and the first steps of Reader Generated Questions (chap. 4) in combination with the district mandated program to promote reading comprehension. This program's activities usually follow the presentation of the text. Bilingual learners can cope with texts better if issues of background knowledge and lan-guage are addressed before they encounter the text.

Thus the approaches included in this book should not be considered an add-on but a way to enhance the literacy activities mandated by dis-

Explore/Discovery Draft					Write first draft	Revise and edit	Final Draft Conference	Final Copy	Publish Share
Choose and explore a topic	Define purpose and audience	Narrow the topic: list subtopics	Consider functional and literate genre and organization	Select information for each subtopic					

FIGURE 2–1   Rhetorical approach within writers' workshop.

tricts. Scaffolding process and language are essential for many bilingual learners.

CONCLUSION

Getting to know students, creating an atmosphere of respect for their languages and cultures, and conducting fair assessments are vital qualities of literacy instruction. Teachers must address them while implementing the approaches recommended in this handbook.

Learning about students and their beliefs about reading and writing helps personalization of instruction.[30] It also helps maintain high but reasonable expectations of students. Teachers working with students in their second language should be particularly careful not to reach conclusions about their students based on their classroom behavior. Some students cope well and quickly flourish and others do not. Unusual performance and behavior, caused by language and culture shock, may lead to incorrect perceptions of their personalities and cognitive abilities. Teachers should ask parents and other teachers about students with difficulties and observe students while they function in their native language in order to form a more accurate representation of such students.

A bilingual—bicultural approach to teaching creates a classroom atmosphere that accepts all languages and cultures as rich vehicles for learning. In such classrooms, languages and cultures connect teachers with students, enhance their learning, and foster linguistic and academic learning. The knowledge the students bring serves as a foundation to further develop that knowledge and to introduce students to new ideas and perspectives. Helping students keep a balance and insuring accommodation between the cultures is a crucial aspect of educating bilingual learners.

A bilingual—bicultural approach is beneficial not only to bilingual students but to English speakers. Awareness of other languages and special work on English for the sake of students who are learning it as a second language enhances the teaching of English for all students.

---

[30]See Sizer (1992) for the importance of considering students as individuals and the different factors that contribute to the differences among students.

3

Approaches with Focus on Writing

The teaching of writing has undergone many changes in the last 25 years. Older students and parents may not be familiar with the new approaches that allow experimenting and creativity. Moreover, parents and students, schooled outside the United States may not be familiar with these approaches either. Teachers need to help students transition to the new ways of learning to write and be clear to parents about their approach and goals. The approaches included in this section help students develop and practice their writing in meaningful ways. There is much opportunity for oral expression (or singing), and reading, as well.

Writing development can take place in the heritage language, in the second language, or in both. Even when developing writing in the second language students can make use of their heritage language. Young beginners go through stages of writing in their heritage language, writing isolated words in English, and lastly writing sentences in English. Most advanced students prefer to write directly in English using an occasional word in their heritage language when they cannot think of the English word. Although some still prefer to plan in their heritage language. The best policy is to set up a classroom atmosphere in which students have the freedom of using either language but they are cognizant of their audience and the language their audience understands.

Besides use of the two languages, another area that needs clear policy is what to do with errors or miscues. Many young learners tend to use invented spelling. They spell according to how the word sounds using sound-letter correspondences from both languages if their heritage language uses the same orthography as English. For example, a Spanish speaker spelled *me* as *mi*, using the Spanish grapheme for the vowel sound in *me*. A Russian speaker spelled *swim* as *cwm* using the Russian grapheme for the first consonant sound. Sometimes students spell a word as it sounds to them which would be different from what it sounds like to a native speaker. For example, *I just to* for *used to*. *There was dey cher oraun* [There was danger all around]. Initial writing also reflects the way students talk and will have the dialect and second language incongruencies of oral language For example, I didn't knew [know] that. The nother [another] reason. I woda [would have].

Educators debate as to what to do with these miscues. Should they be corrected or not? Should students be explicitly taught to avoid these errors? Constant correction can inhibit creativity and the desire to write but if the students are not made aware of how the written language works in the language they are writing, they will never learn it. In this chapter, we present writing strategies that promote the love for writing and the development of the writing process. In chapter 6 we present a number of strategies that help the development of language so that students learn to write accurately for the specific audience and purpose. Students need to learn both that written language is not like the oral one and that language has conventions that must be learned. For example, oral language is more personal while written language is depersonalized. A second grade student explained the growth of a plant in connection to himself: "My alfalfa

---

Suggestions for First Year English Learners

- Have books available in the L1 of the students as models for writing.
- Allow students to write in their L1 until they feel confident enough to write in their L2.
- Have students draw a storyboard prior to writing in the L2 in order to help them organize their thoughts.
- Have students write labels or simples sentences in L2 under pictures or photos.
- Have beginning English learners partner with a bilingual student who is a more proficient English speaker to make a bilingual story.
- Provide beginning English learners with picture dictionaries and/or lists of common words and phrases that they might need to know for the particular writing assignment.
- Have students write about their personal stories, using pictures, film strips, and letting them choose the language.

and grass plant is starting to grow because it has water in it. It has roots, soil and rocks in it." The text made a similar explanation as a generalization: "A plant's growth requires water, nutrients, light, and air."[1]

Writing approaches described in this chapter include:

- Drawing as Pre-writing
- Mailbox Game
- Dialogue Journal
- Rhetorical Approach
- Computers in Process Writing

Drawing as Prewriting and the Mailbox Game are particularly useful approaches for beginners to the writing process. Even older students have enjoyed letter writing and drawing as a way to help expression when working in a second language. It took Debbie, a high school foreign language teacher, much effort to convince her students that drawing was not childish, but in the end, Drawing as Prewriting proved very helpful for her beginner students. For example, a science teacher had students create concept maps with drawings related to the topics covered in her class. Several teachers have combined Drawing as Prewriting and Word Cards (see chap. 4) when initiating students to reading and writing. Drawing is an integral part of initial writing—either in first or second language. For this reason, beginning second language learners should be allowed to use drawing in their initial writing, regardless of age. For older students diagrams, charts, timelines, graphs, photographs and other types of illustrations can also serve the function of drawing.

The Mailbox Game reinforces the notion that writing should be functional and have a real audience. Engaging learners in meaningful writing contributes to writing development "not as a matter of hand and finger habits but as a really new and complex form of speech."[2] To engage the students in writing, teachers need to find real reasons for them to write. They should also find real audiences other than the teachers themselves. This is often a challenging task. Letter writing is a natural and easy task to incorporate in a classroom. Other activities can include entering students in writing contests and writing articles, poems, and stories for the school newspaper. One classroom had the idea of having a "visitors notebook." Students included in the notebook articles that explained what they had learned in the various content area subjects. The principal and

---

[1]Kucer (2001); Schleppegrell (2004).
[2]Vygotsky (1978), p. 118.

other visitors to the class were invited to browse the notebook. In another class students decided to write a book about the social studies topic they were working on to send it to their beloved student teacher who had already finished his field practice. They wanted to show him how much more they had learned after he left.

Dialogue Journals are highly recommended for the first couple of months of the year as a powerful tool to get to know the students and help them lose the fear of writing. Peggy saved the journals and passed them back to her fourth grade students during the last month of school. She felt that writing in their journals again would be not only a good way for the students to reflect on the past school year, but also would provide a way for those students who were anxious about the coming year to express their feelings. Peggy explained to the students that she wanted them to read through what they had written in August and September and then to write what they were thinking about now. The students' reactions to their first months' entries were both comical and inspiring. A few of the students refused to believe that they had really written what they were reading. Some could not even read what they had written! Others remarked on how messy and scattered their writing was then and how much better they wrote now. For their entries in June, several students reflected on how much they had learned that year, and that they felt they had the confidence to succeed in fifth grade. Marcela wrote:

> *When I came in the door I thought that I was dreaming. But then I thought this is going to be a tough year. But Now it's the day before the last day. This year I acomplised 4th grade. Now am like maybe next year every kid (almost) is going to tsay in 1st Kinder 2nd 3rd 4rd and me in 5th.*

Knowing students is key to helping them with their writing because a teacher can more easily interpret confusing sentences to help students revise and edit their work. They can also suggest connections with students' lives, and facilitate integration to class groups by highlighting students' knowledge and particular strengths. For example, as a group of students discussed a topic before drafting, the teacher pointed out that Pedro, a quiet student, had a lot of personal experience on the subject, thus facilitating Pedro's participation.

Many students come to the task of writing convinced that they do not have anything to say and are afraid of being corrected. Lack of interest in the students' personal life and ideas or cultural beliefs about who holds the knowledge may contribute to the belief among students that they have little important to say. Through their questions in the Dialogue Journals teachers can unlock students' ideas, helping in the flow of writing.

Fear of writing correctly may have been developed in previous schooling or in demanding families who based their own knowledge of learning to write in their schooling experience. Dialogue Journals help students lose the fear of writing because this strategy encourages teachers to model but not correct directly the students' writing. Families as well as older students need to understand the rationale for Dialogue Journal. They need to understand that they will be indeed taught to write accurately through other strategies. Teachers should be aware that sometimes students reveal very intimate problems in this written exchange and should handle each case individually. Don, an ESL teacher working with Southeast Asian refugees, invited a professional counselor to the class to discuss the traumas that students were noting in their journals.

Dialogue Journals are harder to use when the teacher and student do not share a language. Teachers can be creative in their adaptations. Lori told a recently arrived Vietnamese student to draw instead of write in his journal. In her response she explained in English what she thought the drawing was about, thus giving him vocabulary for the things he wanted to express.

Dialogue Journals have been adapted for use with a focus on a particular content area or activity. For example, a teacher instructed the students to write about what happened in the subject matter class that was the most difficult for them. She suggested that in retelling what was taught in the class they try to use as much content specific vocabulary as possible. Dialogue Journals are used in Cross-Age projects (see chap. 4) to discuss the tutoring that students carried out with younger students.

Process Writing is a comprehensive way to develop writing. It is good to use after the other approaches that have eased the students into writing. Process Writing allows for more explicit teaching than Dialogue Journal or the Mail Box Game. The ability to improve each writing project increases with time. Using the computer allows students to revise more than once without having to rewrite all over again. The Rhetorical Approach breaks the planning stage of process writing into very clear steps. It can be very helpful in the earlier stages to develop good habits for planning. It helps students develop a topic in depth.

DRAWING AS PREWRITING

Purpose

Drawing pictures before writing allows the students to get ideas down on paper quickly before they struggle with translating their ideas into written language. Children's drawings are influenced by oral language because they are abstract and "tell a story."

> The schemes that distinguish children's first drawings are reminiscent in this sense of verbal concepts that communicate only the essential features of objects. This gives us grounds for regarding children's drawing as a preliminary stage in the development of written language.[3]

Emergent bilingual writers and beginning second-language learners are able to create a story in picture form before committing words to paper and searching for vocabulary that is often unfamiliar to them. As students develop their writing, they naturally skip drawing and write directly. Later, they may add illustrations to their papers. A teacher allowed one student to take pictures instead because she was reluctant to draw. She wanted to write a book about Boston to send to her friends in Japan. Another student used the computer graphics to do his drawings.[4]

Procedure

1. Selecting a theme. This is best done on what is known about the students and their interests, or related to a field trip, or something that happened that day, or a topic that the class has been discussing. At the early stages, very personal things that are close to the students are best, such as "Me" or "Someone Special." Students can also choose their own themes and work individually or in groups.

2. Prepare a book with blank pages and a cover that suggests the topic. For example, have students draw pictures of themselves, or take a Polaroid picture, and paste it on the cover of the "Me Book." If students are older, they can put the book together after drawing and writing.

3. Brainstorm to decide what will go into the book (can use who, what, when, where, and why questions as a guide). The important aspect of this step is to get the students excited about wanting to draw and write about the topic. They also need to plan to keep the thread of the story.

4. Let students draw their stories on each page. If students have access to graphic software, they can use it for this approach.

5. Write captions on each page as the students tell what happened or let them write themselves.

---

[3]Vygotsky (1978), pp. 112–113.
[4]See Gillespie (1990) and Myers (1983) for further information on this approach.

6. Read one or more of the stories to the whole class. Let the students read to each other if they want to do so.

The Approach in Practice:
Writing through Pictures

Susan Drake implemented the Drawing as Prewriting approach with second-grade bilingual students. Of her five students, four were native Spanish-speakers and one spoke Khmer. They were all attending English-only mainstream classrooms, and had been recommended to work with Susan by their classroom teacher. Susan stated that three of the students had been recommended because they were considered bright and deserving of "extra attention." The other two students were sent to Susan because of low academic performance, especially in reading and writing. She felt that the Drawing as Prewriting approach would help these ESL learners, because they would be able to create a story in pictures first that would alleviate problems with immediately thinking about word structure and vocabulary. By drawing pictures first, the students would be able use them as a guide for writing exactly what they wanted to express.

Susan began using the approach by reading to the students a book she had written about herself. They discussed the book and the students then proceeded to fold a paper into a book shape and drew pictures about themselves and their families. Susan purposely did not explain the approach to the students, because she wanted to see what they produced on their own with no pre-stated purpose or introduction. The students were able to write information about themselves modeling some of their ideas after Susan's book, but also including some other personal information about their own families. By having the students write a book about themselves in the first session, Susan was able to learn a bit about each student and the students' backgrounds.

Susan began the second class by reading a passage from *When I Was Young in the Mountains* by Cynthia Rylant. She discussed the meaning of memory with the children, and then had them think about their own memories and wrote the students' comments on the board. At first, none of the students could remember anything about their past, until Jonathan remembered his family's Easter celebration. This prompted the other students to remember past family celebrations. This discussion led the students to think about other events with their families. Seroeut remembered a time when he went to the beach and his brother pretended to drown him. Then, Jonathan spoke about a mountain climbing trip he took during winter vacation.

With some assistance from Susan for ideas, each student began to draw a picture of something that had happened to him or her in the past and then wrote something to go with the drawing. It was still difficult for two of the students, Nestor and Elvin, who did not seem to grasp the idea of drawing about an actual event. Elvin had drawn a helicopter, but when Susan asked if he had ever been in one, he responded that he had not. After a discussion with Susan about his vacation, he began drawing a picture of a baseball game he played with his cousin.

When she first started using the approach, the students orally told elaborate stories to go with their drawings, but only wrote one or two simple sentences that often did not seem to match their drawings. This discrepancy seemed to dissipate over time as the students gradually were able to use their drawings to help write their stories. Alex, for example, had very limited verbal skills in English. However, when he was able to draw a picture first, and then describe what was happening in it, he was able to develop more complex sentences and coherent stories. He needed the drawing to help him develop his written ideas.

During the sessions, the students were allowed and often encouraged to share and discuss their ideas and stories with each other. When they first began the project, they were reluctant to talk or work together. They did not seem to understand the value of sharing ideas. They often covered their papers and would not let anyone, except Susan, see what they had drawn or written. Two students, Alex and Nestor, especially had difficulty working together. They were both brainstorming ideas about animals, but did not want to help each other with those ideas. Gradually, both boys began to see the positive aspects of working out ideas together. Several weeks into the project, the students were doing so well coming up with their own topics and ideas, that they sometimes rejected those suggested by Susan.

The students also had difficulty listening to the texts written by their classmates and contributing helpful comments about the work. Elvin was the first student to read his story. Susan modeled a response to Elvin's story, commenting on what she had liked about it, hoping that another student would want to add something. This, however, did not happen, and Susan had to ask the other students for their opinions. Sarouet offered a suggestion, but the other students had nothing to say. They seemed more concerned with working on their own stories and did not welcome comments or suggestions from the others.

Susan found that the process of sharing ideas and offering helpful comments grew as the students became more confident in their abilities to create their own topics and stories. In one such instance, Elvin did not seem to understand what he had to do. Sarouet showed Elvin his own list of ideas, and then made several suggestions to Elvin, including topics that

Sarouet knew would interest his friend, such as Ninja Turtles. Elvin happily began writing his list, and even contributed ideas to other students.

Eventually, the students were able to offer constructive comments to each other, and the writers listened. After one person finished reading his or her story, each of the other students commented on something they liked about it, and offered a suggestion for a change or addition. The author then decided which, if any, of the suggestions would be used to improve the story.

Susan observed a natural shift from drawing as the precursor to writing, to drawing done second to writing. She noted that when she first began working with the students, all five started their stories by drawing first. Gradually, three of the five students wrote their stories first and then illustrated them. The written word replaced drawing as the initial symbol of ideas. For Alex, however, drawing was still needed to help him create ideas, although he was better able to elaborate in his writing. Susan also noticed an increase in sentences and more complex sentence structure in the stories of all the children as the sessions continued.

The growth in the ability to read and decode words was also developed during the drawing as prewriting sessions. Because Alex was unable to write the words for his stories, he dictated them to Susan. He was not able to read the words back to her, even though they were written exactly as he had dictated them and he did know the sounds for many of the letters. Susan decided to use the Word Card approach (see chap. 3) with Alex and another boy, Nestor, to see if that might help improve their sound—symbol reading ability. Alex did improve his reading ability as time went on. During one of the last sessions, he was able to read his story aloud. He even commanded two of the other students to sit down and listen to him. When he encountered problems in reading some words, the other children crowded around him to help.

This approach proved helpful to all the students in different ways. Some of the students were able to further develop their abilities to select topics and elaborate on their ideas. For others, like Alex, drawing as prewriting provided a means to help develop ideas first in a nonverbal way, so that writing down the ideas later became easier.

MAILBOX GAME

Purpose

The Mailbox Game gives a real-life context for the children's natural desire to write each other notes in class. Letter writing provides an opportunity for the students to write for a genuine purpose to a specific audience. In a bilingual classroom, students are given the freedom of language choice. When used in a second-language context, students are able to work at their individual levels of proficiency. It allows all students to communicate with each other and get to know each other, helping in the formation of a classroom community. Letter writing can be expanded outside the classroom. One teacher had her 6th grade students writing to members of the school staff. This supported the whole school community. Hadaway had second language learners writing to native speakers. The project touched all content areas by creating activities related to the language of the letters, the place of origin of the penpals, as well as shared research activities.[5]

Materials

Materials for the Mailbox Game include the following:

1. One large cardboard box made into a mailbox. You can cover it with blue construction paper and put U.S. Mail in red letters. (This step can be skipped with secondary students.)
2. Individual mailboxes for students and teacher (including teacher assistant, student teachers, etc.) with each person's name written on it. This can be done with liquor cartons containing dividers.
3. Note paper, pencils or pens, and some kind of sealer (stapler, gummed stickers, scotch tape).
4. Literature based on letters. For example Early Childhood (K–2): *Dear Peter Rabbit; Yours Truly: Goldilocks; The Jolly Postman; Dear Dragon; Toot & Puddle; Frog and Toad Are Friends.* Upper Elementary (3–5): *Dear Mr. Henshaw; Love, from the 5th grade celebrity; The long, long letter; The Gardener; Querido Pedrín* Middle School (5–8): *Dear Mr. President: Theodore Roosevelt: Letters from a young coal miner. Abraham Lincoln: Letters from a young slave girl; Griffen & Sabine: An Extraordinary Correspondence.* High School (9–12): *Keep in touch: Letters, Notes and More from the Sisterhood of the Traveling Pants* and *The Color Purple.*[6]

---

[5]See Hadaway (1992) for further information on this approach.
[6]See LeVine (2002) for additional suggestions.

Procedure

Procedures for the Mailbox Game include the following:

1. Introduce students to the concept and format of letters. Explain the different options for the salutation and closing of letters.
2. Read books with letter-writing related themes (see suggested list above).
3. Explain to the students that they can write each other letters or notes when they have some free time. They should "mail" them in the large mailbox. You should also write notes or letters, especially if you want to communicate something to the student, such as: "I was sorry to hear that your mother was sick today . . ." or "I saw you reading 'x' book, did you like it? . . ." Initially, it might be prudent to establish a rule that a student must respond to all letters received to ensure that students who write letters in turn receive letters.
4. One student is nominated the mail carrier (for the day or the whole week). At a set time, the "mail carrier" delivers the letters to the boxes with the appropriate name. This should be done while the other students are busy working on something else.
5. Allow students to pick up their mail without disrupting other activities, for instance, after lunch, or snack (just as people do when working in an office, and so forth).

If students have trouble reading because they are beginners, they can ask the author for clarification. You should not correct spelling or anything else in these letters. If students want to ask how to write something, you can help or teach them how to use the dictionary.

The Approach in Practice: You've Got Mail!

Milissa Tilton implemented the Mailbox Game with a fourth-grade two-way Spanish—English bilingual classroom. The students were a mixture of native English-speakers and native Spanish-speakers who had been together in the two-way bilingual program since kindergarten. She felt that this form of writing would allow the students the opportunity to write for a real purpose on topics that they had chosen to an audience that they had selected. She also believed that it would satisfy their natural desire to communicate with each other and provide an opportunity for building and fostering relationships within the classroom. The educational goals for the project included encouraging better friendships and relationships among classmates, helping students express themselves through writing, improving writing skills, and encouraging students to take more risks in writing creatively and with more details.

Milissa introduced the idea of the Mailbox game to the students. She explained that by writing letters they might get to know their classmates better, and learn the process of letter writing in a purposeful and fun way. The elements of letter writing (date, salutation, body, closing, etc.) were explained to the students. Appropriate and inappropriate topics were also discussed. Students were encouraged to write in both English and Spanish. Samples of letters were written in both languages and displayed on a bulletin board. The single rule established in the program was that if a person received a letter from someone, he or she was obligated to return a letter to that person.

A different person was chosen each week to be the mail deliverer, another to stamp the letters. Class meetings were held weekly so that the students could ask questions about or voice opinions of the Mailbox Game. One student immediately expressed his unwillingness to participate in the project. Milissa encouraged him to try, but did not pressure him into joining the activity.

For a majority of the day, except for lunch, recess, and a 20-minute journal writing period first thing in the morning, the 37 students were divided into two groups (Latitude and Longitude), each working with a teacher. While one group was being instructed in Spanish, the other was working in English, then they alternated. Students did a lot of collaborative group work. For the Mailbox Game, the students were encouraged to write to someone in the group to which they did not belong (i.e., someone from Latitude would write to someone from Longitude).

Letter writing was scheduled as a homework project. However, very quickly it became apparent that some time was needed during the school day for students to write the letters. Students complained that they did not have time after school to write letters because they were busy with homework and other activities. The students were then allowed to work on their letters during the 20-minute journal-writing period. Later, when students became enthusiastic about the project, they wrote letters both during and after school.

The students were given a week to write the letters. Forty-three letters were written during the first week. The teachers made sure that everyone had received at least one letter. If a student did not have a letter, a teacher wrote to the student. Later on, when the mail carriers noticed that some students had not received a letter, they wrote one to them, so their feelings were not hurt.

The students wrote about many topics: friendship, qualities that made the person a good friend, memories of time shared together, music, TV shows, and sports. Elizabeth wrote a letter to Vilmaris about activities that were happening in the class. She was very excited about the duck eggs that were going to hatch. She also wrote about a contest the class was having on naming the capitals of the states, and explained how she was going to try to learn all the capitals.

Most of the letters written that week were in English, however, four were written in Spanish by native Spanish-speakers, and two were written in Spanish by native English-speakers. The letters written by the native English-speakers were addressed to native speakers of Spanish. These students were aware of their audience and had decided to write in that person's first language.

Although errors in the letters were not corrected, Milissa did comment to the class as a whole on the content of the letters, appropriate styles, complete addresses, dates, and salutations. She encouraged the students to refer to the bulletin board display that showed samples of letters and addresses in both languages.

As the weeks progressed, the number of letters sent and received increased. In the eighth week of the project, 132 letters had been written. The students showed progress in selecting topics, increasing creativity, and in the general length of their letters. Some students included poems in their letters, or verses from favorite songs, and another student reflected on the math lesson of the day and included examples of what he had learned. Students wrote to each other about science projects they were doing, and discussed a book that the class had just finished reading. Some students began to personalize their stationery with stickers, stamps, and colorful decorations. Other students wrote letters on their computers at home. Enthusiasm for writing the letters was high. Some students came to school without their homework, but had written a letter! The student, who had initially refused to write letters, finally in the seventh week, after having received a letter from a teacher, wrote back to the teacher, and then to eight other students. Apparently, the enthusiasm of the other students receiving letters had shown him that the only way to get letters was to write them.

The students improved in both their technical aspects of letter writing as well as writing in general. Milissa set the expectation of high standards by reminding students of proper letter-writing techniques during the project. Some of the students also helped each other by writing about grammar mistakes found in letters. Ed, in particular, showed a marked improvement in his format. When first writing his letters, he did not use a salutation, closing, or date. After a few lessons on letter-writing formats,

Ed began to include the opening and closing sections to his letters. By the end of the 8-week project, most of the letters sent by the students had the date and a proper salutation and closing.

The Mailbox Game was a wonderful opportunity for the students to improve friendships, establish new ones, and increase sensitivity to others. A new friendship was formed between a native Spanish-speaking boy and a native English-speaking boy who had not socialized with each other previously. They wrote faithfully to each other in 7 of the 8 weeks, sharing information about each other and their families. Two girls, one native Spanish-speaker and the other a native English-speaker also corresponded, writing half their letter in English and the other half in Spanish. They praised each other for the progress each was making in her second language. Later in the school year, a new student entered the class. She received eight letters from students during her first week telling her how happy they were that she was in their class, inviting her to eat lunch with them and play with them during recess. One girl, who seemed to have difficulty relating socially to the other children in class, was encouraged by letters from the teachers to write to some of the girls in class. She did write to three girls, and then continuously corresponded with them.

Students were able to share joys, problems, and frustrations with each other. At the beginning of the project, one student was writing about her favorite food. By the end, she was writing about moving to a new neighborhood and how the change had affected her. The letter writing also had an influence in some of the students' homes. One mother encouraged her son to begin writing letters to some of his relatives.

The experience was also incorporated into the standard curriculum. Students wrote a business letter to tourist bureaus in different states requesting information on their state. Another letter was sent to museum tour guides thanking them for their assistance on a recent field trip. Some wrote letters while portraying a character from a book they were reading. From the experiences the children had in the Mailbox Game, these "authentic" letters were well written because the students understood to whom they were writing and the purpose of the letter.

At the end of the project, students were asked to reflect on their experiences. Students related that they enjoyed the letter writing because it gave them the opportunity to get to know their friends better. They complained about receiving letters that were messy or not long enough. Some students expressed a feeling of being overwhelmed at times at the number of letters to which they needed to respond. One student suggested that a limit be set for the number of letters sent. Others suggested that each student should write at least once to everyone in the class. Yet others proposed having one partner with whom to write back and forth for a scheduled period of time, and then changing to another person.

The Mailbox Game can be contagious. One student said that she was going to be a teacher when she grew up, and that she would like to "steal" the idea of the Mailbox Game. Another student wrote:

> I really like writing letters. I like to write letters, but I like to get them even more. There isn't anything about writing letters that I don't like. Sometimes I do not have enough time to write, but I try. I start the letter at home and then I finish it either at home or at school. I think letter writing is a great idea because you get to talk to many different people in the class. Even my mom thinks it's a great idea. She thinks she will do it with her class if that is alright with you.

DIALOGUE JOURNALS

Purpose

Dialogue Journal acts as a bridge between oral interaction and the development of composing by providing students the opportunity of a written conversation with a teacher. The journal provides a natural, purposeful means of writing for students. There are no requirements regarding topic and students' writing is not corrected or evaluated. The normal unequal status of teacher and students is minimized, because both parties are equally engaged in the interaction, introducing and elaborating on topics, and so forth. One person does not dominate or control the interaction with directives and questions. The teacher is involved in the content of the interaction, as are the students.

This approach is particularly helpful for bilingual learners when they enter a new class because it enhances their relationship with their teacher, and it provides an individual forum for their needs, such as advice on how to deal with the new culture, problems they are having in classes, specific language concerns, and other helpful hints. In a situation in which they have to express themselves in the second language, students are given time to think about appropriate expression. Oral interaction is often too pressured and spontaneous.

When the teacher is bilingual, there should be flexibility in choice of language. Often students like to codeswitch. One English-speaking teacher who had some knowledge of Spanish, allowed a beginner to write in Spanish introducing the entry with a short statement in English that would help the teacher focus on the topic. She was able to understand and respond in English.

It is important to explain to families the private nature of these journals and the need to respect this privacy. Children sometimes write about personal problems that need to be kept personal. Nicole Montague[7] discussed the aspect of privacy with parents at the beginning of the year.[8]

Materials

Materials needed are a notebook, in which students will write, or a compact disk (CD) or flash drive if using the computer.

Procedure

1. Tell students that:
   a. their Dialogue Journal is a place where they and you will talk about anything they want to talk about;
   b. the journals will not be evaluated or graded in any way;
   c. the journals are private and no one else will read them.
2. Provide each student with a notebook or disk that should be kept in the classroom.
3. A brief handout may be given to older students to clarify concepts and any other requirements. For example, you might want to explain that journal writing will help them write better and will not be used for grading purposes; that it is a confidential correspondence between the two writers. You can also include some basic instructions such as including the date on all entries or writing on only one side of the paper. Some teachers require a minimum number of lines be written.

   If teaching an elementary self-contained class, have students read their journals (your responses to their previous entries) first, then give them time to write their responses. Allow them to return to the journal during the day if they have more to say to you. For high school students, journal writing can be done in class or for homework.
4. Encourage students to write to you about real issues that are important to them, seeking or giving genuine information, solving problems, and so forth. Participants are free to choose topics as they

---

[7]Montague (1995).

[8]See Freeman and Freeman (1989), D'Angelo Bromley (1989), Kreeft Peyton (1990), Montague (1995), Reyes (1991), and Stanton (1988) for further information about this approach.

become important, without fear of censure. You should never pre-determine the topics.

5. Communicate frequently and continuously, at least once a week for at least a couple of months. Although, every day for the whole academic year is optimal, it should be done only as frequently as it is possible to respond to students. Don't overdo it.

6. Keep the communication private. This will help students feel free to express themselves and not fear correction or exposure. Journals become confidence builders and emotional outlets for students experiencing difficulties.

7. Your responses should show interest in what the students have to say. Focus on meaning, not form. Do not correct when responding. It is better to write short responses with few questions. Seek only to clarify meaning. You should ask questions when meaning is unclear. You may model in your responses the correct form of mistakes that appeared in students' entries.

The Approach in Practice—Getting to Know You: Dialogue Journals in Middle School Classroom

Dialogue Journal writing was done by Katherine Darlington's seventh- and eighth-grade Transitional Bilingual Education (TBE) class. The students, who were all native Spanish-speakers, were at various levels of English proficiency. Katherine felt that Dialogue Journals would help her students write for purposeful reasons. Additionally, because her students were at many different levels of English proficiency, Katherine believed that dialogue journals would allow her to individualize the English learning needs of each student.

Katherine introduced Dialogue Journals to her students and explained that they would be writing in the journals twice a week. They were told that they could write about anything, and could write as much as they wanted as long as they had written at least five lines. The students were free to write in either English or Spanish. She responded to the journal entry in the same language. Initially, Katherine scheduled 10 minutes for the journal writing, but soon discovered that some students needed more time to write, so she created a more flexible schedule, allowing students to write for a longer period of time. Those students who finished early worked on an assignment quietly so that the journal writers could continue uninterrupted. Katherine found that the best time for her students to write in their journals was early morning because they were more enthusiastic and there were fewer interruptions. This also allowed her time during the day to respond to the journal entries.

Most of the students were interested in writing in the journals, some even expressing dismay at not being able to finish them in the allotted time. It was for this reason that Katherine allowed students who wanted to continue to do so while other students worked silently for a time on other assignments. Students were also able to write, if they so desired, at other times during the day.

Katherine enthusiastically read all the journal entries that first night. She reported that the next day several students greeted her and stopped to talk before school. She felt as if the students were more trusting of her because she now knew something secret about them, and yet she was still there smiling at them, accepting them for who they were.

The students' development during journal writing varied. Some students seemed to enjoy the process and their entries became longer and more focused, whereas others were still hesitant to share more personally even after several weeks. Katherine did observe that, through her responses to the journal entries, some students were able to write in a more personal, meaningful way. For example, one of the students had only written, "Sorry, have nothing to write." Katherine responded:

> *Do you know I was really surprised to hear you reading in Science today.*
> *Your English is improving very quickly.*
> *How do you like your new seating assignment?*

The student's next journal entry was as follows:

> *I like it, thank you for changing because I was angry with Sharon. and I was going to get in trouble, if I stay near her.*

Some students changed from always complaining about something to asking personal, thoughtful questions of Katherine. One student wrote:

> *What will you say if your sun [son] was in this*
> *shichashon [situation] you wont tell him the same thing*
> *yes or no – why.*

Another student was able to talk about problems she was experiencing since her mother had left home. This student had never spoken to Katherine on such a personal level.

Katherine did an analysis of the topics covered by the students in their journals. The journals were used to question, inform, request, apologize, thank, and report. Results showed that students wrote most about peer and family relationships and self-reflection. Family situations were the most prevalent, followed by conflicts or misunderstandings among friends. They also addressed school subjects, highlights of their school day, and other topics related to their own lives.

The students were asked to complete an evaluation of the Dialogue Journal approach. The evaluation was divided into three parts: self-evaluation, assessment of method, and assessment of teacher's responses. Students indicated that they had learned something from the Dialogue Journals. Many expressed the positive experiences of journal writing such as:

- "getting my feelings out"
- ". . . you gave me insights"
- ". . . I could tell the thing that happen to me to a person I trust"
- ". . . I finally find someone to tell about me and want happen around me"

For the assessment of teacher, Katherine asked the students to evaluate her responses to their entries. Eight students responded that the correspondence was "just about right." Two students felt that Katherine's responses were too short.

In evaluating the success of the method, Katherine felt that the Dialogue Journal approach increased the personal interactions and built a higher level of trust between teacher and student. Because the students were allowed to use either Spanish or English, they were better able to communicate effectively. She also felt that she learned a lot about her students through the journals. Katherine also saw attitudinal changes in the students regarding school and peers. For Katherine, the Dialogue Journal approach was an excellent medium of meaningful, functional communication.

RHETORICAL APPROACH

Purpose

The rhetorical approach is one instructional strategy that supports the writing process. This approach walks learners through the writing process attending to each step in more detail than other process approaches. This process not only helps the students but also orients teachers to the aspects of writing that students have internalized and those that are still a challenge. Bilingual learners' experiences and knowledge about writing vary a great deal. A large number of students tend to be unfamiliar with the expectations of how to carry out writing assignments in American school systems. The rhetorical approach allows for student creativity in each step but scaffolds the process. These scaffolds support the development of writing habits that encourage planning of the content, and choice of purpose, audience, and genre. By breaking the writing process in small steps the teacher has the opportunity to support language development needed for rich writing. This approach can be implemented with different grade levels because the topic and the literary genre will make it more or less difficult. Thus, Mary, a first grade teacher, used it for personal narratives while Liz, a fourth grade teacher used it for non-fiction text, and Valerie used it for argumentative essays with her high school students. Even within a class Liz let two students write narratives because their level of English made it harder to do social studies research.[9]

Procedure

To conduct the Rhetorical approach:

1. Choose and explore the topic. Choose a general topic or have the class choose a topic. Ask students to write a page on this topic (anything they want). Tell them it will not be seen or corrected. Let them discuss in groups what they each wrote about. You can also brainstorm with the whole class.

2. Define the purpose and audience. Have them discuss and list possible reasons for writing about the topic and the different kinds of audiences they would write for. Have them choose one of the situations and audiences. (Either the whole class chooses one, or each group chooses one.)

3. Narrow the topic. Have them discuss and list subtopics from general to particular given the decision made in Step 2.

4. Consider genre and organization. Have them discuss and decide on the genre and organization, considering the content, purpose, and audience they have in mind. For example if the topic is "Penguins," and the purpose is to instruct about them, and the audience is kindergarten students, students may want to write a story that includes factual information about penguins. However, if students decide to write it for their principal to show how much they know about it, they would write an informational paper or booklet.

---

[9]For more information see Brisk, Horan, and MacDonald (forthcoming); Carson, J. F., and Leki, I. (Eds.) (1993); de Alvarado, 1984); Johnson, D. M., and Roen, D. H. (Eds.) (1989).

5. Select information and ideas to be included within each subtopic. Decide specifically what fits given the genre, audience, and purpose.

6. Write the draft. Based on Steps 3, 4, and 5, students write drafts individually. (This can be done in class or as homework.) If the project is long, it can be subdivided so that students or groups are responsible for writing specific sections. The teacher can be available for any questions. Have bilingual dictionaries and grammars available.

7. Revise and Edit Draft. Groups form again to help revise and edit each other's work. The teacher can prepare some questions for the students or he or she can do it with each group to show them how to look at a draft. Clarity of content and organization should be the first order of priority, then comes vocabulary, grammar, punctuation, and spelling.

8. Produce the final copy. Each group is responsible for working on either a group or individual final copy.

9. Publish students' writing. The teacher should look for opportunities for publishing students' writing. Opportunities can include a book for the school library, the school newspaper or a magazine, a district newsletter, or a local paper or contest.

The Approach in Practice: From Mundane Lists to Rich Narratives

Mary Jacques, a first grade teacher, was having trouble getting her students to stick to a chosen topic during writers' workshop. While students had the opportunity to choose their own topics, it was expected that they write stories on those topics everyday including a beginning, a middle, and an end. Mary found that many of the students wrote their stories as a list, usually starting with something that happened first thing in the morning, mentioning their "topic" in the middle and then ending with going to bed.

During a January writing session Peter chose to write about basketball, his story read like this:

> On Saturday I woke up.
> Then I brushed my teeth.
> Then I went to the YMCA.
> I played basketball.
> My team is the Bulls. We won.
> Then I went home and went to bed.

Each sentence was on a separate piece of paper.

Most of Mary's students wrote in this style. As a school the staff had agreed to try to improve the topic and idea development in student writing—an ongoing problem for the whole school as indicated on school wide standardized assessments. Mary decided to try the rhetorical approach to address topic development in writing. Because this was a classroom wide writing issue, and because these students were first graders, she decided to try this approach with the whole class in a shared writing effort.

As a class the students explored possible topics. Amaryi wanted to write about recess. Todd wanted to write about the student teacher. Al wanted to write about gym class. Cori wanted to write about the lunchroom. As students explored many topics the class could write about, Mary wrote these ideas down on chart paper. After a brief discussion, "gym class" seemed to be most popular. She then had them turn and talk to a partner about what they could write about concerning "gym class," and to think about *why* (purpose) they might write this and to think about *who* (audience) might want to read it.

Mary wrote down some of the students' ideas—"we could write a play and act it out for the other first grade"; "we could write an alphabet book, each one of us taking a letter and coming up with a word from gym and give it to the kindergarten"; "we could write a letter to Mr. Marshall (pseudonym), the gym teacher, telling him why gym was our favorite thing." That was it. The class decided they wanted to write a letter to the gym teacher. He would read it, and might even write back!

The next day, Mary drew a web type graphic organizer on the chart paper and had the students brainstorm what they might like to say in the letter. The possible suggestions came out in this order: "We miss you. Playing basketball was so much fun. Thank you for teaching us how to play 'wonderball'." "Have you thought up any new games lately?" "Do you remember when we were playing 'wonderball' and Chi got a bloody nose because the ball hit him in the face?" "Will you write back to us?"

After collecting the suggestions from the students Mary read aloud to them what they had said, and asked the class how they thought the letter sounded. Amaryi commented that "the word could go together better." Mary suggested they reorganize the web by numbering the sentences in the best order. She asked the class for suggestions on the ordering.

During the next class session Mary copied what was on the web onto the chart paper in a letter format.

Dear Mr. Marshall:

Thank you for teaching us how to play wonderball. That game is so much fun. Did you invent it? Do you remember the time when we were playing 'wonder-

ball' and Chi got a bloody nose because the ball hit him in the face? Have you
thought up any new games lately? Write back soon.

From, Room 106

Mary read the letter aloud to the class and they decided it was perfect. As
a class they delivered the letter to Mr. Marshall.

During the next several class sessions Mary had students working on
their individual writing projects using this approach. Students brainstormed topics and ways they might approach the topic. They discussed
this with a writing partner. They went on to create a graphic organizer
and then produced a rough draft and a final copy. Through individual
and group writing conferences, Mary was able to help steer them in the
right direction. In May, Peter wrote his final piece of writing for the year.
He followed the steps of the rhetorical approach in his work:

Last Saturday a strange cat got in my house. It ran into the closet. My dad tried
to chase it out with a broom but the cat didn't budge. I looked in the closet and I
could see the cat's eyes glowing green and red. My dad put on his yellow wash-
ing gloves and turned on the closet light. He grabbed the strange cat by the neck
and threw it outside.

PROCESS WRITING: COMPUTERS

Purpose

Using the writing process students create their writing with the support
of the teacher and classmates. Writing is not a quick product but it is the
result of a well thought process where the author receives feedback from
others. Computers have become an important tool in the writing process.
Revision is basic to good writing, and computers greatly facilitate that
process. Students are more willing to revise when using a word processing program. Printed work looks neat. Even small children's writing has
a book-like appearance. By responding to text written on the computer
screen, teachers of second-language learners are able to correct and explain mistakes, or suggest alternative ways of writing something while
the students are working on the piece. Students are able to immediately
interact with the teacher to ensure complete understanding of what needs
to be revised. The use of the Internet permits students to share their work
beyond the classroom. Exchanges with native speakers of the language
helps second language learners expand the social context in which they

learn the language and as a result they get a broader range of language forms, vocabulary, and expression. Cummins and Sayers found that students' writing "shared with an unknown but knowable faraway audience through the use of classroom technologies — served to foster the discipline and commitment students needed to master the difficult reading and writing skills required" in an academic setting (p. 129). Friedman, Zibit, and Coote used the internet to pair a high school English class — with a number of bilingual learners — and a college Secondary English methods course. The high school students shared their writing with the pre-service teachers who in turn scaffolded the revision process. As a result of the telementoring program and the increased use of computers, students focused more on the revision process. Students benefited from the feedback received from the pre-service teachers and attended to grammatical and spelling errors through multiple drafts.[10]

Procedure

I. Language Choice and Use

Allow students who are beginning to develop writing to choose the language in which they want to write. When students have to write in a particular language, allow them to use either language during planning and drafting to facilitate the flow of ideas. This is especially true when working in a weaker language. For example, when they can't remember a word in one language, they can write it in the other and later look for the equivalent. If they don't know how to start a paper in the second language, let them write it quickly in their native language and then they can try it in their second language. (More proficient speakers usually prefer to do everything in one language.)

II. Genre and Topic Choice

1. Encourage students to write a variety of literary genres, such as narratives, expository pieces, poems, jokes, letters, songs, plays, and so on.
2. Allow the students to choose their own topics. Alternatively, pairs, groups, or the whole class can write about the same topic.

---

[10]Cummins and Sayers (1995); Friedman, Zibit, and Coote (2004). See also Brisk (1985), Daiute (1985), Forcier (1996), Kinginger (2000) for additional ideas on using the computer for writing.

3. Topics for writing can emerge in a number of ways, such as:

    a. Brainstorm with the class suggestions for topics, write them on
        the board, overhead, or directly on the computer using a word
        processing program. You can use the whole list or have the class
        choose 10 topics about which they think they would like to
        write. Make a list and paste one copy on the left hand page of
        each file folder. (If using the computer, copy the file with the list
        of topics onto each diskette.)

    b. If using Process Writing in connection with content area, choose
        general topics that must be covered in the content area curricu-
        lum, and the students individually, in pairs, or groups, can re-
        search and write on one topic. For example, if the general topic
        is insects, each student researches and writes about one particu-
        lar insect.

    c. As a follow-up to reading, ask students to write something com-
        parable (e.g., after reading a fable, have students write a story in
        which one character outsmarts the other).

    d. Ask students to write about the topic that was discussed in a
        sharing time or discussion session, or related to a field trip.

    e. If your students keep a journal, have them circle topics of inter-
        est in their journal and have them write about one.

Any activity that stimulates ideas can then be followed up by writing
about it. The less advanced your students are, the less restrictive the topic
selection should be. It is easier to write about something the students
know and want to express, than about a topic chosen by somebody else
that may be unfamiliar or uninteresting to the writer.

III. Planning for Writing

Several approaches are good to prepare your students to write a particular piece. This is a time to let the learners speak up about the topic.
Ideas should be clarified, vocabulary provided, and further reading may
be appropriate. Semantic Mapping, Drawing As Prewriting, reading, researching in the library or through the Internet, interviewing, generating
questions, finding answers, sharing time and discussion can all help stimulate ideas for students. They can then begin to organize them for the
writing. Also, just writing down everything the learner knows about the
topic can be an alternative. This step can be done individually, in small
groups, or with the whole class. If students have writer's block, talk to

them about things you know interest them, have them read something, or listen to other students' pieces.

Help students define audience, purpose, and genre. For example, use stories to teach reading to younger students, descriptions to explain to a sister class abroad about their town, and so on.

If the class needs to go to a different room to use computers, do brainstorming, semantic mapping, and other prewriting activities on chart paper, which can then be taken to the computer room to be hung up.

IV. Drafting

Drafting and planning are recursive. As students start drafting, they may decide they need to reorganize, read, and research more about the subject. A good practice is to begin drafting by writing for about 10 minutes without interrupting each other. The length of time can vary depending on the age of the learners. You can use this time to also write. Then walk around the room interacting with students. Allow students to consult among themselves. At this stage, students can use either language. Allow students to do their first draft either on the computer or with pencil and paper. Although when they use the computer it is easier to consult with the teacher and classmates because both have better view of the text.

V. Revision

Revisions can be done in pairs, groups, or as a whole class. Students work on one persons' draft. The author reads aloud his or her piece and entertains comments and questions of the other students. Pairs or small groups can sit around one computer to comment on that person's piece. Or students can look at a printed copy. If the teacher has access to a projector, a piece can be projected from the computer for whole class review. Often at this point, the author notices things he or she wants to change. Model how to direct comments to the content and organization. The audience is there to offer suggestions and comment positively on the author's writing. You may want to go first to model the process, including suggestions for changes. It is very common for the author, while reading aloud, to make specific changes. The choice of working in pairs, small groups or whole class depends on the age and personality of the students. Revision focuses on content and organization. Is the content accurate and complete? Does it make sense? Is it appropriate for the audience? Does it follow the organization that the particular genre requires? Demands on revision increase as the students become more experienced writers.

Once students are used to the process, you can have different groups working at different stages of the process. For example, while one group is working on the first draft, another group is revising their first draft, while a third is rewriting their initial draft. These groups *should not* be formed by ability. Move around to help, especially the students who are revising.

VI. Editing

Students produce several partially revised drafts that they keep in their folder and share with you. Periodically, have them choose one piece to develop further and edit to perfection to get published. Editing follows the same procedure as revision, but focuses on grammar, punctuation, and spelling. Many of these errors, however, get corrected while revising for meaning. Use students' errors as the source for needed lessons.

VII. Publishing

Students continue to work to produce a final draft for publication. Each student should decide when the final draft is ready. Stories can be collated into a book with covers, title, date, author and publisher. These books are featured in the classroom lending library. Other places for publication are newsletters, bulletin boards, or web pages. Letters are mailed out to real people, and so on. Let students illustrate either by hand, or by using software programs that produce illustrations.

Routines and structure get students in the habit of writing. For example, students can write one story or paper a week, or they can write for a minimum of 30 minutes each day. If students want to write more, they should not be stopped. Writing is developmental; both the ability to write and to revise will get better with more writing and revising. Therefore, one cannot expect the first final drafts to be perfect. (You need to make this point clear to parents and administrators.) Students should store all their drafts with the date, so that their development over time can be observed.

Tips for better utilization of the computers for Process Writing:

- Have students learn how to touch type.
- For very young children, draw a large keyboard with the capital letters and their corresponding small letter.
- As a reference for those frequently used software programs that are written only in English, it is helpful to write their basic directions

on a poster board in the native language and hang it in the computer area.

- To motivate students, print their first product immediately, even if it is something they have dictated.

The Approach in Practice—Teacher's Responses to Bilingual Students' Writing: The Computer Changes the Process

Charles Skidmore, an ESL high school teacher, adapted his teaching style to incorporate the use of the computer in his writing classes. For 16 Vietnamese- and Spanish-speaking students from Grades 9 to 12, computers became an important element in their writing process.

The students, who were all in Charles' advanced ESL class, had a wide range of writing abilities. They met three times a week in the classroom and twice a week in the computer lab. There were 16 computers and 2 printers in the lab. Students worked on the written piece both in the classroom and in the computer lab.

Topics for the writing assignments were introduced through readings and classroom discussions. Charles integrated the teaching of all aspects of language skills (i.e., reading, writing, speaking, and listening), to interesting topics. He also helped the students become familiar with American literature and themes of Western civilization by relating the ideas to the students' own cultural experiences. For example, Charles introduced the play *The Glass Menagerie* to the students by suggesting that its theme was escape. He then asked the students what escape meant to them. Students were then asked to write an autobiographical essay about escape. After having explored escape through their own experiences, the students read *The Glass Menagerie* and did a character analysis and wrote summaries of the plot. The unfamiliar literature of the new culture was introduced to the students by relating the topics to experiences that the students had had.

Issues and topics in Western civilization and American history were introduced in a similar fashion. The students' voices and experiences were expressed in the different genres of their writing.

Some students preferred to write a first draft by hand before working at the computers, whereas other students typed their drafts directly on the computer. Charles allowed for this flexibility. The students printed some of the drafts so that Charles could comment on them. However, Charles found that students understood his explanations better when he worked directly with them while they were writing at the computer. The final version was shared with the whole class.

Charles actively interacted with the students while they wrote on the computers. He answered questions, read aloud, asked probing questions, pointed out and discussed problems, or simply made a quick comment while walking by a student. Sometimes he focused on one problem or briefly answered questions; other times the interaction between him and the student required more time while together they revised or constructed a piece of writing.

These student–teacher interactions took place throughout every stage of the development of the written piece. The more insecure writers often checked before writing. Elizabeth was writing about the explorer Verrazano. Before writing, she called Charles:

E: What did he do?

C: He was sailing for France, even though he has an Italian name . . .

E: He was Italian, right?

C: Right, but he was sailing for France

E: What's his name?

C: Verrazano

Elizabeth, satisfied that she understood the basic information, went on to write that section of the paper.

Charles reviewed each stage of what most students wrote. Typically, he stopped by a student and read aloud what was on the computer screen. As he read, he pointed out problems and raised questions to help the student find a solution. After helping the student improve what was written so far, Charles gave some direction on how to continue. For example, Charles and Armando were reviewing what Armando had written about Laura, a character in *The Glass Menagerie*. Toward the end of the interaction Charles read aloud:

" . . . when Laura come to dinner . . . "

C: Do you want the present tense there?

A: came (making the change)

C: came . . . good! You're still not ready to end though, you still have to get the part that Laura falls in love and ends up being hurt by Jim. You can finish it up in a couple more sentences. Your basic ideas are there, but use the last 10 minutes to get the last idea, that this loving Jim, that being with him turns out to be very painful for her.

The students dictated the nature of the interaction. Werner usually liked to discuss completeness of content. Elizabeth, a less skillful writer, laboriously checked content, grammar, spelling, punctuation, and every detail of the piece. Charles sat by her side and they read together from the screen, stopping, discussing problems, and confirming every correction that she made.

Depending on the needs and the situation, Charles addressed the whole class, a group of students, or individuals. Normally, it was only at the beginning or end of the class period, and usually for general instruction purposes, that Charles spoke to the class as a whole. More than 90 percent of the interactions were done with individual students in response to specific language or content needs. With the beginning writers these interactions resembled the strategies used with young children developing language or second-language learners at the early stages of second-language development. Mercedes, an emergent writer, raised questions about Magellan while writing her research paper. Charles answered and carried on a long discussion to help her develop one sentence. (Underlining indicates the words that Mercedes decided to use in her final sentence.)

C: for Spain, right!

M: proved that the world was round

C: Explain to me a little bit more. How did he prove it, with a scientific experiment?

M: No

C: No, what did he do?

M: (unintelligible)

C: He and his crew . . . actually he died before he finished . . . but sailed . . . they were the first ones to sail all the way around. So . . . when you make a statement I want you to give me the next piece of information that proves it or shows how. So you can't just say he proved the world was round unless you tell me how. That's what these longer papers are about, a research paper, you are giving me that extra piece of information. I want something like He and his crew, you know crew?

M: yes

C: OK . . . were the first to sail

M: sail around the world

C: completely around the world. OK add it in.
(Mercedes wrote: "He and his crew were the first who sailed around the world for Spain.")

He helped Mercedes by asking probing questions, expanding her language, confirming her suggestions, and providing input that eventually became part of the student's own language. Bit by bit, whole sentences got constructed, using lots of the teacher's language.

Charles helped the students according to their needs. With Mercedes, he had to monitor the process of the initial writing. They made meaning together. With the more advanced students, he discussed the ideas and then left them to write on their own. When helping Armando, Charles raised the problem after reading aloud the text on the screen:

> **C:** (Armando had written "she is shy") . . . All right. You say the way she acts basically as a little girl, when you are telling this you can't just say she acts like it, you have to tell what it is that she does.
>
> **A:** (unintelligible)
>
> **C:** All right, so maybe that's where you want to go from there. What are the things that make her look like a little girl, what are her actions? (Charles started working with the next student.)

Armando wrote "She like to play to recores and play with the Animal glasses." (She liked to play records and play with the glass animals.)

Although most interactions were with individual students, there were times when more than one student took part in a discussion. On one occasion, Charles was discussing how to start a new piece with Tuyet. The sentence they decided on also appeared on Son's screen. Son was sitting at the computer next to Tuyet and had paid careful attention to the discussion. On another occasion, when Charles was helping Son find the appropriate word, Marcial, José, and Tuyet, who shared the same table, joined in the discussion.

Through all the discussions Charles had with the students, the main focus was meaning. Even when discussing other aspects of language, such as text cohesion, a grammatical mistake, or spelling, he showed how it obscured the meaning of what was written. As Charles was reading Them's paper aloud, he pointed to the screen and said:

> **C:** I want a transition here. You've been talking about the Greeks. You can't just start all of a sudden "In Rome . . ." You've got to tell me: As the Greek Empire faded . . . or ended or stopped . . . a new Empire arose, the new Roman Empire. Then you can tell this.

He not only told the student that he needed a transition, but discussed it in order to make sense from the whole text. At another time, as he was reading Tuyet's piece on the computer screen, Charles noticed that "reached" was missing the "ed." He said: reached . . . past tense . . . e, d, because it is past, it was a long time ago.

He read it as it was supposed to be, gave the grammatical explanation, spelled it, and also noted the semantic reason, attacking the problem from different linguistic levels.

With spelling problems, he often sounded out the word until the student figured out the correct spelling. However, besides focusing on sound – letter correspondence, Charles concluded with a brief semantic explanation. In that way, he tried to give students the message that the most important aspect of writing is to confer meaning.

Charles not only helped solve specific problems, but also enhanced the students' awareness of language, how it works, how text is organized, and the purpose of the pieces they were writing, thus developing the learners' metalinguistic awareness.

The responses to the students' work while writing on the computer were very different from the correction of writing done on paper. Traditionally, students write compositions that they hand in to the teacher to be corrected. The teacher then returns the corrected composition to the students, assuming that they read the comments written by the teacher. The teacher was the judge of the students' writing.

In the approach used by Charles, the relationship between teacher and student was more of an editor – writer, in which the teacher discussed problems with the students and together they reached a solution. Therefore, changes are negotiated rather than dictated by the teacher. These "negotiations" can be quite long, but because they are oral, they are quicker and less cumbersome than most written responses. Teachers spend between 20 and 40 minutes responding to each student's paper.[11] Charles, on the other hand, reached an average of 10 students in a 50-minute period. He was also able to use many other strategies not available in written responses, because of the ability to interact orally with the student.

The students often shared the printed drafts of their work with Charles. However, they often found the written comments ambiguous and requested clarification. Tomi called Charles because he had circled the word "widow" in the printed draft.

Tomi: Amanda is a widow?

C: She is not, because her husband is not

---

[11]See Zamel (1985).

Tomi: Not married

C: They are married. What makes a woman a widow?

Tomi: When a husband dies.

C: All right, but he is not dead; he left, but he is not dead

Tomi: So they are divorced.

C: They are divorced. Exactly. So she is a divorcee (he spells it while Tomi types. Tomi types "divorced") No. The person is called divorcee

Tomi: e,y?

C: No, e, e.

Through this 10-turn interaction, actual teaching was taking place. Tomi learned the difference between "widow" and "divorcee," as well as "divorcee" and "divorced."

Often students reacted negatively to Charles' written comments, whereas they were more accepting of his oral remarks. For example, Charles had returned comments he had made on Elizabeth's first printed draft. It had many correcting marks, making the paper look messy. There was a note stating: "Elizabeth, you did a very good job!" Nevertheless, Elizabeth asked Charles if she should throw away that version and start anew. It took some convincing to make her realize that the corrections were all minor ones, easily fixed. In contrast, during a previous session, she and the teacher had thoroughly revised another piece directly on the computer screen. Elizabeth painstakingly worked at improving it, never suggesting that maybe she should clear the file and rewrite the paper.

The students also, in some instances, seemed to conference better when they did it at their computers. Charles came to them, and stood at their side, so the students, in a sense, were still in charge of their piece, making the teacher's role that of a helper. Conferencing at the computer seemed less intimidating for some students.

The conferencing that did take place was highly individualized and accommodated to the language of the learner. The students set the agenda for the interactions, which were directed to the language needs of the moment. They focused mostly on content; on helping students make meaning. Charles patiently continued the interaction until the students arrived at what they wanted to say. Charles was also able to expand on the language of the beginning English students. He modeled correct language forms and confirmed correct usage. There was much talk about language and writing while the pieces were being revised.

Charles has found that using the computer in his writing process classes has changed the way he teaches writing. Before using the computer, students usually did their writing at home. They handed in their papers to Charles, who commented in writing; then the students produced a second, and usually final, version. Through the use of computers, the students write in class, actively interact with both teacher and other students, and revise their papers as many times as they want or need to. In this process they learn much about English and writing.

The students' writing and revising strategies greatly improved. Their questions became more sophisticated. They became more aware of reaching an audience with their writing and were more excited about publishing. They entered contests and submitted their work to school magazines and newspapers. Three students won honorable mention in a statewide essay contest. Charles had never entered students in the contest before. Using the computer as an integral part of the writing process converted the task of writing into a pleasurable activity for both Charles and his students.

4

Approaches with Focus on Reading

When teaching reading to bilingual learners there a number of considerations to keep in mind. Reading is not only a cognitive and psycholinguistic process but also a sociocultural endeavor. Readers must process the language from print to the reader's conceptual bank going through phonological, syntactic, and semantic processes.[1] During processing bilinguals have access to their two or more languages and may use aspects of one while reading in the other. Acquisition of reading is also influenced by community uses of reading and the cultural beliefs, attitudes, and uses of reading in families and communities.[2]

Learners must become emotionally engaged with the texts to become enthusiastic readers. Choosing texts that help spark interest in reading and strategies that help students go beyond the text to explore ideas and feelings increase interest in reading per se. Books that reflect students' cultural experiences engage students and their families (see Appendix B). When a class has students of many different cultures, it is not always possible to find books that reflect each of the students' background. Looking into the broader themes within the literature, however, can raise students' enthusiasm. For example, Angela read *Baseball Saved Us* with her Spanish-background students. Although the story is about a Japanese boy in the internment camps, students explored foreign relations and treatment of immigrants. These topics were very much part of their life experience. In addition, they became extremely interested in learning more about World War II.[3] This example also illustrates that reading literature

---

[1]See Birch (2002).

[2]Perez (1998).

[3]For full description of this lesson see Brisk, Burgos, and Hamerla (2004).

can be a good segue to develop interest in reading and to facilitate understanding expository writing.

Teachers may encounter three different situations when teaching
reading. Their students may be young learners being initiated to reading
in one or two languages, they may be literate in their heritage language
and need to learn to read in English, or they may be in upper elementary
or above needing to learn to read in any language. The easiest task is to
teach reading to a bilingual child who is already literate. All they need is
to learn to do it in a different language. Children either young or older
who are becoming literate, especially if it is done in their weaker language
have a much harder time. They need to be taught literacy as well as language. The approaches presented in this chapter can be adapted to various levels of proficiency and literacy ability.

When teaching reading, teachers must decide on the purpose, the
grouping, and the materials to be used. They should also make sure that
the purpose of reading is meaningful and connected to what students are
learning throughout the curriculum. Teachers should consider using materials found outside the school as instructional materials. Georgette, a
high school teacher, used the booklet to study for the driver's license test
with her high school second language students. The motivation to read
and understand the text was very high.

Choice of language to introduce reading is another decision that
teachers or programs need to make. Bilingual programs initiate reading
in the home language and then move to the second language. Other programs initiate students in both languages simultaneously. And yet others
start in the second language and then move to the first. The type of student and purpose of the program define the choices. Many classrooms,
however, start students in the second language and never introduce the
first because schooling is only in the second language and the personnel
are often not fluent in another language. In this case, sometimes families
teach literacy in the heritage language or send children to after school
programs to learn to read and write the family's language. The interaction
between the type of program and background of students presents different degrees of challenges. For example, it is easiest to introduce reading
in the strongest language to a young student who comes from a literate
family and it is hardest to teach reading in the second language to older
students with limited literacy background. Teachers often do not have a
choice and have to adjust to the context in which they are teaching. It is
recommended that teachers seek help from volunteers and college students to support their efforts (see chap. 8). Even when teachers use the
second language, they can take advantage of the heritage language to
check comprehension and discuss the text. If teachers do not know the

---

Suggestions for First Year English Learners

- Have books available in the L1 of the students. Bilingual books (in the students' L1 and English) are also helpful.
- Have students draw major events of a story as a way of retelling it.
- Have students match words, phrases, or sentences to pictures of story read.
- Write sentences having to do with story problem or main idea on sentence strips. Cut the sentence into its individual words. Have students put words in order to reform the sentence.
- Partner a less proficient English speaker with a more proficient English reader when reading.
- Introduce important vocabulary words/concepts prior to reading. Provide drawings or pictures to support the learning of the new words/concepts.
- Have a volunteer who speaks the L1 explain key point of the reading to the student.
- Do Cross-Age projects (see this chapter) pairing older and younger students of the same language background
- Increase wait time for beginning English readers to respond.
- Allow students to respond in their L1 if other students can translate.

---

native language, they can let the students use it or arrange for tutors and/or cross-age projects with older students who do.

As we explained in chapter 1, to become literate in a second language a student needs knowledge of language, knowledge of literacy, and content knowledge. This knowledge assists learners to comprehend and decode text. Although approaches described in chapter 6 focus on the knowledge of language, the ones included in this chapter address all of them to different degrees.

The approaches presented in this chapter provide a variety of ways to develop and enhance reading ability. Teachers can combine them and adapt them to address different needs and age levels. The following approaches are described in this chapter:

- Word Cards
- Shared Reading

- Reader-Generated Questions
- Response to Literature Strategies
- Cross-Age Project

Holdaway[4] proposes that to introduce reading teachers should model, read with, and encourage independent reading. However, when reading in the weaker language, there should be an additional step: Scaffolded independent reading, where students are taught language and reading strategies. Reading Aloud (see chap. 8) is a good way to model reading. It can also scaffold independent reading by letting students read independently after the teacher has read the text aloud. While using Word Cards and Shared Reading, teachers both model and invite students to read with them. The Reader Generated Questions approach scaffolds independent reading. Scaffolding text is crucial for initiation to literacy and facilitating reading in a second language. Independent reading can be unproductive without scaffolding for students either new to reading or new to the second language. Scaffolding also facilitates coping with material where the second language level is too challenging for the reader. Response approaches encourage independent reading as well as independent response activities. The Cross-Age approach incorporates all by modeling what older students will do with the younger ones, rehearsing reading with teacher and classmates, and reading independently to the younger students. Thus, the Cross-Age approach is particularly appropriate for older second language learners because it incorporates modeling, reading with, scaffolded independent reading, and independent reading without making students feel that they are back in first grade.

Word Cards and Shared Reading are effective approaches to initiate students to literacy in their native or second language. Word Cards was primarily developed for children to learn the sound – letter correspondence using their own words. It is also a good way to get to know the students and their interests. Often students are introduced to the written language through flash cards with words that come from a textbook, or prepared by teachers. Word Cards allow students to learn through the words of their interest. It is a particularly useful approach for students who are learning a different writing system. Word Cards can also help students with their spelling. A teacher used it with a second grader who could not read his own writing because of his spelling. After implementing word cards, the student improved his spelling and his reading fluency.

---

[4]Holdaway (1984).

Some teachers have adopted the idea of using students' words for other vocabulary activities. Paul, an English language arts teacher with a good number of bilingual students in his class, used words suggested by his students for the weekly vocabulary list. Another teacher used the students' words for her weekly spelling tests.

Shared Reading has been associated with young children and big books. It can be adapted for older students using overheads as a way to share a reading passage. Shared Reading gives students the opportunity to internalize the rich language of experienced authors. It is extremely helpful for students learning a second language because the language is modeled and repeated for them before they try reading aloud by themselves. Shared Reading offers a good complement to reading aloud to the whole class. Hearing *and* following the text facilitates reading comprehension. Only hearing the text makes it much harder to comprehend for students without proficiency in the language of the text.

Response to Literature Journals and Reader-Generated Questions are useful for students who have gone beyond initial literacy. Response Journals are particularly good for fiction and Reader-Generated Questions is helpful with expository reading. However, they can both be used with either genre. The Reader-Generated Questions approach requires time to implement because it has a number of steps. This approach teaches students the different steps of the reading process, fomenting good reading habits. Cross-Age Projects are appropriate for developing many literacy skills. Because older students practice skills in order to teach them to younger students, it is an ideal approach to remediate skills for upper grade students. The older students master material below their grade level, but they do not feel humiliated because they are preparing to be teachers. Thus, the content is below grade level, but the process is challenging. These projects have been used for literacy in general, reading, writing, math, and even to redevelop the native language of students who, by high school, had mostly lost it.

Other approaches included in this volume that enhance reading are Anticipation Guide (chap. 5), Dictogloss and Language Experience Approach (chap. 6), and Jigsaw and Situational Context Lessons (chap. 7).

WORD CARDS

Purpose

The Word Cards approach helps the students understand the sound—symbol connection of words. Words initiated by the students are used to learn decoding skills. This approach promotes phonemic awareness because the teacher in sounding out the words while writing them down demonstrates how words break up into smaller units. This approach also teaches the alphabetic principle, i.e., letters stand for the sounds in the spoken words. For students in the upper elementary grades and on, adding word families illustrates how English spelling patterns are also constrained morphological and not only by sound-letter correspondence. For example, if a student gives the word *capable*, the teacher with the help of students can add *capacity*, *capability* and so on. In these words the sound of the first "a" changes but the spelling does not because they belong to the same word family. Word study improves spelling and writing as well.[5]

The words from the word cards can be used for other activities that promote phonemic awareness (see below under follow up activities). Griffith & Olsen suggest a number of books that use "playing with sounds" to promote phonemic awareness.[6] For beginning English language learners these texts may be confusing unless the teacher clearly explains that they should try to "play" with language rather than understand everything.

For bilingual students, the use of Word Cards can also help increase and enhance vocabulary and language use in both the first and second language.[7] These words should be the main source of words for word walls often found in early childhood classrooms.

Procedure

Following is the procedure for the Word Cards approach:

1. Prepare strips of strong cardboard or index cards. The younger the students, the bigger and stronger the cards should be.

2. Every day have each student give a word. Write it down on the card. As you write, sound the word out and let students watch as you write. Make sure the students are facing the card. If students are reluctant to give a word, write down words that would represent something close to them. (Talking to the student might bring out some ideas.)

---

[5]Williams and Hufnagel, 2005.

[6]Griffith and Olson (2002) summarize the importance of phonemic awareness, explain what it is and is not, and provide resources.

[7]See Ashton-Warner (1963) for further information about this approach.

3. Give the cards to the students. Let them read them aloud and on their own. (Have kindergarten students trace the letters with their fingers.)

4. Keep a file box in which to place the cards. You may write students' names in the corner of the cards to keep track of whose words are whose. (You can also let the students keep their cards in individual envelopes.) If students give words in both languages, put them in separate boxes, labeling the boxes by language.

5. Every day have students find their own words, sit with a classmate, and read their words to each other.

6. If students fail to remember how to read their own words, help them by sounding out the letters. (Although Ashton-Warner recommends discarding them, we have found that students get very upset if this is done.)

7. Once students have between 10 and 30 cards, use the cards for follow-up activities such as:
   a. Taking a few and checking to see if students remember them.
   b. Choosing one to elicit discussion of a topic by the whole class or a group. Have students write about it.
   c. Having the students write their word on a large piece of paper and make a drawing.
   d. Spreading cards on the floor, reading one word, and asking students to locate it.
   e. Using them for spelling tests.
   f. Having students put together a dictionary, organizing cards alphabetically, and keeping them handy as reference when they are writing.
   g. Creating games with the words.
   h. Promoting phonemic awareness by matching words that rhyme or finding new words that would rhyme with those in the original cards; segmenting initial, final, and middle sounds; replacing sounds to form new words. Once students have collected a number of cards, the teacher can ask such questions as: Which words rhyme? Which of these words doesn't rhyme? Which words don't have the same medial sound? Which words start with the same sound? And, which words have the sound /t/?
   i. Using Elkonin boxes as recommended by Clay[8] with the words in Word Cards for students who are having difficulty breaking up words into units of sound.

---

[8]Clay (1985).

Two adaptations of the word card approach were successful given the context. In one case, a teacher worked with seventh grade Vietnamese students who were not literate in their native language and were just learning to read in English. The teacher asked students to bring each day a word that they had seen written somewhere. They had to copy the word on a card and draw a picture of the context. As they worked with the words they also added a sentence using the word in the back of the card. In another instance, Liz worked with a fourth grader who was good at comprehending reading but had difficulty with words in the text. She asked the student to find words in the text that he either did not know or could not pronounce. As he pointed to the word she would write it on the card and pronounce it.[9]

The Approach in Practice:
Kindergarten Students Learn To Read Chinese

Musetta Leung used the Word Card approach to assist her Chinese bilingual kindergartners understand the word—symbol relationship in Chinese. Musetta found, in her work as a bilingual teaching assistant, that many of her students did not have experience with Chinese print. She wanted them to learn to read by using words that they had purposefully asked for and that were relevant to them.

Six children worked with Musetta three times a week. She began by having the students each give her a special word to write on an index card. In the beginning, there were some students who could not think of any word they wanted written down. When this happened, Musetta prompted them by asking questions about their family, the weather, food, and so forth, so that she could elicit some sort of response from the children. As the sessions continued, however, the children were usually able to supply their own words.

Musetta usually had each child stand by her and say the word that he or she wanted her to write on the index card. The children then traced the characters that Musetta had made to form their requested word. There were other times when Musetta simply had the children say the word while sitting with the rest of the group. Musetta then wrote the word while sounding it out. Although she was concerned that the children would not pay as much attention when she did the activity this way, Musetta found that the child who had offered the word to her always watched her as she wrote the word. The cards were stored in the students'

---

[9]See Brisk, Dawson, Hartegering, Macdonald and Zehr, 2002.

individual cubbies. When the children returned the second day, they were very excited about retrieving their cards. Some of them had remembered their word and were able to say it. After each student had said the word, Musetta had them trace the word. One of the students, Edward, asked Musetta where to start tracing, so she guided his finger to the first character of the word. When working with the whole group, often the children seemed bored while waiting for each child to say the new word. Musetta suggested to the students that they draw a picture of their word while they were waiting for their turn.

The students were then asked for another word to add to their packet of words. When the students had trouble thinking of a word, Musetta asked what they had eaten for breakfast, which prompted such words as *ice, milk,* and *egg.*[10] There were occasions when there was no word in Chinese. For example, Dennis could not think of a word, so Musetta asked what he had eaten that morning. He replied, "Cereal." Because there is no Chinese word for cereal, Musetta asked what he had with the cereal. When he offered the word *milk,* Musetta asked if he wanted that word added to his pack, Dennis agreed. Although the students did need help in thinking of words sometimes, Musetta found that the words elicited with her help were often the words that the children did not remember. Dennis, for example, did not remember the word *milk* the next day.

On one occasion, the children were asked to create sentences using their word cards. After modeling an example, Musetta asked the children to make their own sentences. Dennis, who is not usually quick to answer, was the first to offer a sentence. The other children also created phrases and sentences, such as: *four airplane, fall rain* (acceptable in Chinese), *five cookies, seven glasses of milk.* Musetta took all the phrases and sentences created by the children and made a book out of them. The children were very attentive when Musetta showed them the book. On each page she had written the phrases or sentences created by the children and had drawn a picture to go with the words. She pointed to the words on each page while she read them to the children. The children then spontaneously repeated the sentences. The book was a great success. One of the children even took the book to his homeroom to show to his classmates and to his third-grade reading partner.

A few days later, the children enthusiastically read their book. They were able to read the words even without picture cues. They then played a game with the book and the word cards. While Musetta reread the book,

---

[10]All words were said and written in Chinese. We are using the English equivalent for convenience.

each child raised his or her card into the air when he or she heard the word read by Musetta. After the children had learned more words, they were very eager to make another book. For this book, Musetta wrote the words on the top of the page, and the children illustrated each page. On the suggestion of one of the students, each child illustrated the page on which his or her own word had been written.

As the weeks progressed, and the children were used to the word card procedure, they developed a routine. When Musetta held up a card, the children first identified its owner. Then, the owner of the card, usually with a big smile on his face, said the word. Musetta praised them for their "super memory," to which the children smiled, or replied, "Of course!"

Musetta had made individual folders with two pockets into which she inserted the word cards of each child. On one pocket was a picture of a "happy face" into which the children inserted the words they knew; on the other pocket (with a sad face), the children placed the words they still did not know. The children were very happy to receive the folders, and became very possessive of them. They enjoyed taking out their word cards, studying them, and counting them to see how many they had accrued.

The use of word cards also helped to involve the children's parents. Fiona once approached Musetta and sadly told her that she had asked her mother to write the word *turtle* in Chinese for her, but her mother was unable to. Musetta suggested that she use that word on one of her new word cards. Fiona smiled at this suggestion. Fiona then asked Musetta to write the word *turtle* on another card so that she could bring it home to show to her mother. She did not want to use her own card for fear of losing it at home! Seron also asked if he could take home his folder and "teach" his father his words.

The children had a take-home book in which they wrote two of their favorite words. They drew pictures to go with the words they had written. The children took the books home and read the words to their parents.

Although some children were still having difficulty remembering their words, by the end of the word card project, Musetta found that many of the children were able to read all of their words as well as many of the other children's words. She notes that some of the difficulty the children had in remembering the words might, in part, be due to the problem of translating words from spoken Cantonese to written Chinese. For example, Seron had given the spoken form of the word *home*, which is different from the written form. Although Musetta explained this difference to Seron, he was still not able to remember the word when he saw it on his card. She was, however, confident in saying that the Word Card approach was effective for teaching beginning Chinese literacy skills.

SHARED READING

Purpose

This approach teaches reading through modeling and coaching using authentic literature, and introduces decoding strategies in context. Students are exposed to authentic literature in either their first or second language. They learn, through practice, the formal language of written text. Teachers model the enjoyment of reading and the process and strategies readers use to understand and think about text. To familiarize learners with various text structures, teachers should use a variety of texts when reading with students. This approach helps second language development by providing repetition in an enjoyable and low pressure context. It helps in developing confidence because learners internalize language patterns that they can apply to their own language use. An important component of this approach is choral reading. Choral reading has been shown to help diction, fluency, reading rate, and prosodic reading. It decreases oral reading miscues and increases understanding. In addition, for beginning second language learners, choral reading allows them to behave as readers in a low pressure environment by just mouthing words while they become familiar with the sounds and rhythm of English. As they gain confidence, they can join the reading by sounding out the words that more experienced peers and the teacher model for them. Poetry and songs can also be used with this approach. It is especially appropriate for older learners.

This approach is widely used in many schools. It is not totally new, since Brigham Young used it in the 19th century to teach reading to his own children.[11] However, most omit the last step, having students create their own book following the patterns learned. This is very important added practice to help second language learners develop writing and reading proficiency in the new language. It does not have to be done with every book read but it is an effective way to scaffold writing.

Although Shared Reading is usually done with text that has repetitive language, it can be helpful to do with informational text. For example, Angela used it to read the science 5th grade textbook. Her students were having trouble with the text. Shared Reading with constant interaction and clarification of terms and concepts helped students understand the text, become very familiar with it so they could refer back when discussing any topic, and become conversant with the language of the text. Reading books together expands children's vocabulary. Repetitive read-

---

[11]In the Beehive House Museum in Salt Lake City, Utah, there is an example.

ing increases the number of responses, the length of responses, the infer- ences, connections to self, and the level of engagement with the book.[12]

Materials

Choose stories with repetitive patterns, songs, or poems. When working with a large group of young children, obtain or produce big books; when working with older students, transparencies can be used. The following are some books and poems appropriate for shared reading. For grades K–2: *One Monday Morning; Goodnight Moon; Ask Mr. Bear; Too Much Noise; Brown Bear, Brown Bear* (as well as many other books by Bill Martin, Jr.). For grades 3–5: *Hailstones and Halibut Bones; Oh, the Places You'll Go!* For high school students *Woman Work* by Maya Angelou as well as other poems and songs.

Procedure

Following are the procedures in the Shared Reading approach:

1. Read aloud a story from an original book. Students listen only.
2. Read the story from the big book or transparencies using a pointer to show where you are reading. Read with fluency and expression.
3. Allow students to join in if they want to. Repeat this procedure as many times as needed. Prepare response activities for students who do not need to continue to participate in the repetitive reading of the text. For example, students can write about their favorite char- acter in the book, write a different ending for the story, and so on.
4. Let individual students read to the class also using the pointer.
5. Have small versions of the original available so that the students can borrow it to read on their own or in pairs. They can also borrow the books to take home.
6. Use the reading to do different types of exercises, such as the cloze procedure, looking for specific words, letters, etc.
7. Have students develop their own big books using an original story as a pattern.

The same procedure can be used with a poem or song. It is best to write them on large chart paper so that the whole class can see.

---

[12]See Holdaway (1979); McCauley & McCauley (1992); Mooney (1994); and Peregoy and Boyle (2005) for further information on this approach.

Production of the Big Book

Students enjoy participating in the production of the big book. For students working in the second language, it provides added practice in reading and vocabulary recognition in that language.

1. Obtain 5 to 10 pieces of stock (32 × 42) or a large pad; felt pens (black, brown, and other colors).
2. Trace lines 1½ inches apart for the story line. Copy wording in the book exactly as the original in format and content. Leave space for margins and illustrations.
3. Copy or trace illustrations from the original (you don't need to do them all) or have students draw them on separate piece of paper, then paste it to the book.
4. Staple together or thread the pages through rings, including a title page.
5. Place on an easel for reading.

The Approach in Practice:
Bilingual Students Produce a Big Book

Peggy Yeh selected the Shared Reading approach for the five Chinese bilingual students with whom she was working. Because Chinese is the main language spoken in these children's homes, Peggy felt that this approach would provide the students with the opportunity to enjoy stories in English and also increase their English reading skills.

Peggy worked with the classroom teacher to select an appropriate book to share with the children. They chose *Paper Crane* by Molly Bang; a book that they felt was especially appropriate for the children because the crane has a special meaning in the Chinese culture. (It represents longevity and is symbolic at birthday celebrations of Chinese elders.)

Peggy started the first session by placing a paper crane in front of the children. This sparked their interest and there were many questions about what it was, what were they going to do with it, could they have one, and so on. Peggy then talked to them about the crane and its meaning of longevity and good health in the Chinese culture. She explained to the children that cranes were a popular symbol at the birthdays of elders. One of the children remembered having seen a crane at her grandmother's birthday.

When the discussion of the crane and birthdays had ended, Peggy then read the title of the book and the author, and asked what they saw on the cover of the book. The cover showed a picture of a young boy holding a paper crane. This led to a discussion and many questions about birds.

Although not directly related to the book, Peggy felt the discussion was important in order to elicit background knowledge from the children. She then continued by asking the children to predict what they thought the story was about. Edward believed the story had to do with "a little boy who gives his grandma a paper crane for her birthday." Another student predicted that it was a story about a boy who had lost a paper crane.

During the reading, Peggy modeled skills she wanted the children to use while reading. When she came to a word that she thought the children might not understand, she paused and asked them what they thought the word meant. For example, when she read the word *unusual,* she asked the children what it meant. One child replied, "It means something you do everyday." Peggy reminded the child that usual is something you do everyday, and then asked the children what happens when you "undo" something. Another child responded, "You don't do it," after which another student replied, "It's something you don't do everyday."

All through the reading of the story Peggy encouraged the children to make predictions about what would happen:

Peggy: Why do you think the stranger is back?

Tyrone: Maybe he's still hungry.

Peggy: Maybe . . .

Feona: I know, I know, he wants the crane back!

Peggy: Hmmm, could be, let's read more to find out.

While reading, Peggy made sure that she used a different voice for the different characters in the story so that the children understood that there was meaning to what she was reading; that reading was not just decoding words. She was also careful to point to each word with a ruler as she read it. She felt that pointing with a ruler was especially important for the children, because directionality in reading Chinese (right to left and vertical) is quite different from English (left to right and horizontal).

When they had finished reading the entire book with Peggy, the children were invited to make their own big book version of the story. Peggy copied the text onto large paper. The students then illustrated each page. Peggy saw many opportunities for learning and skill building during these sessions. When the students weren't sure what to draw or had some questions about the drawing, she referred them back to the story to reread and discuss the section about which they had questions. They also practiced sequencing, decoding, and comprehension skills while they compiled their illustrated pages into a big book. Because the pages had been mixed up during the drawing process, the students had to reread and put the pages in the correct sequence.

When the big book was completed, the children enthusiastically read and reread the book. For the first reading, Peggy had them all read together just for the practice of reading aloud. Peggy had the students work on their intonation in the second reading. The students read a third time, each taking turns going up to the easel to read a page. From the repeated readings, Peggy saw the students' confidence and fluency increase. One student in particular, who was usually quiet and not very vocal, read confidently and with a loud voice. Students were also able to remember many of the more difficult words because of the time they had spent discussing them during the readings.

Peggy found the implementation of the Shared Reading approach to be a valuable tool for the ESL students with whom she was working, and an effective approach to teach reading strategies to those students. She felt that her students had learned a great deal about story structure and had gained confidence in reading aloud.

RESPONSE TO LITERATURE

Purpose

The purpose of this approach is to have students think about what they have read, reflect on it, and relate it to personal experience and knowledge. It helps students better understand the text they are reading, while at the same time, making it personally meaningful to them. Bilingual learners are able to relate text to their unique experience as bilinguals. Students' background knowledge maps their interpretation of text. When reading text in a second language, students respond commensurate to their level of understanding. They have the opportunity to respond in their native language.[13]

Procedure

There are several ways to respond to literature. Following are three possible approaches:

Journals

1. Introduce the approach by modeling your own responses to a book the students have just read. Brainstorm with the students the kinds

---

[13]Peregoy and Boyle (2005) and Peterson and Eeds (1990) for further information about this approach.

of things they could have written about. Use questions to help. For example: "How do you wish the story had ended?" "What did you think of the characters?" "What did you like and why?"

2. Give students a notebook.

3. Ask them to write their reactions to the book or chapters assigned, for example, one elementary school teacher told the students to write "letters" to her about their readings. Tell students not to write a summary of what they read, but write their personal reactions to the readings (i.e., feelings, ideas or questions). For students who are good in oral language but have difficulty writing, the teacher or a tutor may write down the oral reactions the student gives.

4. Respond to the students' writings. Focus on what they are saying and on their questions. Do this activity twice a week, on days that you don't discuss the readings orally. It is important to schedule the activity so that you will have time to respond to each student's journal every time he or she writes. Therefore, do not schedule the activity with more frequency than you can respond.

Double-Entry Journals

This approach is similar to the previous one, but instead of reacting to the whole text in general, students react to selected sections. They copy parts of the book that they like on the left-hand side of the notebook and write their own reactions to that section on the right-hand side. This process can be scaffolded by the teacher. The first couple of times the teacher can choose a few sections that carry the main ideas and give suggestions for the students to write their thoughts about. The next couple of times the teacher selects a few and the students select others. Finally they select all the sections on their own.

Point-of-View Pieces

Students write something as if they were actually involved in the book. For example, they can write a letter as if one of the characters had written it; with another student, each taking the role of one character and writing a dialogue; they can write a diary entry, a speech, or have a phone conversation as if they were one of the characters; and so forth. Positioning students in relation to the text encourages students to engage deeply with the text and go further in their thinking about characters and events.[14]

---

[14]Long and Gove (2003).

Literature/Learning Logs

As they read a book, either fiction or non-fiction, students stop to write down their thoughts, questions, and observations. They bring these logs to discussion about the books. The teacher can respond in writing to clarify questions or difficulties.[15]

The Approach in Practice: Response Journals in a Bilingual Classroom

Angela Burgos implemented the Response to Literature Journals approach with her class of fifth-grade Spanish bilingual students as part of the English literature curriculum. She hoped that by using the method the students would become more actively engaged in English reading activities, and would be encouraged to share their own viewpoints and interpretations of the texts.

Angela started the method in conjunction with a unit on folk tales. During a 10-week period the students read and studied nine books:

The Giving Tree

Why Mosquitoes Buzz in People's Ears

The Legend of the Indian Paintbrush

The Legend of Scarface

The Weeping Woman/La Llorona

The Village of the Round and Square Houses

The Luminous Pearl

Mufaro's Beautiful Daughters

The Legend of the Food Mountain

She began by reading the book The Giving Tree by Shel Silverstein to the class. She then shared thoughts, impressions, and questions about the book to the entire class, writing her impressions on an overhead projector as she thought aloud: "I enjoyed the special relationship shared by the boy and the tree. They loved each other very much. I noticed the different stages of the boy's life in which he would ask the tree for something. I wondered why the tree never said no." She then invited students to share their thoughts about the story while she wrote them on the overhead.

---

[15]See Peregoy and Boyle (2005) for further description and uses.

Carla asked, "Why weren't there any other people in the story?" Jorge suggested, "What you do if you were in that situation?" Another student asked, "How about what we learn from the book? Like a *moraleja* [the moral]."

Angela also modeled how to relate the story to one's own life. She told the students that the tree in the book reminded her of her mother, and how her mother, like the tree, gives because it makes her happy. The children immediately understood the connection Angela was trying to make.

After the entire class had formulated questions together, Angela broke the students into groups to collaborate on additional questions to add to the list. She felt that in this way, students who were too shy to speak during the whole class discussion would have an opportunity to share in a smaller, less intimidating group. When the activity was done, Angela compiled a list of open-ended questions from those suggested by the students:

What do you learn from reading the book?

Why did the author write the book?

Did you like or dislike the story?

How do you feel about the story?

If you could change anything about the story, what would you change and why?

What would you do if faced with the same situation?

How do you feel about the characters?

She explained to them that many of the questions could be used with any story and would help them in their response to literature assignments. Nevertheless, she encouraged the students to respond in whatever ways they wished.

The students were then given a notebook and asked to write to Angela about their reflections on *The Giving Tree*. Angela stressed the importance of writing personal reactions to the story and not a summary of what was read. She also emphasized that they should be more concerned about what they wrote than how they spelled what they wrote. They were able to write in either English or Spanish.

Initially, Angela noted that the students' responses were brief, but they did write about their personal reactions to the story. For example, Carla wrote in response to *The Giving Tree*: "the tree churent give so much to the boy because they boy is greaty." (The tree shouldn't give so much to the boy because the boy is greedy.) For the next lesson, Angela introduced the African tale *Why Mosquitoes Buzz in People's Ears*. Again, Angela modeled how to make connections between what happened in the story to one's own life. She related how when she was young she had told a lie and gotten her brother in trouble. The students understood the connection and wrote about similar experiences in their lives. For example, Susana wrote:

Dear Ms. Burgos,

The day I got in trouble was wen I was in quindergarden that a teacher tease my had and I BAit the teacher and skeeam and Rand to my mother and she say That y Bait her hand and she drent twish my hand. so then I had to brenger to th hospital. (The day I got in trouble was when I was in kindergarten. That a teacher squeezed my hand and I bit the teacher. I screamed and ran to my mother and she said that I bit her hand and she didn't twist my hand. So then she said that I had to bring her to the hospital.)

In her response to Susana's entry Angela again makes a connection to the story:

Dear Susana,

I could understand why you got in trouble. Your mother didn't know the teacher had twisted your hand. Now you know how the animals felt.

Several different activities were used throughout the 10 weeks to present the various books. For several of the books, *Why Mosquitoes Buzz in People's Ears, The Weeping Woman/La Llorona,* and *Mufaro's Beautiful Daughters,* Angela conducted a whole class-guided reading activity. She began by reading the title and author, showing the cover of the book, and then asking the students to predict what the plot of the story might be. The students made predictions based on what they saw on the cover of the book. After a discussion of possible plots and characters, in which all answers were accepted, Angela read part of the story aloud while the students followed along in their own copies of the book. She paused while reading to ask for more predictions as the story developed. After reading the story, the students responded in their journals.

The students also read one of the books independently. Angela gave them a choice of one of three books, *The Legend of the Paintbrush, The Legend of Scarface,* or *The Legend of the Food Mountain,* to read by themselves. She provided a brief description of each of the books so that the students would make a better decision about which book to select. The students were allowed to either read alone, or with other students. Angela provided index cards for the students to write down any words they did not understand.

At first most students sat with one or two others discussing the cover of the book they were reading, or looking at the illustrations in the book. When the students did begin to read their books, however, many did so alone. When the students had finished reading their books, they responded in their journals.

The students wrote in their journals, to which Angela responded, twice a week. Although, initially their entries were brief, the students were able to relate what they had read to something meaningful for them. As they continued reading the folk tales and responding to them in the journals, the students' responses were more detailed and they referred more often to the events and vocabulary of the text.

Mini-lessons were also conducted from time to time to help the students understand the process of the approach. Angela sometimes modeled a response to the book they had read. At other times, she copied a response from one of the students to use as a model and shared with the whole class using the overhead projector. Carla had made an analogy between the character in *The Legend of the Indian Paintbrush* and the mosquito in *Why Mosquitoes Buzz in People's Ears*:

Dear Teacher,

I really like the story because it says a lot of the things that happened and I feel very good for him because its really good idea you now smashing to make some paint. I think that his favorite thing is do is paint like the mosquito he like to bugg on people's ears so the man like to paint and the mosquito like to bugg can you see the diffents.

For some of the folk tales, Angela showed a video version. The students were then able to compare and contrast aspects of the book with what was presented on the film.

Angela found the journals to be a valuable resource for helping the more introverted students. Carmen was a student who rarely participated in class discussions. Angela saw growth in Carmen's confidence and abilities to relate to literature through her passages in the journal. She also used the journal for clarification and to ask further questions about the stories read. As an additional resource for evaluating the literacy development of the students, Angela used a Response to Literature Checklist.[16]

The Response Journals approach was an important component of the reading program for these students, because it allowed the students to

---

[16]See Peterson and Eeds (1990).

respond at their own reading and writing ability without fear of peer judgment or criticism. It also helped both Angela and the students keep pace with students' individual learning. The students were able to express themselves.

READER-GENERATED QUESTIONS

Purpose

The purpose of this strategy is to facilitate reading comprehension and foster recall by walking students through the steps of the reading process: stimulating background knowledge, predicting, actual reading, and synthesizing. This approach develops good reading habits. The activities preceding the actual reading also provide an opportunity to teach vocabulary, teach how to produce questions, relate the topic to students' personal experiences, learn about students' background knowledge on the topic, and clarify possible contradictions with the author's intended meaning when students' and author's cultures contrast. A key step in this approach is the self-generation of questions by students. Not only comprehension is facilitated but also teachers get a glimpse of students' knowledge and understanding of the topic. Other benefits of asking good questions are enhanced ability to predict, to recall information, and to answer test questions. Teachers may give students practice in generating questions before using this approach. They can have students read a story or expository text and generate two good questions. Good questions usually start with a question word and focus on general text ideas. Students should learn to ask factual as well as inferential questions. Before asking students to ask questions it is good to model the different types.[17]

Procedure

This activity has six different steps. When the text is in the students' second language, the native language can be used for the first three steps. Throughout the steps you should teach vocabulary, text structure, and other language skills that will facilitate the process of understanding this particular selection. These steps can be applied to a whole text or, in the

---

[17]See Cohen, R. (1983), Davey and McBride (1986), and Rosenshine, Meister, and Chapman (1996) for ideas on training students to ask good questions. See Henry (1984) for further information about this approach.

case of a longer text or chapter book, the steps can be applied to sections or chapters. Steps in this activity include:

1. *Stimuli.* Introduce the topic of reading through:
    a. pictures, graphs, maps, time lines;
    b. semantic map;
    c. real objects;
    d. title of the reading (and initial sentence); or
    e. statement of the general theme.
    f. Teach two or three key words that relate to the theme of the reading

During this step, explore the students' background knowledge on the topic, relate it to their own experiences, and clarify any misconceptions.

2. *Generation of Questions.* Ask the students to generate from one to ten questions (depending on ability) about this topic. This can be done in several different ways:
    a. Write questions on the board or chart paper as students suggest them. (Put the name of the author by the question.)
    b. Let students generate and write down questions in small groups.
    c. Let students write questions individually.
3. *Responding to Questions.* Have students guess responses to the questions. Depending on the size and level of the class, do it as a whole class or small group activity. Different groups can work on different questions.
4. *Presentation of the Text.* Depending on the age and level of students and text difficulty, present the text by:
    a. Telling the story or content of the text to the students.
    b. Reading aloud the text.
    c. Letting the students read the text individually or in groups, either in class or as homework.
5. *Checking Out Responses.* Ask the students to check the accuracy of their responses.
6. *Final Activity.* Have the students write a summary, prepare a graph, outline the content, draw a picture, or some other activity that will help synthesize the content gained on the subject.

Follow-up

If some of the questions the students asked were not answered by that particular text, take the students to the library or bring resources to the room, so that individually or in groups the students can look for responses. Another possibility is to have students interview experts to find out the responses.

The Approach in Practice:
Sixth Graders Cope with Science Texts

For many second-language learners, content area study is a very complex, and often frustrating, process. Renate Weber Riggs felt that the Reader-Generated Questions approach would be helpful to bilingual students studying science. Renate worked with four sixth-grade Spanish—English bilingual students enrolled in an integrated Spanish—English bilingual program at an urban elementary school. Spanish was the first language of all four students, although three of the four students indicated that they preferred reading and writing in English to reading and writing in Spanish.

Renate decided to use this approach because she felt that the students would benefit from the cooperative learning atmosphere this approach incorporated. It would also be an opportunity for the students to use language for meaningful purposes. She followed a six-step plan for the five topics that she (with input from the classroom teacher) had wanted to introduce to the students. The topics were: Green Plants, Plant—Animal Cycle, Fungi (Mushrooms), Fungi (Molds), and Skeletal System.

In her introduction of the approach, Renate explained to the students that they were the ones who would be asking the questions about the specific topic, and that afterwards, they would investigate and research answers to those questions in the texts read during the classes. She felt it was important to show the students that they already had some knowledge about the topics. Renate encouraged group work and the use of Spanish in the students' discussions, even though she herself did not speak Spanish. She made every effort to help the students realize that their first language was a valid, viable, and important means of communication. Renate also functioned as the scribe during the sessions. She felt that writing for the students created a less stressful situation for them and facilitated the flow of the discussion.

The Study of Green Plants

The first topic introduced to the students was green plants. A semantic map was used to organize information students already knew about green plants. The students were given books with photographs and sentences to help stimulate ideas and formulate questions about green plants.

Renate wrote the words "green plants" in the middle of a 9 × 12 paper and asked the students to say as many words as they could related to the subject of green plants. As Renate wrote the words on her paper, the students copied the words on their own papers. After there were a number of words on the paper, Renate explained to the students that they would categorize the words. She pointed to words such as *trunk, fruit, roots, stem,* and *leaves,* and asked the students what could be said about those words. One student replied: "It is a tree." Renate wrote *Parts of a Plant.* She then pointed out *soil, water, sun,* and the students correctly responded, "Need to grow." She continued categorizing the words until the students eventually understood the idea and began volunteering words from the map to fit into categories.

During her next session with the students, Renate explained to them that they would come up with questions that they wanted to learn about green plants. She began by writing two sentences on the board that the students were to copy on their papers: Green plants make their own food. All living things depend on plants. She then had George read the sentences aloud, and then explained that they would use those two ideas to help stimulate ideas for questions they might have.

Angel began by asking the question: "Why do trees have brown trunks and when they little the stem is green?" Renate was writing down Angel's question as he said it. With a little coaxing from her, Angel added the word *are* and corrected his question to ". . . when they are little the stem is green." Renate wrote the question on chart paper, and then had Angel reread it and write his name next to it. Other students contributed to the list of questions, following the same routine of dictating to Renate, rereading their question, and writing their name next to their question. The students copied the questions on their own paper. This was a perfect opportunity for Renate to see how they were writing their questions on the paper. She noticed that many had forgotten the question marks at the end of the sentence. When she asked what was needed at the end of all questions, everyone yelled, "Question marks."

When the students had generated six questions, Renate told them that they would now try to answer the questions to the best of their knowledge. The students enthusiastically began responding to the questions. Renate wrote down all their answers. She had forgotten to tell the students to leave a space between each question in order to write the specific answers related to that question later on, so the students had to write the answers below all of the questions.

When the students had answered all the questions, they opened their science textbooks. Renate read two paragraphs from the text and explained to the students that they were reading the book to find any answers to their questions. Renate used this approach as reading to learn, rather than reading to comprehend a story. Students, therefore, used several sources, in addition to the class text, to read about the topic.

Jorge found that two of the questions were answered by the text. Renate asked him to read the question first: "Why are plants green?" Jorge then referred to the textbook and read the answer: "Plants use chlorophyll to make their own food." As Renate was reading this answer to write on the chart paper, Jorge realized that that did not fully answer the question, and added: "Chlorophyll makes these cells look green."

Strategies Used for the Different Steps

Renate used different strategies for each step depending on the topic. For the first step, Renate used semantic maps to stimulate ideas for the green plant and skeletal system topics. Pictures and photographs from both science textbooks, as well as other books, were used when working on the plant—animal cycle and fungi—mushrooms topics. When the students were studying about fungi and mold, Renate brought in moldy cheeses, breads, and even a bottle labeled penicillin.

To produce questions for the plant—animal cycle topic, students looked at a drawing from a book about photosynthesis. The students worked in groups to discuss the drawing and come up with questions. Students discussed in their groups in both English and Spanish. After a few minutes, Renate called the groups together and wrote down the questions they had formulated.

Responding to questions was the third step in the process. The students used the resources available to them to find the answers to their questions. The students dictated the answers to Renate, who wrote them. On one occasion, as Renate was writing down what one student had said, he, Albin, noticed he had made a mistake and self-corrected. Albin had said, "Because when the animals breathe out oxygen, um, the plants breathe in carbon dioxide in." As Renate was writing his response on the chart paper, Albin realized his error and corrected himself: "Because when the animals breathe out carbon dioxide and the trees breathe in carbon dioxide."

The fourth and fifth steps in the process allow the students to verify the responses they made to their questions by investigating textbooks and other sources for their information. For example, on the lesson *Fungi/Mushroom*, Renate read about fungi from a biology book. The students then read through the passage again looking for answers to the questions they had generated. One of the questions the students wanted answered on this topic was, "Why is the bread blue?" George responded, after looking in the book, "Because it says—They send threads (pronounced threeds) of mold into the bread. Maybe that's not the answer." Renate explained to George that he had given part of the answer and that it could be added to the answer they were formulating for the question.

Renate stressed the importance of the format of the texts used. Texts with subheadings helped the students focus more quickly on what they were reading and where possible answers to their questions might be. As the students were looking through the books to find the answers to their questions, they were also learning the formats. For example, when reading the passage on the skeletal system, "The skeletal system functions in four ways," the students found a chart on the page explaining the four ways.

Renate also found it was important to ask students to explain their answers further if they did not seem to make sense. In one instance, one of the students answered the question, "Why does that have something black?" (the fungi topic), with "Because it doesn't work." Instead of asking for an explanation of the response, Renate simply wrote what the student had said. She later discovered, while speaking to a Spanish-speaking teacher, that the student had translated the Spanish phrase "no sirve" (it's no good).

To complete the cycle of the Reader-Generated Questions, various activities were implemented in order to review and ensure an understanding of the topic. At times verbal review of the material was conducted, or other teachers asked questions about the topics. For the topic of fungi/mold, the students were asked to draw pictures of what a mold looked like. Some students also wrote captions under their drawings. For that particular session, students from a mainstream class had joined Renate's group. Michelle, one of the more shy students in the bilingual group, was able to discuss and explain the concept of molds to the students from the mainstream class.

Renate believes that Reader-Generated Questions is an excellent approach for development of academic language and recall of content material. She found that the quality and quantity of the students' questions improved during the activity. As the weeks progressed and the students were more involved in the activity, they began to realize that they could ask different types of questions and that there may be more than one answer to their questions. Renate also saw an improvement in how the students focused on the text when looking for answers to their questions. The students who participated in this activity recalled better than the rest of the class the topics covered in the science curriculum.

CROSS-AGE PROJECT

Purpose

The purpose of this approach is to help older students with learning difficulties by making them teachers of younger students in precisely the area they are experiencing difficulty, such as reading in the native language or English, math, science, and so on. The students are actively involved in their own learning as they practice reading, asking questions, and internalizing the strategies they use to work with the younger children. This approach is helpful for bilingual learners because it allows them to focus on the development of literacy in one of their languages based on their needs. Older students can work on basic skills without feeling that they are being treated as slow or beginners. In learning how to be teachers, they familiarize themselves with learning strategies.

This approach provides a natural setting for integrating students of different language backgrounds. Teachers of older bilingual students can arrange a Cross-Age Project with a class of younger monolingual students. Also, older bilingual students can serve as role models when working with younger bilingual students. Both these contexts make bilinguals proud of their language skills. This approach also gives the younger students individual attention. The most crucial aspect of this approach is to give the older students the chance to prepare well before they start working with the younger students.[18]

An alternative described by Bromley, Winters, and Schlimmer[19] is to carry out such projects between university pre-service teachers or high schools students through journal exchanges. After choosing your "buddy" and exchanging letters of introduction and pictures, pre-service teachers or high school students discuss books appropriate for the younger students through journals. They use graphic organizers, questions, and others strategies that facilitate comprehension. One person is in charge of physically carrying the journals between college or high school and the elementary school. With Internet this can also be done electronically. Working in pairs increases students' enthusiasm about reading, writing, and exchanging ideas. It provides learners with a different and authentic audience.

Procedure

Follow these steps to conduct a Cross-Age Project:

1. Choose two classes, one with students older than the other.
2. Explain to both classes what the project is all about. Introduce the classes to each other through an activity.

---

[18]See Freeman and Freeman (1998), Juel (1991), Labbo and Teale (1990) and Urzua (1995) for further information about this approach.

[19]Bromley, Winters, and Schlimmer (1994).

3. Start working with the older students by doing the following:
   a. Model the chosen method or approach.
   b. Train, explain, and discuss the method with students.
   c. Let them rehearse with each other and do any preparation needed.
4. At all times, the older learners should keep a journal in which they reflect, first about the training, later about the actual experience as teachers.
5. Read and respond to the journals. Steps 1–5 should take a minimum of two to three weeks to ensure that the older students are ready.
6. When the "teachers" (older students) are ready, start implementation.
7. Pair the older with the younger students. If the classes are uneven, some groups may be larger than two. Divide the two classes into two groups. Each group stays with one of the two teachers involved.
8. Allow for follow-up activities as they naturally develop at the initiative of students.
9. Plan other activities such as parties or field trips that they can do together.
10. Meet with the "teachers" periodically to discuss how the implementation is going, as well as the content and process of learning. Focus especially on the older learners' needs.

The Approach in Practice: Bilingual Fifth Graders Become Reading Teachers

A Cross-Age Project was initiated between Mary Eileen Skovholt's fifth-grade transitional Spanish bilingual classroom and a monolingual English first grade. The main purpose for the project was to create an atmosphere for authentic reading and writing activities in the second language (English) for the fifth graders, while giving individual attention and opportunities for hearing stories read aloud to the younger children.

The fifth-grade students were in the last year of their bilingual program, many of them having been in the program for less than three years. All their subjects were taught in English in order to prepare them for mainstream classes the following year. Although the students' listening and speaking skills were advanced, their average reading grade level was 3.7. The first graders were students who were in a "readiness" class that could be considered a transitional class between kindergarten and first grade. It was felt that both classes would benefit from the Cross-Age Project.

The teachers began the project by introducing the idea to the fifth graders who responded enthusiastically to it. They had already worked on making a big book with that particular first-grade class, so a relationship between the students had already been formed. They were told how important their preparation was for the success of the project. The teachers began by reading children's stories to the fifth graders. The children listened to the teacher reading a story aloud and then wrote in journals about various aspects of the project (i.e., the stories read to them, being read to aloud, and so forth). The teachers then responded to the journals.

The classroom teachers chose folk tales as the stories they would read to the fifth graders to prepare them to become the teachers. They felt that the content of the stories was appropriate for both age groups, that it would hold the interest of the older students, and that the illustrations would help elaborate the meanings of the tales. During these read-alouds the teachers concentrated on modeling techniques that the older students would use when they were the "teachers." They asked questions to monitor comprehension, help make predictions, elicit prior knowledge, and make the important connections to the children's own experiences.

Although hesitant at first to read aloud to the fifth graders, thinking that they would not enjoy such an activity, the teachers soon discovered that fifth graders reacted positively to listening to stories read aloud. Excerpts from the students' journals corroborate this finding:

> *Today we listened to a story it was called* Who's in Rabbit's House. *I liked the story because of the frog and how he laughed. I also like when the caterpillar came out of the house. I really liked that story and I hope I hear or read a good story like:* Who's in Rabbit's House. (Mitchell)
>
> *I liked the story because it was good and it was sad because they didn't have food at the end and I would like to read it again to the little kids. Someday I would like to read this book again. Can you read it again?* (Gisela)

The students wrote in their journals after each story read aloud. This activity allowed the students to not only reflect on the story, but also to relate the story to their personal experiences and feelings. They were able to critique the stories that were read, suggest alternative endings, and so on. The teachers found that the journal entries were rich with discussions about the favorite parts of the story, whether the story could be true, and how they could relate what happened in the story to their own lives, an important connection for comprehension and the joy of reading.

Mitchell wrote in his journal about his liking scary stories:

> *Today I checked out a book.* Ghost's Hour, Spook's Hour. *I liked beautiful stories but one of my favorites is scary stories. I like scary because I like to be scared. I don't know what's inside me that makes me feel that way.*

By writing in the journal, Mitchell was able to reflect on his feelings about the story, and share his reaction to the stories read. Another student, Ana, connected the story of *The Ugly Duckling* to experiences she had when living in Puerto Rico:

> I liked the part when the duck didn't know that he was a swan and he saw his reflection on the water. And I thought he was going back with his mom. In Puerto Rico I had a man chicken and a hen and I have ducklings but they were all beautiful . . .

Efrain became the expert when he was able to explain to the class, because of his experiences in Puerto Rico, why the mother hen sits on her eggs.

The teachers continued the read-aloud modeling twice a week for five weeks. They felt that each student needed the time to prepare for his or her role as teacher. The help of the school librarian was solicited during the fourth week of the project to show the fifth graders appropriate books for first graders. She showed them examples of appropriate children's literature and explained how to look for suitable books (e.g., predictable books, rhyming books, and picture books). She also modeled for the students, showing them different techniques they could use when reading aloud, and explained why the strategies were important. The students displayed their understanding of the modeling done by the librarian through their journal entries:

> The book I picked to practice is Three by the Sea. . . . the book they read in the library was a good story. We have to read easy books to the children so that they could understand and phrases repeat and sound and pictures so that they enjoy the book just like we enjoy a book. (Wanda)
>
> Today I was in the library. I learned how to express my feelings when I read a book and how to show them the picture and tell what's happening in the picture. It was nice to know about books. (Marta)

During the fifth week of the project the fifth-grade students began to read to each other for practice. They had selected the first book they were planning to read with the younger children. They asked their partners questions using the strategies they had learned from the teachers when they were reading aloud. The partners being read to also had the opportunity to role-play and ask questions of the reader. This experience provided the students with authentic purposes for reading and a deeper awareness of the purpose of reading. Many students expressed that they learned more and enjoyed reading more when they were able to share the experience with a peer.

When the students were ready to read to their first-grade partners, each class was divided into two groups. One half of each class read in their own classroom while the other half visited the other classroom. It was planned that halfway through the project the groups would switch so that everyone had the chance to visit both classrooms. The teachers decided to let the children "naturally" pick their partner. Because each class had the same number of students, there was no problem with pairing up. The fifth graders seemed to just walk over to their partner. The students spent 30 minutes reading. After returning to their classes, the fifth graders spent another 20 minutes writing about the experience in their journals. The journal entries reflected many positive feelings that the fifth graders had about the read-aloud. They expressed a sense of responsibility to their charges:

> *I like reading to Luis because he listens to me and he gave me some sentences. He drew me a dinosaur and I taught him how to write the word "strong."*
>
> *The book I read the is* Little Monster's Neighborhood. *It was about little monsters and Luis laugh and he was very happy. I drew him a bird and he said, "You are my best teacher." So I was happy to read to him. I hope he won't be absent.* (Raul)

They also understood the importance of selecting appropriate reading material, that is, books that their partners preferred:

> *I read to BJ All My Toys are on the Floor. I like the story and BJ did not kind of like it so next time I will read him a better thing than that.* (Efraín)

As the project continued, the confidence of the students increased and they began to initiate other activities with their partners. They had the first graders pick out the book they wanted read, or had the first grader act out part of the story. Observations of the first graders showed that they were beginning to mimic the modeling techniques done by their fifth-grade partners.

Writing became part of the activities. The first graders drew a picture related to the story after having heard it read aloud. Some first graders even wrote about the story, or dictated a sentence to their partner.

The project proved to be enjoyable and important for the first graders as well. During a class assignment, the students had to respond to the prompt: "I have a good day when . . ." Most of the students responded by saying, "My partner reads to me." When interviewed at the end of the project as to whether they liked being read to, Christina replied, "I think it's nice for kids who know how to read to show little kids how to read."

The culminating activity was a field trip for both classes to Boston Public Gardens, which has a special tour designed around the book, *Make Way for Ducklings* by McCloskey. Each student received a copy of the book that was signed by their partner as a remembrance of the special bond between them.

Through an interview done at the end of the project, the fifth-grade students expressed that they felt that they themselves had become better readers by reading to the first graders. They explained the strategies they used to help them become better readers. For example, Gisela stated: "Well I used to read very fast and I learned how to stop when there is a period, etc." And Juan said: "How the little kids learned helped me myself to read better." Edison clearly shows satisfaction with his progress: "To read with expression, to get into books, learn words, made me happier."

Eileen noticed an increase in the quantity of reading done by the students once they became involved in the Cross-Age project. They became more interested in books for their own pleasure, and were more careful in selecting books. She attributes this to the increase in self-confidence and motivation the students gained by working with the first graders. Efrain comments: "I learned to read better. I took two books, one for me and one for the little kid."

The students also demonstrated a better understanding of the writing process and its relation to reading. Juana commented in her journal: "Writing helped me think about things because you write down everything that happened with the little children." Melissa stated: "Now I understand more about reading. After when I write it, I read it again."

The Cross-Age Project is a win—win situation. The older students learn the importance of reading, and can increase their confidence and skills in both reading and writing. The younger students are given some "special" attention and also have excellent role models in the older students.

5

Approaches with Focus on Oral Discourse

While second language classes have often emphasized the development of the oral language, first language classes (either in English or in another language) have neglected oral language in favor of literacy development. In reality, students need both oral and literacy skills to succeed in school. Both social and academic settings require the ability to listen and speak. Moreover, oral and written language support each other in development. Students may come to school with different levels of proficiency in the oral language (first or second). Most children will have the basic social skills in their native language. Their ability in social settings in the second language will vary depending on the amount of contact they have had with native speakers. Oral ability for academic purposes will depend on the kind of talk used at home or the amount of previous schooling the students have had.

Students need oral language to relate informally to peers and adults during play, lunch time, and other non-academic activities. They also need proficiency in listening and speaking to understand directions and instruction, to be included in group work, and to respond during classroom discussions. Oral language helps students learn both by understanding instruction and constructing knowledge.

Oral language and literacy learning support each other. Phonological awareness, or the notion that language is separated into segments, is a strong predictor of reading ability. In turn, reading and writing can help phonological awareness.[1] Knowledge of vocabulary facilitates reading and writing while lots of reading increases knowledge of vocabulary.

---

[1]Dickinson, McCabe, Clark-Chiarelli and Wolf (2004).

Teachers need to facilitate students' listening comprehension, especially in the second language and scaffold speaking proficiency. Explanations in English are difficult to understand when students are still in the process of acquiring the language. The teacher can facilitate it by speaking clearly, enunciating well, paraphrasing complex terms and supporting explanations with visual organizers and nonverbal clues. Reading Aloud by the teacher (see chap. 8) and when using Reader-Generated Questions (see chap. 4) presenting the text orally helps students develop listening comprehension. Group activities, such as Jigsaw (see chap. 7), encourage students to listen to their classmates. For newcomers speaking is often a frightening task. Teachers should give students time to develop confidence. Using tutors (see chap. 8) helps students gain this confidence by rehearsing the language before using it with the whole class. Ethel started her literacy class with a major question written on the white

---

Suggestions for First Year English Learners

- If some students are unable to participate in a discussion in English, allow them to share their thoughts in their L1 and have another student (if available) translate what was said.
- Have students participate in small group discussions instead of whole class. For some beginning English learners it is easier to speak in a smaller group.
- Provide sentences starters for students. For example, when discussing reaction to a book or story, model appropriate statements, such as: I thought the character was . . . because . . .; I wonder why the author wrote . . .; I think the setting of the story was . . . because; I didn't understand why . . ., etc.
- Have students draw their reaction to or understanding of an assignment before having to explain it orally.
- Increase wait time for students' oral responses.
- Have students teach native language words to share their cultural background and practice their oral language
- Teach students basic questions such as Can you help me? Can you repeat that? And teach them when to use them.
- When students give a response, paraphrase their response and encourage them to expand their responses so they can hear their ideas and practice expressing ideas.

board. She asked the question orally and let students volunteer answers. For the silent ones, she walked to their seat and let them whisper their answer in her ear.

The approaches presented in this chapter help students practice their oral language in particular for use in academic contexts. They include:

- Student-Directed Sharing Time or Group Discussions
- Anticipation Guide
- Talk-Write

Student-Directed Sharing Time or Group Discussions are done completely orally, but enhance literacy development because they require students to discuss and think around a topic. Through discussions students develop and clarify concepts. Teachers may assume that students know a concept, but in oral discussions the depth and accuracy of knowledge is revealed. For example, Liz asked students to define immigration. Two-thirds of her class were either immigrants or children of immigrants yet the discussion revealed confusion as to whether you had to move from another country or another state to be an immigrant. A lengthy discussion scaffolded by the teacher through questions led to an understanding of the concept. These approaches can be easily integrated with reading and writing activities. It is easier for students to carry out this activity in their stronger language or bilingually. If the instruction is only in English, students' second language, teachers should not pressure beginning students to speak. The nature of the activity changes with the age of the students. Younger children discuss spontaneously in relation to things that have happened to them, need more rules of behavior, and the leader is chosen as the activity starts. Older students can relate the discussion to issues in the curriculum, can do research in preparation for the discussion, and the leader can be assigned ahead of time.

Students also have an opportunity to discuss and deepen their understanding of topics and concepts related to a reading when they use the Anticipation Guide approach. By analyzing statements related to a reading prior to the actual reading, students orally share with each other their ideas about the topics and concepts presented. Their background knowledge can be activated and pertinent vocabulary can be introduced. Through discussion, students can begin to understand important concepts of the reading, so that when they read the material comprehension is enhanced. A mainstream teacher with lots of second language learners worked collaboratively with a bilingual teacher. They implemented the Anticipation Guide before reading a book. The bilingual teacher helped a group of newcomers in the mainstream class discuss and fill out the anticipation guide. All students were engaged in the full class discussion.

The Talk—Write approach is an excellent way to develop listening and speaking proficiency and to give students practice in being critical and helpful about each other's work. It is a useful approach to implement prior to writing a piece, because it focuses on the development and clarity of topic through talking and writing. It can also be helpful when students have different strengths. A mainstream teacher paired José, a Spanish-speaker fluent in oral but not written English, with a native speaker of English. José acted as the questioner, leaving for the native speaker the role of modeling the oral and written language.

STUDENT-DIRECTED SHARING TIME AND GROUP DISCUSSION

Purpose

Student-Directed Sharing Time and Group Discussions give students the practice of talking about something to an audience. Reading and writing activities can be done either before or after the oral activities to help students research information or reflect on what was discussed. It can be an opportune time for bilingual students to discuss issues relating to culture and language, for example, the struggles of living and studying in two cultures. This approach is easiest when students can use their stronger language. When they must speak in the second language, teachers have used helpful strategies such as deciding on topics ahead of time, letting the students have notes to help the oral expression, and starting with a Semantic Map about the topic to provide vocabulary.[2]

Procedure

To execute the Sharing Time approach:

1. Choose an area of the room where the participants can sit in a circle. Explain to the students that every day they will gather around a leader and talk about something. It can be something that happened to them on the way to school, over the weekend, or a television program they saw, a newspaper or magazine article they read, and so forth.

---

[2]See Savignon (1983) and Michaels and Foster (1985) for further information about this approach.

2. Choose the leader of the day and have that student sit in a special chair. Start with those students who are surer of themselves. The first day, you may want to model the role of the leader by taking the leader's chair and telling something that happened to you personally.

3. Give the rules (which should be reviewed occasionally):
   a. one person shares at a time
   b. leader chooses the person who speaks
   c. students have to raise their hand if they want to talk
   d. if students misbehave, they will get a warning (given by the leader, who also decides what "misbehaving" is)
   e. if given a second warning, students go to their seats.

To execute Group Discussions:

1. Divide the class into groups of 6 to 10 students, or work with the whole class.

2. Let the group decide on a list of topics that they would like to discuss for the term, or the month.

3. Before beginning the actual discussion, they may want to outline the topic. This outline, as well as reading and research, can be assigned as homework in preparation for the oral discussion.

4. Let students start the discussion. Give them a fixed amount of time to carry out the discussion. Assign a leader to help the flow of the discussion. If it is conducted in the nonnative language, students should feel free to ask a question, insert a word, or ask for a translation in their native language.

Follow-Up Activities:

Have students write an essay or summary of the topic discussed.

Have students read more on the topic discussed.

Tape record and transcribe sections of the discussion. Have students analyze their language. Follow up with lessons on specific language skills.

It is better to implement the discussions in cycles. For example, the group chooses four topics for the month. Each week they deal with a different topic. They discuss for 15 minutes every day for 3 days, the fourth day they write a summary, and the fifth day they bring their summaries for a final discussion. Leaders can be preassigned.

The Approach in Practice: From Silent Spectators to Active Learners

For Alice Kancl's 12 sixth-grade Haitian students, the Student-Directed Group Discussion approach provided a nonthreatening environment in which they could overcome their discomfort of speaking in public, and develop or increase pride and interest in their native culture. Alice implemented the Student-Directed Group Discussion Approach with the students, ages 11 through 14, twice a week during their Haitian Culture class. Because there were not many materials available in the school for that particular subject matter, Alice assigned the students a topic on which they researched using newspapers from Haiti, listening to radio programs, and interviewing family members. The topics to be covered included religion, family, life in Haiti, education, and politics. On the first day the students carried out a discussion session on the topic, then on the second day, Alice expanded on the topic using notes she had taken during the first day's discussion.

During the first session, the two speakers, Bervelyne and Nancy, spoke about religion and voodoo. Both stood in front of the class to make their presentations, Nancy speaking for about five minutes and Bervelyne nervously reading from a paper. Because there were no questions asked by the students after their presentation, Alice felt the need to add more information and ultimately took over the session. It was not until later that she realized that she had participated more than she should have, and had not encouraged the students to participate more. For the next session, she had the students sit in a circle. Although Alice made sure she did not take over the discussion, she still felt the need to monitor behavior and order in the group. Other students did participate in the discussion sharing their own thoughts and experiences on voodoo spirits. Esther shared her experience of living next to a person apparently possessed by voodoo spirits, and how she used to look through the keyholes in the door to see because children in her family were not permitted to look at such things.

Esther was the presenter at the next session. She spoke about the structure of the family as it is now in Haiti and how it was in the past. She explained that, in the past, the notion of family was different from what is thought of family nowadays. In the past, family could consist of father, mother, children, grandparents, aunts, uncles, and even longtime friends. She explained that at present, when one talks about family, it is usually mother, father, children and grandparents.

Esther also talked about the lakou system (i.e., several small houses are together on one piece of property and everyone lives like a family).

She also talked about the previous monetary system, about which she had learned from her grandmother. The other students seemed very interested in her presentation and asked many questions. Occasionally, during the discussion, students directed their question to Alice, who suggested that the questions be asked of another student.

Even though this particular session was a bit more integrative and participatory, Alice believed that the sessions were becoming question and answer periods with the presenter being seen as an expert on the topic, or being challenged for what she had said. Alice, therefore, reviewed the idea of Student-Directed Group Discussion, went over the protocol of the discussion (i.e., raise your hand to make a comment, wait your turn to speak, and so forth). She also decided to have a monitor for each session who assisted the leader in making sure the discussion was orderly and everyone had an opportunity to share.

As the Student-Directed Group Discussion sessions continued, the students became more comfortable with the format. They observed the rules of the group, turning to the monitor when they wished to speak. They joined in on the discussions, relating the topic to their personal experiences. Darline and Jean Ralph spoke about life in Haiti. Because neither was well prepared for the topic, other students took over the lead. Hans explained that there were two classes of people in Haiti, those with lots of money and those with no money. He went on to explain that because the poorer people did not have money, they exchanged goods and services instead. He told the group that people in the village helped each other during bad times. This statement reminded Jean Ralph of a good friend he had in Haiti with whom he shared many things. Other students then spoke about their experiences living in Haiti. Sometime during the discussion, Esther began to talk again about voodoo. The monitor interrupted and reminded the group that religion was not the topic currently being discussed.

It was during the topic of education that Alice saw growth in how the students discussed issues, and how comfortable they were in expressing their opinions. The students were speaking about schools in Haiti, and in particular, teachers in Haiti and their use of corporal punishment, which was allowed by law. Darline spoke about her first-grade teacher:

> I will never forget that teacher I had in (*preparatoire* I) first grade. She was so mean, she used to hit us with a ruler on our knuckles.[3]

---

[3]All discussions were carried out in Haitian Creole.

Esther had a different opinion of the schools in Haiti. She stated:

> In Haiti the teachers are very strict but the students respect them. But here in _____, the students say anything they want to the teachers. They are so disrespectful.

The discussion of schools and the Haitian education system continued. Alice learned a lot about the students just from listening to them talk about their experiences in school in Haiti. She learned that many of her students were from rural schools, where the school experience is quite different from students attending school in the city. She was surprised that the students even admitted having attended a rural school, because they usually were embarrassed to say that they were from the country. Alice believed, however, that the sense of community and trust was strong enough in the group, that the students did not hesitate to talk about their lives.

The political situation in Haiti at the time was also an important topic of discussion for the students. They were involved in discussing the election that was to take place soon in Haiti. Nancy began the discussion by talking about what she had heard on the radio about the election:

> I heard that twelve of the candidates were eliminated. There will be an election on November 29th where people will be going to the polls for the first time in 30 years to elect a new president. A few months ago the Junta said that they will allow Haitians who live outside the country to vote, but now I think they have changed their mind. My parents said they don't think the election will take place because of all the turmoil . . .

Others joined in. Sandy stated:

> Well, I hope there is an election so they can stop killing people.

Hans then remarked:

> If we had a revolution this would not have happened, everything would have been fine by now. It is two years, two years since Duvalier left and nothing has changed.

Jean Ralph replied:

> Well, it is the same for the C.N.G. (National Council of Government). The Haitian people had no objection at the beginning but when they realized the C.N.G. was a continuation of the Duvalier's regime they turned against it.

In reviewing the overall effects of the Student-Directed Group Discussion approach on the goal of increasing students' ability to speak in public, Alice saw a marked improvement. The students no longer waited for her to initiate a discussion. They expressed their opinions about a topic, and challenged the comments of others. One of the students even asked Alice if she would take them to the library so that they could better research their topics. Alice believed that the Student-Directed Group Discussion encouraged the students to become more interested in their native culture and the politics of Haiti. This project involved the families as well. Much of the information was secured through interviews with family members.

Once the students in Alice's other classes heard about the discussions that took place, they also asked Alice if she would conduct that type of lesson in their classes. The students began to see Alice as a person they could trust and approached her frequently to discuss many other issues.

ANTICIPATION GUIDE[4]

Purpose

The Anticipation Guide Approach can assist in reading comprehension. It encourages deep-level discussions of topics of a text prior to reading. It helps readers "anticipate" what the author's message may be or what the relevant material of the story is. It can also assist students in responding better to text.

For bilingual students it provides an opportunity to elicit background information that may help in comprehension or to be introduced to new topics prior to reading. They are able to discuss relevant topics and expand their thinking about the topics. When reading in their second language, they can begin to use new vocabulary pertinent to the content of the material.

Procedure

1. Read the text and select one or two major topics or concepts you want the students to learn.

---

[4]Readance, Bean, and Baldwin (1981) and Tierney, R., Readance, J. E. and Dishner, E. K. (1995).

2. Write three to five *general* statements about those concepts. They should be concepts with which the students are familiar and about which the students can either agree or disagree.

3. Make a chart with four columns. In the first column write the statements you wish the students to consider. In the second column write "Me," then agree and disagree underneath the word me. In the third column, write "My partner and I," then agree and disagree underneath that. In the fourth column write "author," then agree and disagree under that.

4. Have students indicate whether they agree or disagree with the statement by checking agree or disagree.

5. When the students have completed their "Me" column, have them discuss and debate their answers with another student. Have the partnered students then try to come to a consensus about the statement and mark their decision in the "My partner and I" column.

6. Direct the students to read the text. When they have completed the reading, have them fill in the "Author" column.

7. Follow-up activities can include a post-reading discussion, a reflection response to the reading, or a written reflection about the statements in relation to the reading.

The Approach in Practice:
The Author and I Agree!

Peggy (co-author of this volume) was hoping that the Anticipation Guide approach would help her students grasp the deeper meaning of the stories they read. The students were fourth and fifth graders in a transitional bilingual program. The students were all native speakers of Spanish, with a beginning level proficiency in English. Peggy was responsible for teaching Spanish literacy and English as a Second Language to them. Many of the students were on a third or fourth grade reading level in Spanish, but their comprehension of stories was very literal. They didn't seem able to respond more deeply to the author's message in a story.

She introduced the Anticipation Guide to the students as an activity prior to reading *La Moneda de Oro* by Alma Flor Ada. Juan, the main character of the story, is a thief who overhears Doña Josefa, a "curandera" or healer, remark that she was the richest woman in the world. Juan decides to rob Doña Josefa of her money and follows her as she roams the countryside healing the sick. However, in his pursuit to rob the money, Juan changes and begins to realize that there are other ways to be rich besides having a lot of money.

Peggy passed out the following anticipation guide in Spanish to the students:

Anticipation Guide

	I	My Partner and I	Author
To be rich means having a lot of money	Yes ____	Yes ____	Yes ____
	No ____	No ____	No ____
People who do bad things can't change	Yes ____	Yes ____	Yes ____
	No ____	No ____	No ____
It is important to have a lot of money.	Yes ____	Yes ____	Yes ____
	No ____	No ____	No ____

She explained to the students that they should read the three statements and then indicate in the box marked "I" whether they agreed or disagreed with the statement. When the students were finished, they were to discuss their responses with another student, and then both those students should try to come to a consensus about the statement. In other words, if both students agreed or disagreed they would indicate that on their paper. However, if one student agreed and the other did not, they would defend their point of view and try to convince the other to change his/her mind. After a good five minutes of discussion, Peggy called all the students back to review what had been discussed. Interestingly, all the students had agreed that being rich meant having lots of money and that having money was very important. In the discussion, some students expressed the idea that it could mean having elaborate, expensive possessions. Most also agreed that people who did bad things could change, if someone helped then. During their discussion, Marcos and Nelson had not agreed about people being able to change. Marcos felt that if someone was bad, they would always be bad; however, Nelson was able to convince him that some people might change if they had help and encouragement. When the discussion was completed, the students read the story. They had the option of reading by themselves or reading with a partner.

The next day, Peggy had students complete the anticipation guide by indicating what they thought the author believed about the three statements. She then had students write written commentary on the three statements. The students' responses were well written and well thought out. Most had understood the author's message and the moral to the story. For the first statement (Being rich means having a lot of money), Anthony responded: "*La autora no[s] muetra que tener mucho dinero no es rica. Por que doña jocefa tenia una moneda de oro pero eso no quiere de sil [decir] que eso e cel rica. La riqueza que tenia doña josefa era la amita de toda la persona."* [The author shows us that to have a lot of money is not being rich. Because Doña Josefa had a gold coin does not mean to be rich. The richness that Doña Josefa had was everyone's friendship.] In response to the second statement (People that do bad things can change) Cristina wrote: *"Yo pienso que la persona que asen mardade pueden canbiar porque Juan canbio porque el sedaba cuenta que la persola loque rian ale asi como el es."* [I think that the person that does bad things can change because Juan changed because he realized that people loved him for who he is.]

In reflecting on the exercise, Peggy felt that the students' responses to the reading were of better quality than previous ones they had written. They wrote their statements of belief and then provided evidence from the story to support their reasoning.

TALK–WRITE APPROACH

Purpose

This approach gives students the opportunity to talk to someone about what they are writing before committing it to paper. It gives them a real sense of audience. Listeners, by asking questions and offering suggestions, help the writers focus on what they intend to write before actually writing out a story. It is helpful for bilingual and second-language learners because they are able to practice orally what they will later write. By talking to someone before writing, bilingual and second-language learners are able to "work out" vocabulary and linguistic structures that might impede their writing. It also provides a partner in the revision process.[5] One teacher adapted the approach by having each student talk about what they were going to write while the other asked questions. Then they both wrote and continued consulting with each other.

Procedure

1. Pair or let students pair themselves: one will be the talk-writer, the other the questioner.

---

[5]See Zoellner (1983) and Wixon and Wixon (1983) for further information about this approach.

2. Give them felt pens and large sheets of paper, or have them use a computer.

3. Suggest a topic to write about, have students choose their own, or suggest a broad topic and have pairs choose subtopics.

4. Start the process of talking, writing, and reading:
   - The writers first talk about what they want to write, the questioners encourage, ask questions, seek clarification, and so forth.
   - Once they feel they have discussed enough, the writers start writing. The questioners help the writers include all information and organize thoughts and compose the sentences, being careful not to dominate the procedure.
   - When completed, the questioners read the entire piece.

5. Circulate through the groups making suggestions when necessary or providing positive encouragement.

6. When all groups have finished, have students tape products on the wall; point out a few examples that demonstrate positive features of writing, or that may focus on a specific skill that is being taught.

Talk–Write assignments should be short, considered first draft, and not be graded.

The Approach in Practice—That's Right!: Talk–Write Approach for Bilingual ASL Students

For Paul's[6] students, the Talk–Write approach proved to be a helpful tool for improving the depth and clarity of their oral and written summaries and reports. Paul, a bilingual English–ASL teacher, adapted the Talk–Write approach for four students (ranging in age from 16 to 18 years old) in his "substantially separate" English class in a public high school. The students are with Paul for 45 minutes each day. During other periods, the students are in mainstreamed classes with 25 to 30 hearing students, a content-area teacher, and a sign language interpreter. Two of the students, Debbie and Lakeysha, are profoundly deaf. They are both bilingual in ASL and English, although Paul stated that they are not completely fluent in ASL, and use a type of sign language called Pidgin Signed English (PSE) when they speak to each other in his English class. Both Debbie and Lakeysha are reading below grade level (fourth-grade

---

[6]Not the real name because we were unable to communicate with the teacher who implemented this approach to obtain permission to use his name.

reading level on standardized testing) and have trouble with vocabulary and grammatical elements in writing.

Another student, Briana, has a mild hearing loss. Her reading comprehension is good, and she has good control of English grammar and syntax. Her main area of difficulty in writing is developing and organizing her thoughts. The fourth student, Robert, is hearing, but has a history of severe language delays. Because of the language problems, Robert attended a school for deaf students and learned sign language. Robert also demonstrates difficulty in organizing his thoughts when writing.

Paul hoped that by using the Talk–Write approach, the students would see the importance of planning and thinking out what they intended to write before committing to paper. He felt that the approach would help the students to better clarify, redefine, extrapolate, infer, draw conclusions, defend and debate in their writing. He also wanted to change the teacher-directed, teacher-centered writing classes in which these students were used to working.

Paul first tried to incorporate the students' reading lessons into the approach. He had planned to assign readings to the four students and then have them work in pairs, and by using the Talk–Write approach, write summaries of the stories read. Briana and Robert were assigned a chapter from *The Outsiders* to read. They were excited because both had seen the movie version of the book. Debbie and Lakeysha were given a chapter from a book whose main character is deaf. When they met again, Paul found that Briana had not read the chapter that was assigned and was therefore not able to contribute to any discussion or summary of the chapter. She was, however, able to help Robert with his summary by asking questions that helped him expand his ideas and elaborate on the summary.

Similar problems were encountered with Lakeysha and Debbie, who complained that they did not really understand the story they were reading. This experience made Paul realize that the students were probably intimidated by the length and complexity of the stories, and also that they should have been able to choose what they read and wrote about. He then allowed the students to decide on their own writing topics. Both Debbie and Lakeysha expressed interest in reading biographies of deaf people, Briana chose to read about musicians from the *Rolling Stone* magazine, and Robert expressed an interest in writing about "heavy metal" bands. Paul noted that the students were then more willing to work on summarizing the articles they had read. Once the students had read their articles and stories, they worked with each other on the summaries, adapting the Talk–Write approach.

While working with Robert, who had read an article about a musical band, Briana was having difficulty in getting him to express more than the basic factual information obtained from the article. She was finally able to encourage him to reread the article and explain why the band about which he was writing was so famous. Robert was able to write a more comprehensive summary with Briana's assistance. Briana also seemed to have gained something from her experience, because she wanted to take Robert's article home to read!

Debbie and Lakeysha had more difficulty critiquing and offering suggestions to each other's signed summaries. Lakeysha, especially, was not comfortable questioning any of Debbie's remarks. Debbie seemed to have a better idea of what the focus of a biographical summary should be. Lakeysha, on the other hand, was not able to focus on the main point of the biography she read. However, after both Debbie and Lakeysha had reread Lakeysha's article, Debbie was able to help Lakeysha improve her signed summary. Neither of the girls, however, felt comfortable correcting or critiquing each other's written summary. They expected Paul to intervene and correct their writing for them.

Debbie had attended a lecture given by Reginald Redding in which he talked about his experiences of being deaf and African American. For another writing assignment, Debbie chose to write a letter to Reginald Redding. In keeping with the Talk–Write approach, Briana worked with Debbie and helped her organize her thoughts before writing. Debbie told Briana in ASL that she wanted to focus on Mr. Redding's experiences as the only African-American deaf student at a school in New Jersey. Because Briana, acting as the questioner, had not attended the lecture, the questions Briana asked Debbie were authentic. She was seeking information from Debbie that would help her understand the main points of Redding's lecture. Briana asked about Mr. Redding's feelings on being the one African-American deaf student in a school that traditionally educated only White deaf students. She stated that Mr. Redding told them that he had to work very hard. Although Debbie did not seem to want to express her own feelings about the issue when talking to Briana, she did mention them in her letter to Redding.

Debbie wanted to begin her letter by introducing herself; Briana suggested that she include information about the topic of the letter and where Debbie had heard Mr. Redding's talk. Debbie accepted Briana's suggestion and included that information in the first paragraph. In his lecture, Mr. Redding had also spoken about his experiences with racism. Debbie alluded to that in her letter, and was able to relate his experiences to her own as an African-American deaf person. Paul felt that Briana's collaboration with Debbie, through her asking questions and offering suggestions, helped Debbie write the following more comprehensive and meaningful letter:

Dear Reggie Reddish

Hello, my name is Debbie _____, and I went to your lecture about Black History month in Public Boxton liabiry at Copley place. We had been ejoy you in there about black history month. I understand your own past because I almost same experience yours owns about other people rasim to yo also I got too from white people. I am sore tht we had same feel about rasim. now there are change law because of Martin Luther King. Jr. for right now I feel like I am share in world with any people. I only depend on other people is there are good people so I can beam friend with each other thank lord that i am still friend with any peole in the United State.

I am 16 yers old, I am deaf black girl because when I am twenty-two months old, I got high fever i call spinal menigtis. I went though all hearing mate in school only not middle school only deaf and for right now I am in _____ High School it is for hearing mate classroom. also I want to go college and my goal to become a lawyer or psychrlogist or eye doctor. I am not sure because I am in 10th grade now I will be two year later to gradute from high school.

We go visit to Gallaudet college on April 13th and 14th. We want be our guide of M.S.S.D if that okay? Okay thank you for your pleasure to listen us and I hope you will have nice day.

Sincerely

Debbie _____

Lakeysha, who had also attended the lecture, decided to write a summary of Mr. Redding's talk. Unlike Debbie, Lakeysha was not able to incorporate the suggestions of her classmates into her writing. She preferred to sign her ideas to either Debbie or Briana who then wrote them on paper. Once Lakeysha looked over her written ideas, she elaborated and expanded on them using sign language. She still was not comfortable with the writing stage of the Talk–Write approach.

Although each of the four students progressed differently through this Talk–Write approach, Paul believes it helped them all become better writers. He felt that the approach especially helped Lakeysha and Debbie, the two profoundly deaf students, who demonstrated better writing skills when first given the opportunity to express their ideas to others in sign language. This approach also helped students to remain on task. When one felt like chatting, the other would remind him or her of the task at hand and the work proceeded in earnest.

6

Approaches with Focus on Language

An important component of teaching literacy to second language learners is to teach language. Students need language to access and express ideas. Depending on age, level of proficiency, and extent of stay in the country, students will have different needs. Older more recent arrivals may have difficulty with phonology (sound system) while younger learners master this aspect of language early on. Teachers should be aware that nativelike pronunciation does not mean full mastery of the language, especially the academic register required in schools. This academic language develops through reading (chap. 3), writing (chap. 4), oral language (chap. 5), and content area (chap. 7). In this chapter we focus on approaches that support development of vocabulary and grammatical structures. Students who are new to English will have to develop this language from scratch. Those who have some fluency in English or who are native speakers of the language of instruction, will need the vocabulary and complex structures more typical of literacy events, either oral or written.

The acquisition of the sound system becomes more difficult after age 7.[1] Although phonology may improve, older students may never acquire native-like pronunciation. Many of the phonological errors at these early stages of development are the result of transfer from the native language. For example, Japanese L2 learners have difficulty distinguishing the /r/ and /l/ sounds and may pronounce *row* as *low*. Spanish speakers have difficulty with initial consonant clusters that include /s/. They often add an initial vowel, pronouncing /student/ as /estudent/. Russian

---

[1]Genesee et al., 2004

130

speakers have difficulty with the initial th- sounds pronouncing thin as sin and then as zen.[2]

Most important is helping students make their speech comprehensible. Researchers and practitioners recommend global instruction of pronunciation, including: word and sentence stress, intonation and rhythm, projection, and speech rate to enhance comprehensibility. Materials such as *Jazz Chants* by Graham (1978) and *Sounds Great* by Beisbier (1995) were successful in improving these more global aspects of pronunciation. Focus on just individual sounds improves the pronunciation of difficult words but does not render the speech of L2 learners more comprehensible.[3]

Vocabulary acquisition is crucial to the language development of students. It is especially important for second language learners who need to interact socially with their monolingual peers as well as acquire academic vocabulary that will assist them in understanding major concepts in various subject areas. Studies with both monolingual and bilingual populations have shown that there is a correlation between vocabulary knowledge and reading comprehension, that is, those readers with a larger repertoire of words comprehended text more easily and efficiently than those students who had a poor knowledge of vocabulary.[4]

Vocabulary acquisition is difficult because of the sheer numbers of words L2 learners need to acquire to catch up with native speakers. At the start of elementary schooling a native speaker may already have five thousand words, while at the beginning of secondary education they may have 40 thousand. Children acquire an average of three thousand new words every year.[5] L2 learners with a strong education background acquire words in the second language at great speed because they already have a lot of the concepts in their first language. Learners new to the English language should be introduced fairly quickly to the list of approximately 1,500 to 2,000 high frequency words.[6] To assist second language learners in learning content vocabulary, Echevarria, Vogt and Short (2004) suggest selecting several key terms from a lesson's material that will facilitate concept development. They also advocate providing explicit teaching of what they call "school language," for example words such as: identify, define, compare, summarize. The use of real objects, pictures,

---

[2]For a thorough review of the various areas of difficulty for L2 speakers of a variety of language backgrounds see Swan and Smith (2001).

[3]Derwing and Rossiter (2003).

[4]Proctor, Carlo, August, and Snow (2005); Tan and Nicholson (1997).

[5]Nagy (2000).

[6]Nation (2005).

movement, rephrasing ideas, and role-playing are other suggested strategies for vocabulary development.[7]

To compensate for the limited vocabulary, L2 beginners may resort to gestures. For example, a kindergarten student eager to participate in the discussion of the book *David Goes to School* said, "David . . ." and proceeded to act out what he wanted to express but lacked the words in English to do it. Another productive strategy is to paraphrase indicating the meaning. For example, a child, who did not know the word for zoo, said to the teacher, "My mother brought me to the animals. They live there." In these situations, teachers and fellow students could assist in the language development by recasting in words what the student wanted to express. For example say, "Your mother brought you to the zoo." And then write the word on a card and put it up on the wall or in a vocabulary notebook.

Students need to acquire different types of words. In addition to the words used in daily life and familial conversation (my father *drives* a big machine), students need to acquire more sophisticated words (my father *operates* heavy machinery) found in written text as well as domain specific words (have you completed the *operations* required to solve the math problem?) required in different content areas. They also need to learn the multiple meanings of words which differ in English from their heritage language. For example, *table* in English and Spanish (*tabla*) refer to a type of graph (the information is included in this *table*). In English it is also used for the piece of furniture (in Spanish *mesa*) and *table of contents* (in Spanish *índice*).

Sound, spelling, and structural complexity create difficulty in vocabulary comprehension. Some of these sources of difficulty include:[8]

- Spelling (laughed, Wednesday, picture, business)
- Acoustic similarity (teacher said: *equality*; students understood: *a quality*)
- Same sound, different spelling, different meaning (eye/I)
- Different sound, same spelling, different meaning (tear/tear)
- Same sound, same spelling, different meaning (scale/scale)
- Length: (word: *competition*; child read: *comption*)
- Syntactic class (child said *I'm boring* for *I'm bored*)

Teaching students about cognates is helpful for vocabulary development. English language learners, especially those with knowledge of

---

[7]Cary (2000); Herrell and Jordan (2004).
[8]See Birch (2002) for a complete analysis of vocabulary difficulties.

Greek, or Romance or Germanic languages, can often draw on their linguistic backgrounds to determine words' meanings in English. Andrew was pleasantly surprised to learn that his recent arrival high school student was able to handle what he thought would be difficult vocabulary because her background knowledge of Greek helped her understand English words with Greek roots. Many students, however, do not readily see the connection between their first language and English. They need to be encouraged and taught how to use what they know in their L1 to learn new words in their L2.

The grammatical difficulties that learners have when using their second language are multiple. At the discourse level connectors (*however, nevertheless, therefore*) that mark relationships between sections of the text are problematic and usually overused.[9] Conjunctions or pronouns connecting sentences create difficulty, especially because the referent is unclear (The police caught the thief. *He* was hurt). Errors in word order, which can differ from language to language, are mostly transfer errors. For example a Spanish, French, or Vietnamese speaker will say "the house white" following the Spanish, French, or Vietnamese rule to put the adjective after the noun. Although the possessive constructions *the car of my father* and *my father's car* are both accepted in English, the latter is more natural for native speakers. Beginner French or Spanish-speakers prefer the first form because it matches how possessive is done in their languages. Other typical sources of difficulty are using *she* for *he* and vice versa. Often L2 speakers omit the auxiliary to do in negative structures (*I no want money*) and questions, indicated with rising intonation (*Where put the book?*).

Second language learners often use incorrectly or omit grammatical morphemes. Below is a list of the most common errors of grammatical morphemes in young L2 learners:[10]

- be-copula: I dunno if she my grandmother [*is* missing]
- be-auxiliary: Women and children working in the farm [*were* missing]
- Past –ed: I open my eyes [opened]
- Irregular past: I take my sleeping clothes [took]; I didn't sawed [see]
- Past tense form + auxiliary *do*: I didn't knew [know]

---

[9]See Hinkel (2002).

[10]This list is extracted from the research reported by Genesee et al., 2004. (An extensive list of examples can be found on pp. 124–127). Teachers of students of many ages throughout the world report similar errors in learning English.

- Prepositions: "no eating bus" [*on* and article missing]; "I have two Zach on my classroom." [used *on* instead of *in*]
- Plural –s: "I need two book." [*books*]
- Determiners: "and it gots basement" [*a* missing; gots for has]; "I can eat the ice cream" [*the* unnecessary]
- Possessives: "Sleeping beauty dress was . . ." [*beauty's*]; ". . . if I let them borrow something of mines I will expect to get it back." [*mine*]
- Third person –s: "in the picture it show train, cotton mill and desk." [*shows*]; "my dad don't wanna watch TV" [*doesn't*]

As children develop their second language they make fewer of these errors. At times, they may use morphemes correctly and incorrectly in the same sentence. With proficiency, when used incorrectly, they know how to repair the error. Teachers need to understand that the acquisition of these features of the language is developmental. Depending on the age

---

Notes for First Year English Learners

- Conduct mini-lessons to provide language needed for a basic understanding of the lesson.
- Introduce important vocabulary on the topic of the lesson orally and in writing before the lesson.
- Write sentences with important words or phrases in context
- Concentrate more on communication skills than grammar skills.
- Incorporate beginning English language objectives into lessons.
- Provide books in English on tape so that students can see written language structure.
- Don't use synonyms or a lot of idioms for known words.
- Label objects in your classroom
- Provide instructions and steps of tasks in writing. Point to them when saying them orally
- Beware of sarcasm and indirect speech.
- Slow down speech and use shorter and simpler sentences.
- Keep passages short and monitor comprehension as you go along.
- Use pictures, lists, charts, Venn diagrams, graphic organizers, objects, maps, graphs, body language, experiments, and lesson related video clips to support language explanations.

when the students started intensive exposure to the second language, they may or may not ever acquire some aspects of the grammar. When students focus on the message and want to elaborate, often their grammar and spelling or pronunciation suffer. Teachers must, on the one hand, search for the richness of meaning within inaccurate language. On the other hand, they must help students reach accuracy or at least the ability to repair language, particularly in writing.

The approaches included in this chapter help students focus on language in more detail. In addition to the approaches included in this chapter, taping and analyzing portions of the students' language during group discussion (chap. 5) can be helpful in language instruction. They are particularly useful for second language development, but they can help students with limited literacy in their first language as well. The following approaches are presented and illustrated with a case study:

- Dictogloss
- Vocabulary Connections
- Language Experience Approach (LEA)
- Show Not Tell

Dictogloss exposes students to academic language in a context where they must notice language. By working in groups recreating the academic text, students support each other. Although the approach was developed for high school students by choosing age/grade level appropriate material, it can be adopted to various grade and language proficiency levels by using text for different levels of proficiency. It is especially useful to make students familiar with the language of content areas and a good way to introduce a topic.

Dictogloss and Reformulation (see chap. 8) encourage language learning because students have the opportunity to notice and discuss language. The following rich conversation on language occurred between James and Mark when working on Mark's sentence "here are the reson why I pike that they won of my best day ever." Afra, the teacher, used the Reformulation strategy to help students notice language.

James: You need to write capital *h*.

Mark: *here are . . .* (writing)

James: No, no . . . capital *H*. You need to write capital *H*.

Afra: Why do you need to capitalize?

Mark: Because it's a beginning of a new sentence.

James: Here are the reasons why I . . . (dictating as Mark writes)

Mark: (Tries to spell reason out loud.) It is *r e s o n*?

James: No, it's *r e a s o n* . . . and it's *picked* not *piked*.

Mark: *Here are the reasons why I picked . . . this day?*

James: . . . *that day* . . . because it's in the past.

Mark: *I picked that they* . . . oh, OK it says that right here (referring to the reformulation) *that day* . . . I probably changed *they* to *day*.

James: Let me read it all. (Looks at what Mark has been writing.) *Here are the reasons why I picked that day one of the best day ever* . . . See that doesn't make sense.

Afra: What doesn't make sense?

Mark: . . . *why I picked that day one of my best days* . . . no the best day ever.

James: I think we should cross this out . . . (*one of the best day ever*), and then must leave *the reasons why I picked that day*. Then you start writing about it.

Mark: Yeah, telling why it . . . was the best day ever.

Afra: So, how would you write it? (Mark is writing.)

Mark: (Reads what he has written.) *Here are the reasons why I picked that day one of my best days ever.* Sounds better? *best day ever* . . . yeah, that sounds good (answering himself).

Vocabulary is key to successful literacy acquisition. Vocabulary is a major predictor in reading comprehension. Vocabulary knowledge in the first language is also a predictor of vocabulary development in the second language. There are many ways to teach vocabulary. The approach included in this chapter (Vocabulary Connections) is particularly sensitive to students' cultural backgrounds. Much clarification and cross-cultural explanations can be done during the discussions on how students associate the words to their lives. Because of the importance of vocabulary development, a number of additional suggestions for teaching vocabulary follow the section on Vocabulary Connections. Teachers should incorporate teaching of vocabulary into every lesson. Vocabulary development is an important component of the Read-Aloud Approach (see Chapter 8). Methods used to teach vocabulary from context include: choosing words that may be unfamiliar to the students, but are used often in texts, discussing them in context and then having students create their own sentences using the words;[11] choosing words that the learner is unable to

---

[11]Beck, McKeown, and Kucan (2002).

recognize or pronounce and repeatedly reading the text and signaling recognition of the words;[12] highlighting pictures, motioning or paraphrasing during reading.[13]

The LEA approach was developed to initiate children to reading. We have used it with students of all ages to introduce the first and second language for reading, writing, and language development. It is particularly helpful to introduce literacy in the native language to older students with limited or no schooling. LEA is good to help students develop language structure, vocabulary, and spelling. When working in the second language, students could express themselves in either language and then work on rendering the whole piece in English with the help of more fluent bilinguals.

Show Not Tell is a very specific approach to improve something the students have already written. It helps students develop rich expression and should be coordinated with other writing approaches. By enhancing the detail of their text, students learn words that more precisely describe what they want to say. One of the aspects of language that needs to be developed in the academic discourse is to be explicit and precise. Students are so used to interacting with people with whom they share context that they do not realize that unless they are more precise they are not going to be understood by others. For example, their science procedural recount may read "I put it there" rather than "I put the colored water in the beaker."

DICTOGLOSS[14]

Purpose

In the Dictogloss approach students hear repeated, fluent readings of text, which in many cases would involve academic language. Teachers can choose text to target specific aspects of language. It is best to carry out this strategy with short text. If the text is long, it is best to select small sections. Each section should be done at a separate time with the students reading the rest of the text on their own, pairs or any other way deemed appropriate. If the selection is too long the students may feel overwhelmed.

---

[12]Li and Nes (2003).

[13]Freeman and Freeman (2000).

[14]Gibbons (2002); Jacobs, G. and Small, J. (2003); Wajnryb, R. (1990).

Students take notes as they hear the dictation and then rewrite what they thought they heard from the dictation. It helps students learn note-taking skills as they focus on the main ideas of text.

Bilingual students benefit from this approach in that it combines language learning with content learning. All four language skills (listening, speaking, reading, and writing) are integrated in this approach. This strategy engages students in talking about language. By comparing notes and revising students notice language. Noticing facilitates language acquisition, especially of details of language. This strategy provides students with good models of written language and helps them try to use such language.

Procedure

1. Present the topic of the text to be studied. It's best to use material the students know something about.
2. Read a short passage at normal speed while your students just listen.
3. Reread once or twice at normal speed. Students write as much as possible, particularly key words and phrases. The aim is to get as much information as possible.
4. Have students work in pairs discussing and improving their notes. Then they work with another pair improving the notes further and writing a final product. They should aim at producing a coherent and complete text using as much as possible the words from the text. For the final version they should also work on grammar and spelling.
5. Compare original with student produced text to show differences and praise ways that students expressed themselves differently.

The Approach in Practice:

When Peggy (co-author) learned about this approach she thought it would be an effective way for her Spanish bilingual fourth grade students to work both on improving their English language skills and learning how to listen to and understand important academic language.

She decided to use the approach during the students' social studies period. The students had been studying about the 13 original English colonies in North America. The next unit of study was the Revolutionary War. The students had already done an activity on taxes and learned that the colonists felt that the taxation laws that they were under were too harsh. Peggy began the Dictogloss Approach by reminding the students about the taxation activity and explained about the impending war. She then explained the Dictogloss Approach to the students and told them that they would be learning to take notes to help them understand the topic they were about to study.

Peggy chose to read a few passages from the social studies book. For the first reading, she read the text at a normal speed and instructed the students to just listen. She read the text again at normal speed, this time instructing the students to write down (in bulleted form) anything they thought was important information.

When she had finished reading the second time, the students formed pairs and discussed what they had written down. They rewrote their notes to reflect what they had discussed in their pair. Another pair then joined them and the four discussed what they had written. Peggy explained to the groups of four that they were to try to rewrite the original text using their notes as a guide.

Most of the groups had difficulty getting started. However, they were able to settle down and negotiate with each other about what and how to write. Peggy worked with two groups who didn't really seem to understand the instructions. Once she clarified the directions they were able to get to work. One group of students, the majority of whom were at the beginning proficiency level in English, was allowed to write in Spanish.

While the groups were working, Peggy walked around to help any group that needed assistance. As she was walking around, Peggy noted that students in the group were trying to clarify meaning. For example, in one group Emily had stated, "all of the African-Americans had died." Catherine quickly corrected the statement to "one of the dead was an African-American." In another group, Jason expressed his confusion about whether the colonists actually threw tea into the harbor.

In other groups students were helping each other on grammatical and syntactical aspects of what they were writing. While Nelson was writing one of the sentences, Kelvin stopped him to make sure he has written an "s" on the word soldier to indicate plural. In her group, Sharinna was writing a sentence about the Boston Massacre and asked her group if what she had written made sense.

Peggy repeated the Dictogloss approach for the remainder of the social studies chapter. When the students had finished their rewriting of the dictation, she had them write a summary of the main ideas of the chapter. The results were very encouraging. The students had really seemed to capture the crux of the chapter. To make sure that all students understood the chapter, Peggy had them individually write the main idea of the chapter along with three details supporting the idea. Again, the students showed that they had understood the chapter well. Andrea wrote: "The George the 3rd sent governers to the colonist so they cuod get taxes and the colonist didint like it. A) the colonist made protest B) They droped the tea on the ocean C) The king didint listen." José, a beginning English learner, chose to write his assignment in Spanish: "Los coloni estava enfogenados porque aria una nueva regal que ellos tenian que pagar tax. 1) peliando por libertad 2) atuando como indios 3) botando el tee al agua." (*The colonists were angry because there was a new rule that they had to pay tax. 1) fighting for liberty 2) disguising themselves as Indians 3) throwing tea into the water.*)

For Peggy, the Dictogloss approach was a great way to introduce a new history chapter to her students. She felt that they were learning how to hone their listening skills when hearing English academic text. She also believed that the collaborative effort when the students were working in groups helped the students who were less proficient in English understand the concepts better. Students also worked on specific sentence construction and grammatical accuracy.

VOCABULARY CONNECTIONS

Purpose

Vocabulary is the single most important area of second-language competency when learning content.[15] This approach to teaching vocabulary makes the students active learners and allows them to draw on their own cultural backgrounds and knowledge to establish meanings of words. Students make connections between the vocabulary and their own life's experiences before reading a selection, thereby validating their prior knowledge.[16]

Procedure

Following are the procedures for the Vocabulary Connections approach:

1. Choose a reading selection.
2. Choose 5 to 10 words crucial to understanding the selection, preferably in no more than one or two semantic fields.

---

[15]Saville-Troike (1984).
[16]See Torres-Guzman (1992) for further information about this approach.

3. Ask the students to look up the definitions of the words in the dictionary. (This can be done as homework.)
4. Have students discuss the definitions as well as give examples in their own lives of the selected words and their meanings. Clarify added meanings the words may have in the cultural context of the author.
5. Have students read the selection.
6. Have students retell or write a summary of the selection. Encourage them to use their new vocabulary.

The Approach in Practice: Students' Background Knowledge in the Classroom

For the seventh graders in Antolin Medina's Spanish bilingual history class, the vocabulary approach helped the students relate words from their history text to their own lives. The 16 students in the class were from six different Latin American countries. The students had varying literacy abilities in their first language.

The students' history book was a Spanish translation of a book written in English specifically for students in the United States. Antolin felt that his students were at a disadvantage, because they might not be as familiar with U.S. history as what the authors of the text had assumed. He felt that the students needed extra support in understanding the vocabulary of the text, because the context of it in the history text might be incongruous to their experiences.

Before reading the chapter on the American Civil War (1861–1865), Antolin listed eight words that he felt were important for a true understanding of the chapter. The words selected were:

alocución (address)

abolicionista (abolitionist)

guerra civil (civil war)

emancipación (emancipation)

plantación (plantation)

proclamación (proclamation)

estrategia (strategy)

táctica (tactics)

The students first looked up the meaning of the words in the Spanish dictionary. The students worked in groups and wrote down the meaning of the words as one student read aloud from the dictionary. Students then discussed the meanings of the words until all were sure that they understood the meaning as explained in the dictionary.

Antolin then had the students try to find examples from their personal lives for which they could use one of the vocabulary words. The students willingly participated in the discussion. They related the terms to many aspects of their own lives from personal experiences in school to international politics. For the word *address*, one student used the example: "Principals address the whole school sometimes." Another student said, "Presidents do it all the time."

Many students were able to provide personal examples for civil war. A student from El Salvador, whose family owned land in the rural region of the country, related how his family had to leave their property and move to the city because they were "tired of being between two fires." He explained that his grandfather (the head of the family) had to supply food and other materials to both the government army and the guerrillas whenever they crossed his property. They were also constantly being warned not to help the other side of the conflict.

Although the students did understand the general meaning of *plantation* (i.e., a planted area farmed by paid workers), Antolin felt the need to explain its significance in the American Civil War period. After his explanation, students were able to relate it more easily to their experiences. One student saw a similarity between the plantations of that era and the situation of many Haitian laborers in the Dominican Republic.

When the students were not able to provide examples, Antolin explained the concept. When the students could not relate the term *abolitionist* to anything in their lives, Antolin explained how the abolitionists were opposed to slavery and were named so because they wanted to *abolish* it from in North America and the Caribbean Islands.

When the discussion of the vocabulary had finished, the class read the assigned chapter. Students took turns reading the selection. Following the reading, students answered general comprehension questions about the selection. For homework, the students wrote a summary of the major events of the civil war. In the summary, they had to include the vocabulary words that had been discussed prior to the reading.

Antolin noticed a great improvement in the summaries done by the students on this Civil War chapter. Previously, many students tended to copy sentences directly from the textbooks for their summaries. No student did that in his or her Civil War summaries. They showed an understanding of the main events of the Civil War and were able to use the vocabulary correctly.

Students in Antolin's class improved comprehension of their social studies text by learning relevant vocabulary. Internalizing new words required more than just looking up the dictionary definition. Students needed to associate the words with their personal experiences and background knowledge, to understand the cultural context of the words, and to discuss topics associated with these words.

Additional Vocabulary Approaches

What follows are examples of how teachers and tutors incorporate the teaching of vocabulary in their lessons. It was evident as they were working with their students that lack of vocabulary was inhibiting reading comprehension and fluency. The approaches used to teach new vocabulary ranged from direct instruction in the meaning of words found in stories to teaching students how to independently determine the meaning of unknown words.

Caroline Clark tried several approaches for teaching vocabulary during her Read-Aloud activities with a ten-year-old native Spanish-speaking fourth grader that she was tutoring. She chose words from the texts she was reading aloud that were common either in academic or informal language situations, were not as familiar as other words, or were repeated in the story. For the first two sessions, Caroline introduced the words to her student before the reading. After the reading she reviewed the words again with the student. To assess whether her student remembered the meaning of the introduced words, Caroline had him use the words in sentences. Both times he was able to provide appropriate responses for 2 of the 3 words learned.

For the next two read-alouds Caroline did not discuss the vocabulary words before reading, but rather presented them after the book had been read and then showed him the words in context. A third type of vocabulary method was used for the last read-aloud. Caroline chose to teach the words that her student had problems pronouncing or was not able to define when asked.

At the end of all the sessions with her student, Caroline gave a culminating vocabulary quiz. His accuracy level on that quiz was approximately 75 percent. She found that although all three approaches helped increase her student's vocabulary, the more effective approach seemed to be words that were taken from the text based on the student's inability to pronounce or recognize them.

For Ciara O'Connell role-playing was an effective way of helping Marie, her first-grade Haitian second language learner develop the vocabulary she needed to express her emotions and handle conflicts with her classmates. Ciara's school had adopted a conflict resolution curriculum that had a role-play component. Teachers and peers model (role-play) concepts that help children deal with conflict in their daily life. Since the children in the class were not yet able to write, not able to create a skit of their own, Ciara decided to role-play words for the students.

She chose six basic emotion/feeling words: happy, sad, angry, scared, surprised, and disgusted. For each lesson, she showed a photograph of a child expressing the emotion word that she wanted the children to learn that day. Ciara elicited examples from the children of their experiences with each emotion as it was introduced. She then explained to the children that they would be doing some role-playing. She associated role-playing with pretending and imagining hoping that the children would make the connection between the words. The Haitian student seemed to be able to grasp the concepts as they were introduced. She was even able to role-play her expression of sadness when asked what she would do if her sisters teased her.

More telling of her comprehension of new vocabulary was that this student was able to use the new words spontaneously. For example, one day she complained to Ciara that one of the other students was "frustrating" her because he had taken her spot on the rug. On another occasion it was the Haitian student who was told by a fellow student that she had made her mad by taking her crayons. Ciara helped both girls resolve the conflict by using their newly learned vocabulary to express their feelings.

Ciara believed that introducing vocabulary through role-playing reinforced the learning of the words for her student and helped her gain more confidence in speaking up when conflicts arose. She also showed more confidence when attempting new words.

Along with teaching new vocabulary words from books they were reading together, Nicole wanted to ensure that her tutee would be able to use helpful strategies when she was reading independently. She taught her how to preview a book before reading so that she could activate any background knowledge she had on the topic of the book and make connections to the story.

Nicole saw her student using this strategy as she was reading a book about a student starting school. As she was previewing the text, she told Nicole that the book reminded her of when she started school in the United States. She was scared but excited starting school. While she was reading the story, she encountered the word *frightened*. She didn't know the word and tried to read on. Nicole observed that by reading the word in context and connecting what she had read to her own experiences starting school, she was able to discern what the word *frightened* meant: "Junie was frightened of starting kindergarten. What if nobody wanted to be her friend?" On the other hand when her student encountered <u>fossils</u> she thought it was <u>pictures</u> because they were found in a museum. Pictures can also be misleading. Her student thought that the word <u>tepee</u> meant sister because the picture showed a sister waving good-bye. The tepees in the background were barely discernable.

She also secured a children's dictionary for her student and spent considerable time teaching her how to use it. Although it took some time for her to learn how to utilize the dictionary when reading, Nicole felt that over time it helped her student with her reading comprehension. Additionally, since it was the student herself who chose which words to look up, she was becoming more responsible for her own learning and selected words that were important for her to know.

LANGUAGE EXPERIENCE APPROACH

Purpose

The Language Experience Approach (LEA) helps develop reading and writing through the use of students' own language, thoughts, and ideas. Students are able to read the stories with minimal cuing because they already know the meaning. The LEA does not require a specific level of proficiency in any language. Students working in a second language are able to develop at their own pace, using language they know and use in their own lives. It also opens a window to their cultures and ideas. It provides the teacher with a baseline for assessing the individual needs of the second-language learner. In a bilingual classroom it allows for choice of language.[17]

Procedure

This activity can be done with the whole class, a group, or individual students. Students will dictate a story to you. Follow these steps to execute the Language Experience Approach:

1. Conversation may suggest experience stories. The students may retell a news item, give a description of a job, game, toy, or an event happening in their life, or a sports story. A picture book with words covered is another resource.

---

[17]See Dixon and Nessel (1983), Peregoy and Boyle (1996), and Rigg (1989) for more information on this approach.

2. The entire story is written (on the board, chart paper, overhead film, or computer) as the students speak. Alternatively, sticky notepaper can be used to write the story and students can arrange sentences afterward. When working with the whole class or group, let students volunteer sentences. The name of the students can be placed next to their sentences.

3. Although the original approach recommends writing exactly what the students say, you can intervene on particular occasions to seize the opportunity to teach language. For example, Pedro dictated: "If I had magic, I will not clean the floor." The teacher, realizing that he was going to dictate other sentences explaining what else he would do, decided to teach him the use of the conditional. Before writing it down, she repeated the sentence correctly "If you had magic, you would not clean the floor?" and asked Pedro if he agreed. Because he nodded affirmatively, she wrote it correctly. For the following two sentences Pedro still used *will*. The teacher repeated the process. By the fourth sentence, Pedro, on his own, used *would*. Second-language learners need feedback if they are to learn the language.

4. Read the entire story to the students, point to individual words. Remember that precision in pointing is very important.

5. Reread a sentence, pointing to the words; then have the students read that sentence, pointing to the words.

Follow-Up Activities

1. Pick out the meaningful words in the story. These words may be underlined. Write a word card for each of the words selected. Teach these words as sight words.

2. The students match their word cards with duplicates in the story, reading each word.

3. Either you or the students mix the cards, and the students read word cards independently. If they have trouble, they may match the word cards again with the story until they know several of them. Be satisfied with a reasonable number of words learned, depending on the students' abilities and learning paces.

4. Other word games can be played with these or other words or sentences from the story. These words may become a part of the students' vocabulary card-pack to be reviewed at your discretion.

5. The students may take their story and the word cards home.

6. You make a set of word cards.

The Approach in Practice: Teaching Reading in the Special Education Resource Room

The LEA proved to be a helpful approach for Laurie Whitten's first-grade student Teddy. Although Teddy was born in the United States, his family speaks Greek at home, and Teddy attends a Greek-language school in addition to attending a monolingual English public school. Teddy had been referred for special education evaluation by his classroom teacher because of problems he experienced maintaining on-task behavior. This lack of attention was very evident during reading activities. He had difficulty with reading fluency and decoding, and lacked knowledge of strategies to use when encountering such problems. Laurie felt that the LEA might help Teddy increase his fluency and build up his sight-word vocabulary.

Laurie began her sessions with Teddy by showing him several picture books. She told him that he could pick whichever book he liked and that he was to write a story about it. So that Teddy would not be distracted or intimidated by the words on the page, Laurie covered the text of the story. Although the use of a book is not necessarily part of the LEA, Laurie felt that it would help Teddy maintain focus and develop a story sense. She also felt that using picture books while covering the text of the story helped second-language learners focus on making their own meaning for the story. Often, students new to United States culture do not understand the content of the story.

After a few minutes discussing several books, Teddy chose *Milton the Early Riser*, by Kraus and began dictating his own story to Laurie, who wrote on yellow sticky papers. By writing the story on the sticky papers, Teddy was able to change the order of his story if he so chose. Both Laurie and Teddy read and reread portions of the story as it developed. Laurie was careful to make sure that the words were pointed to as they were read. This first story and session with Teddy gave Laurie a good deal of information on words and sounds with which Teddy was having difficulty. She was able to note the sounds she should work on with Teddy and the words (such as *want, went,* and *with*), which he often confused. Because the focus of reading lessons in his classroom was a phonics-based approach, Laurie decided that she would work on context-based approaches to help Teddy with word identification.

In the following sessions, Laurie began transferring the sentences from the yellow sticky papers to sentence strips. Teddy participated by dictating the sentences to Laurie from the sticky papers. He was very motivated as he saw his story being displayed. He also made changes to his story, adding details and personal pronouns. For example, when adding the sentence "but the bear friends didn't answer him," to the story, Teddy changed it to "but *his* bear friends didn't answer him." If Teddy had difficulty with the words in the sentences, Laurie worked on using context clue strategies for him to read the words. Many times by reading the remainder of a sentence, Teddy was able to go back and read an unfamiliar word. Laurie found that an added benefit to Teddy's learning to read difficult words from context clues was that he was more inclined to read the sentence again, which increased his fluency skills. The rereading of the sentence was not what he usually did when he tried to decode a word. He usually just said the word and went on, but did not really comprehend what he had read.

Laurie did work on decoding skills with Teddy when he was very close to reading the word correctly. She sometimes cued him with the beginning sound. On words he confused frequently, she pointed out the differences in the beginning or ending sounds of the words. For example, he consistently confused the word *announcement* for *compliment*, probably because he had learned the word *compliment* and would say that word whenever he saw the "ment" ending. Laurie reminded him to look at the beginning sounds of the word, so that he would see that the word *announcement* could not be *compliment,* because it did not begin with a /k/ sound. After looking at the first two syllables, he was able to remember the word *announcement.*

She also used decoding strategies in helping Teddy distinguish between *want, went,* and *with*. He often needed to be cued to look at the letters and say the sounds. During one session, Laurie had Teddy go through the story he had written and color code the three words. After looking at all the words he had marked on the paper, he expressed how much work he had done! They then talked about the similarities and differences in the words, and Teddy began focusing on the middle sounds in each word. To reinforce the lesson, Laurie dictated sentences from the story, but omitted the three problem words. Teddy was to hold up the word card containing the correct word needed to complete the sentence. He was able to correctly use the word *with,* and improved his accuracy using the words *went* and *want*.

When they had completed transforming the story from the yellow sticky papers to sentences strips, Laurie used the text for cloze[18] and sequencing exercises. Teddy was able to fill in the missing words without having to refer to the story. She also made a smaller, typed version of the story in which Teddy drew illustrations.

---

[18]This is a technique in which words (usually every fifth or seventh or so forth) in a sentence are omitted. Students are required to provide appropriate words to complete the sentence.

When they had completed their book, Teddy read the original *Milton the Early Riser* book. He was able to read the first 12 pages with no problems, reading quite fluently, and easily recognizing many of the words. Teddy was also very interested in comparing his version of the story to the original.

In evaluating the success of the LEA with Teddy, Laurie found that there was a decrease in his guessing at words and that he was using decoding skills more. He also demonstrated an increase in the use of context clues to help him in his decoding. She observed better fluency in Teddy's reading, both of his own story and the original version of the story. Another positive outcome of the approach for Teddy was that he was able to stay on task for an extended period of time, 40 to 45 minutes.

Laurie believed that Teddy's reading abilities were better than what had previously been thought. What Teddy needed was a text and an environment that would motivate him to read. When provided with a text reflecting his ideas and language patterns, along with the encouragement to use other strategies beyond initial consonant sounds, both Teddy's fluency and interest increased.

SHOW NOT TELL[19]

Purpose

The Show Not Tell approach helps increase students' use of detail and clarity in story writing. Students learn to clarify detail and draw a picture or scene with the words they write. For example, students write: "The movie was fantastic because it was so real." What is meant by "fantastic" and "real"? When working with bilingual students, the approach shows how students from different cultures picture something. Show Not Tell can be applied to writings the students produce through the use of other approaches.

Procedure

1. Practice for about 10 minutes daily having students expand a general statement into a paragraph. Examples:
    The room is vacant.
    Lunch period is too short.
    She has a good personality.

---

[19]See Caplan (1983) for further information about this approach.

Have students write so that the reader can *picture* what they mean. Share some of the pieces with the class each day. Read them aloud and have students comment only on the content of the writing.

2. Apply the approach to revision by having students work in groups. The "editors" underline sentences they think are underdeveloped or unclear. The writers then have to work to improve the sentence by expanding it and clarifying it. They then resubmit to the group for further comments or suggestions.

3. Daily writing can be used to improve specific techniques, such as persuasive argument—debating the pros and cons of a short lunch period; or comparison and contrast—showing similarities of school in native country and school in the United States; or sequencing—listing the steps for making a dish native to students' countries, and so forth.

The Approach in Practice—"She was Dazzling": Making a Picture With Words

It is often the experience for children learning a second language to be removed from their classroom for a certain time during the day or week to work with another teacher or assistant in a small group on various language skills, a program often referred to as a pull-out program. This was the case for the three children with whom Elizabeth (Beth) E. Morse worked. They worked with an ESL teacher who saw the children twice a week for 45 minutes. Beth, a graduate student volunteer, was working with the ESL teacher to help improve the writing skills of the three fourth-grade students, two girls (Misha from Russia and Min from China) and a boy (Andre from Russia). All three students were considered advanced English learners, although Misha was a less advanced writer than the other two.

Beth's role was to support the ESL teacher in teaching Process Writing to the students. Students initiated writing with their ESL teacher, so Beth decided to work on teaching the students to add more detail to their stories. Beth felt that the Show Not Tell approach would help her accomplish this goal. Because she met with the students only once a week, she had to adapt the approach.

In their ESL classroom, the students had been studying fairy tales and were working on writing their own. Beth first reviewed their knowledge of the five senses and the importance of the who, what, when, where, why, and how questions in writing. She felt that the introduction of these two concepts would give the students a framework from which to work when adding details to stories they had written. Beth explained to the students that they should picture in their minds what the characters looked like and then write down a description. Initially, Andre had written a simple sentence about the setting and characters in his story:

There was a castle and there was a king with his son.

His son was a prince. He hated peas. The king hated peas too.

King's name was Francis and the prince name was Christopher.

After working with the students on mentally picturing the characters and setting, Beth saw some improvement in the details of the descriptions. Andre revised his description of the castle to include that it was made of straw. When Min was having difficulty mentally visualizing her characters, Beth suggested that she draw a picture of them first, then write a description from the picture she had drawn. Min drew a picture of a king and queen and then described them: ". . . She was pretty, She had brown hair and a betuflul smeles." And, ". . . a wicked king he was ugly, and had red big eyes."

Beth taught the students to *show* attributes of their characters rather than just *tell* what they were like. She assisted students with difficult vocabulary. She helped them find words they needed or correct those they had attempted. While reviewing with Andre his story, Beth asked:

How does the reader know that the king and prince were poor?

Andre: They have those, you know, things in their clothes.
Beth: What?
Andre: You know. How do you say? (makes a circle with his hands)
Beth: A hole?
Andre: Yeah, a hole. How do you spell it?
Beth: I'll write it here for you. What do you want to say?
Andre: They wore clothes that was old and had holes.
Beth: Okay.

Beth then noticed the word *drizzeling* on Andre's paper

Beth: What do you mean here?
Andre: Um . . . The princess was like shiney.
Beth: Do you mean dazzeling?
Andre: Yeah. That's it. How do you spell it?

Beth also tried to show the students the importance of adding more information in their stories by using the "wh" (who, what, when, where, why) framework. Andre had written a story about a king and a princess, who at the end of the story had died. He had not, however, given any explanation as to the princess' death. Beth reminded him that the readers might want to know why the character had died, so he added: ". . . pea got alive, it got teeth too and the pea ate the princess and no one knew what happen."

Of the three students, Misha seemed to be having the most difficulty writing stories. She had moved from her native Russia to Israel when she was four years old. She had fond memories of Israel and talked about returning there when she was 16. There she learned to read and write Hebrew, which she liked learning. She did not show the same enthusiasm for English.

She was very reluctant to work in class and often balked about having to write, complaining that it hurt her hand. After two sessions of her leaving in tears and refusing to revise, Beth thought about having Misha use the computer instead of writing by hand. When Beth suggested this to Misha she was very excited. When Misha was living and going to school in Israel she used the computer frequently. It seemed to change her whole attitude about writing. While checking on her progress during one session, Beth thought that Misha had cut one of her stories and left out some important parts. When she questioned it, Misha explained that she was reorganizing her story so "that it sounds better." Misha was becoming more conscious of chronological order in her story.

Although the students clearly did increase the number of details in their story writing, Beth would like to have seen more growth and more carryover to their work in the ESL classroom. She saw the importance of close collaboration between tutors and classroom teachers in order to effect the best instruction for the students.

7

Literacy in the Content Areas

Literacy in the content areas is challenging because it often assumes prior knowledge, it requires students to use the materials in ways consistent with the theories of learning of American education, and it uses a form of language very different from the conversational discourse that students use in their daily interactions.

Ability to read a text or to write about a topic in content area classes in the second language depends on the knowledge about the topic. Educated students bring their wealth of background knowledge to the task of comprehending and producing text. The topics, however, are sometimes difficult because they may represent aspects of curriculum that were not necessarily covered in their previous education. A major source of difficulty for some students in social studies and English literature is the assumption of prior historical, social, and geographical knowledge. For example, many students from tropical countries do not have a good understanding of the changes in the four seasons and its affect on people living in different environments. Many students coming from tropical countries know only about rainy and dry seasons.

Different cultures have different philosophies and attitudes toward knowledge. In the American academic context students are seen as independent learners who are supposed to analyze, question, and critique the knowledge contained in texts. Some cultures believe that knowledge is handed down from learned people to the students. They "worship" every word from texts or teacher's discourse wanting to understand and take down everything. They are not supposed to analyze and critique but rather memorize and internalize the knowledge. Such students address reading and writing in ways that do not fully serve them in the American school context.[1] For example, Elsa, a good high school student in her home country, tried to take down every word teachers used in content area classes. When given a text to read and study, her note taking consisted of practically copying the whole book with little understanding of the content or the important points.

Given the specialized nature of academic language, either English or the heritage language, students may have difficulty using it orally or in written form. The vocabulary, structure, and function of language vary in the different contexts where language is used. Conversational language assumes shared context resulting in unexplained events, cropped sentences, and known vocabulary. Academic language, or the language used in school and textbooks to address content area, is explicit, sentences are well formed and use complex structures, and the vocabulary is domain-specific, i.e. specialized for each content area. Grammatical structures are complex and unusual. Phrases or subordinate clauses rather than conjunctions are used to develop argumentation, making the text more difficult and requiring knowledge of vocabulary that can signal relationships (*The attack on the Twin Towers influenced the decision to pass the Patriot's Act* to mean *The Patriot's Act was passed because of the attack on the Twin Towers*). In history books participants are rarely expressed as individuals or people but rather represent categories or collectives (*Americans, Congress, authorities*) or even whole concepts can be the subject of a sentence (*The attack on the Twin Towers*). Definitions often appear in apposition (*Buenos Aires, the capital of Argentina, . . .*) rather than connected by the verb to be (*Buenos Aires is the capital of Argentina*). Rhetorical connectors such as *in addition, however, obviously,* and others are very difficult for second language learners to follow and to use. Usually students overuse them when they write.[2] The vocabulary is precise and often abstract and hard to understand and explain. The sheer number of new words is a challenge. Vocabulary is best acquired when it is used frequently but content-area vocabulary is mostly used during the limited time dedicated to each discipline. This limited practice makes it harder for students to acquire and recall words. Moreover, vocabulary in the content area may be similar to the one used in ordinary conversation but has a different meaning in the former context. For example, *plane* in geometry is different from the *plane* in which we fly to other places. Even within the content areas students have to learn different meanings for the same word: the *revolution* of the earth around the sun is quite different from the *revolution* of the colonists in North America against the British. Additionally, often in content-area

---

[1]Ballard and Clanchy (1991).
[2]See Hinkel 2002 for more detailed explanation.

textbooks, authors change vocabulary words within a paragraph or chapter. For example, students may have learned the vocabulary word *voyage* and understood its meaning in a passage about the Pilgrim's trip to Plymouth, however, they may not have understood the word *journey* that was used in the same paragraph.[3]

Text organization and content can be confusing in different content areas. For example, the language of mathematical word problems is a major obstacle for L2 learners who could be quite capable of solving the problem otherwise.[4] The mathematical problem is usually embedded in a story that contains concepts often unfamiliar to students. For example, the following problem presents difficulties with the names of the breeds and the word *altogether* to indicate sum. "Terrie has three house cats. The Siamese weighs 4.5 kilograms, the Tabby weighs 3.6 kilograms, and the Persian weighs 2.3 kilograms. How much do the cats weigh altogether?"[5] It also contains the number three, which is irrelevant to the problem, and may increase the confusion. Words used ordinarily with a certain meaning are frequently used with a specialized meaning (*rational, irrational, column, table, operation*). A concept can be expressed with many different words (*sum, add, plus, combine, increased by*). Prepositions, which are difficult for L2 learners, carry key meaning (*divide into, divide by*). Other grammatical structures that can complicate comprehension are comparatives (*Maria earns six times as much as Peter*), passive voice (*Each student in Mr. Lincoln's class was given a card with an equation written on it*), logical connectors (*If . . . then, such that, consequently, if and only if*).

Academic writing develops over the school years, as children become socialized to produce it in school. Immigrant students with education in their country of origin have developed academic writing. However, different cultures have different rules based on their own philosophical ideas of the purpose of writing, and the responsibility bestowed upon writer and reader. Their writing style transfers to English, making teachers judge them as unclear, not to the point, and "disorganized." In reality, they are applying text structures used in their culture. Teachers need to explicitly point out the characteristics of Anglo-American text and how the students

---

[3]See Schleppegrell, Achugar, and Oteiza, 2004 for a detailed analysis of the language of history books. See Gibbons (2002); Menyuk and Brisk (2005) and Schleppegrell (2004) for additional ideas about academic language.

[4]Dale and Cuevas, 1992, Chamot and O'Malley, 1994.

[5]Daily Math Practice (1999) p. 752.

can "translate" their text to this new form. Some researchers feel that the end result should reflect both cultures to a degree. The differences in text structure across cultures may be one of gradation depending on genre. Traditional literature stands at one extreme showing the greatest contrasts with scientific writing at the other sharing the most features.

In Anglo-American text it is the responsibility of the writer to make the text clear to readers. Ideas must be explicitly developed. Usually the main idea is stated initially and the rest of the text attempts to convince the reader of the validity of this idea. In contrast, Japanese text gives the reader the responsibility of interpreting text, thus the writer does not have to be explicit or clear. Vagueness and indirectness is considered desirable and respectful of the reader's ability to interpret. In Anglo-American text logical proof and justification of the writer's position aims at persuading the reader. Ideas are presented in a logical way, showing their connection and purpose of the text. Ideas are clearly developed in separate paragraphs. Connectors help in text cohesion. In contrast, romance languages and Russian include additional material that deviates from a linear logical argumentation. Asian texts tend to be inductive with arguments preceding the presentation of the thesis. Persuasion is not overt but subtle. Ideas are strung together sequentially and not clearly separated in paragraphs.

Arabic writing is characterized by parallel constructions, high frequency of coordinating conjunctions, and extensive use of adjectives and relative clauses. Ideas are expressed and then repeated. For example, a Lebanese student wrote an idea, followed by a sentence that started with "in other words" where the original idea is paraphrased. Amplification and exaggeration are considered acceptable means of persuasion.[6]

The acquisition of academic language is developmental and continues through the high school years. It comes with exposure and linguistic maturity.[7] A number of the approaches presented earlier, as well as those included in this chapter, help students cope with content, cultural, and language difficulties of content area study.

This chapter addresses the following approaches:

- Graphic Organizers: Semantic Mapping
- Cooperative Learning Strategies: Jigsaw
- Situational Context Lessons

---

[6]For a good analysis of the characteristics of ways of writing by members of different cultures and the controversies involving this research see Hinkel (2002) and Connor (2002).

[7]See Menyuk and Brisk (2005).

Suggestions for First Year English Learners

- Start the lesson making sure that everybody understands the topic of the lesson.
- Provide visual aids for learning such as maps, globes, graphs, real objects, and videos.
- Conduct a "walk-through" of the text to be read, highlighting title, subtitles, captions under pictures, graphs, maps, process steps, etc.
- Keep a list of key vocabulary words and phrases hung in the classroom during the unit of study.
- Provide instructions and steps of tasks in writing. Point to them when saying them orally.
- Break down larger chunks of information to help with comprehension of content
- Show/model to students how to take notes when teaching content lesssons.
- Incorporate cooperative learning with more fluent bilingual peers.

Graphic Organizers require thinking and discussion that can be done either in preparation to read or write or after reading or writing. Using Graphic Organizers before reading helps students explore their background knowledge, develop relevant vocabulary, and make predictions. Graphic Organizers are helpful to plan writing by organizing thoughts, establishing knowledge and gaps, and rehearsing the language. After reading, students can synthesize the content of the readings using Graphic Organizers. It helps with checking comprehension and fostering recall. This approach can help with clarity of ideas and organization when revising drafts. Graphic Organizers are very useful when working in a second language, because they display ideas concretely using a limited number of words. They also help them focus on what is important about a text that they will read or have read. Even beginners can participate by offering just one idea.

Jigsaw is one of a great number of cooperative learning strategies. It can be easily adapted to develop one or several literacy skills for students of different grade levels and literacy abilities. The nature of the materials and the task dictate the level of difficulty. A science teacher efficiently covered her unit on human organs using Jigsaw. She provided extensive materials in the native and second languages of the students according to availability and quality. Students had to read, write, and create visual props to support their oral explanations of what they had learned about the organs. A foreign language teacher used simple directions for a game as reading material for beginners. The students focused on reading and playing the game to demonstrate comprehension. Jigsaw is very helpful for students who are afraid of using a second language. While in the expert group they rehearse their ideas and language with a limited amount of material. During sharing they can participate on an equal basis with others.

The Situational Context Lesson is a more complex approach that gives students practice in academic oral language, reading, and writing, while using a number of other approaches recommended in this book. Most teachers have used this approach to fulfill interdisciplinary requirements. Students do not write a traditional autobiography, but write about the issues that are affecting them as bilingual – bicultural individuals. Teachers have used Situational Context Lessons from first through twelfth grade. This approach has been successfully implemented in bilingual, ESL, and mainstream classes. For mainstream classes, teachers chose topics that enriched the curriculum or that affected all students, not only bilingual learners. For example, a first grade teacher introduced differences in writing systems among languages. She invited relatives of Japanese, Chinese, and Spanish speaking children in her classroom to present their writing systems to the whole class. A teacher working with older learners preparing to take the state high-stake tests prepared a whole unit that included the history of the legislation of such a test, the reasons for having created it, and how to go about addressing the various types of items in the test.

Some teachers have paired to implement this approach. For example, a mainstream social studies teacher worked in coordination with an ESL teacher to implement units of the social studies curriculum and develop language and literacy to a combined class of English-speaking and bilingual students of different language backgrounds. This approach helps teachers familiarize themselves with the situational factors that affect bilinguals.[8]

In addition to the approaches described in this chapter, several approaches described earlier can be successfully used to develop literacy with content area materials. The Rhetorical Approach is an excellent way to scaffold academic writing and encourage research. It allows the teacher

---

[8]For a complete analysis of situational factors see Brisk (2006, chap. 3) and Brisk, Burgos, and Hamerla (2004).

to help students create pieces following the organization expected in an Anglo-American text. Liz, a fourth grade teacher used it to develop a whole social studies unit. As the students wrote about it they also learned about it by discussing and researching.[9] Valerie used it with her high school students to write essays. Shared Reading helps students understand difficult text. Angela, a 5th grade teacher, often read aloud from the science and social studies textbooks while the students followed along in their own copies. They interacted activating background knowledge, clarifying vocabulary, and relating concepts with their own lives. As we saw in chapter 4, Renate successfully used Reader-Generated Questions with the science textbook. Sharing Time can be done around a topic students researched. Alice (see chap. 5) used it to explore issues related to the Haitian culture with her middle school students. Marla used it after introducing a new topic in her advanced fifth grade class. Students went off to research subtopics of the subject. A leader for each subtopic directed the discussion. The Anticipation Guide (chap. 5) is an excellent way to help students understand difficult text. Lidia used Talk-write as a way to explore how much students knew about the social studies topic she was starting to cover. Peggy used Dictogloss (chap. 6) with her social studies textbook to develop students' understanding and production of academic language in that content subject. Similarly, Antolin used Vocabulary Connections (chap. 6) with complicated readings in Social Studies.

GRAPHIC ORGANIZERS:
SEMANTIC MAPPING

Purpose

Graphic Organizers help students arrange information by utilizing the most important aspects and concepts of a topic into a visual representation. In addition to Semantic Mapping, described in this section, there are many other types of Graphic Organizers, such as Venn Diagrams, story maps, main idea — supporting details, and sense matrices. Semantic Mapping stimulates vocabulary development and activates background knowledge. The maps display words, ideas, or concepts in categories and show how words relate to each other. Mapping helps students to visually organize information and can be an alternative to note taking and outlining. It is a very helpful prereading — prewriting practice. The organizers can also

---

[9]Brisk, Horan, & MacDonald (forthcoming).

be beneficial as a postreading activity through which the students demonstrate and increase their comprehension of a topic (see chap. 9).

For second-language learners they are a tool for scaffolding knowledge and increasing vocabulary. When used as a pre-writing activity, students will need support while writing about the concepts they have in the graphic organizer. Students may have the ideas but not the language to show the relationships among the various ideas noted it in the graphic organizer.[10]

Procedure

Follow these steps to execute Semantic Mapping:

1. Brainstorm a topic with the students. Write the topic on the board or on paper and have students write it on their paper as well.
2. Brainstorm other words related to the topic. These become the secondary categories written around the central theme or topic. Connect them with lines to the topic. The students write them on their papers.
3. Be creative: use words, pictures, phrases, geometric shapes, or colors to portray the map. Once the students have the idea, they can create maps in a variety of ways.
4. Discuss the ideas generated on the map. Ask, "What do these ideas have in common? How do they relate to each other?"
5. As the students answer these questions, group the words into categories; the groups can be labeled.

This activity can be done before reading a selection or in preparation to write about a topic. It can also be used after reading to check on comprehension or after writing to improve organization and completeness of a topic. Figure 7–1 is an example of a semantic map.

The Approach in Practice:
Mapping It Out for Reading

Semantic Mapping proved to be a successful approach for the three second-language learners with whom Judy Casulli was working. Judy worked with three siblings (a sister and two brothers) from Chile as a tutor. The

---

[10]See Buckley and Boyle (1981), Homza (1996), Flood and Lapp (1988), Peregoy and Boyle (2005), and Perez and Torres-Guzman (2002) for further information on this approach.

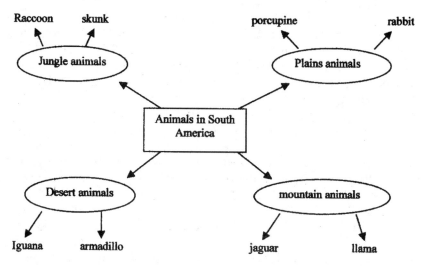

FIGURE 7–1   A semantic map.

children's parents had requested that Judy help the children with their homework, but after a few initial sessions, Judy felt that she would be more helpful to the children by increasing their English proficiency. The oldest child, Nancy, was 10 years old; the brothers were Pedro, 9 years old, and David, 5. She worked with the students two days a week in their home after school. Although David was quite young and only beginning to read and write, he was able to actively participate in the lessons. In the beginning he volunteered words and then usually just drew pictures or circles when needed, but by the end of the sessions he was able to write some words, and copy others.

Judy decided to work with semantic maps because she felt it would help increase the vocabulary of the children. She also believed that using semantic maps was an effective way to stimulate conversation about a particular topic and was a good prereading and prewriting activity. The Semantic Mapping lessons were precursors to reading books and writing stories with the children.

Judy usually asked the children beforehand which topic they wanted to discuss during their next session together. In that way, she was able to find resource materials and books related to the topic in which the children were interested. The first topic chosen by the children was Halloween. The children had been in the United States for less than a year, so this was to be their first Halloween. Judy asked the children in English what they knew about Halloween. They replied in one-word answers such as *pumpkin, skeleton,* and *witch.* Judy wrote down the words on chart paper as the children said them, and they copied the words into a notebook. Some of the words were said in English, and others were stated in Spanish. When a word was said in Spanish, Judy told the children what the word was in English and then proceeded to write it in English on the chart paper. If it seemed as if the children did not understand the concept of a word, Judy first tried to explain the idea in English, and then explained in Spanish when necessary. Once a good list of words was generated, Judy and the children discussed the more unusual ones. By discussing some of the words in a little more detail, Judy was able to see exactly what the children understood of the concept, and the children were able to practice more English.

When the discussion of the words had ended, Judy put up a clean piece of chart paper with the word *Halloween* in the center. She asked the children to think of how the list of words could be grouped into categories. The children understood what Judy wanted, and Pedro noticed that many of the words were names for animals. Pedro wrote the word *animals* to the lower left of "Halloween" and the children took turns calling out words that belonged to that category. When all the animal words had been written, David, the younger brother, drew circles around each word. The activity continued until all words had been placed in one of the four categories: Animals, Monsters, Pumpkins, and Trick or Treat. The discussion that took place during this activity was done in both English and Spanish with the children usually saying the key word in English, but explaining their reasoning in Spanish. Pedro tried to form simple sentences in English with the key word. Nancy did not want to say much in English. Judy followed this activity by reading a story about Halloween, *Rotten Ralph's Trick or Treat.* If a word from their map appeared in the story, Judy asked a question to further reinforce their new vocabulary.

The children had picked the topic of work for the second time they did Semantic Mapping. Judy began by asking the children to tell her some words that had to do with work. Nancy replied in Spanish *secretaria* (secretary). Pedro then offered the word *teacher.* Nancy objected because she wanted to continue thinking of other categories beside the specific name of a worker, for example, the place they work, the job they do, and so on. Judy tried to explain that the idea was to just write down whatever came to mind, and that they would organize it later. However, Nancy was quite adamant about organizing as they went, so Judy conceded. The children were able to skip the initial step of listing and worked right away at organizing their words into categories, because they had a good grasp of the concept. One problem with this particular mapping session was that the topic was too broad, which caused some confusion for the children. They ended up with a somewhat organized listing of words. They then worked on organizing the map by workers, under which was identified the place they worked and what they did at work. Again, after the session, Judy read a book to the children about people working.

On one occasion the children had told Judy that for their next topic they wanted to discuss *airplanes*. However, Judy was unable to find a book suitable to discuss with the students, so she changed the topic to *food*. Although the students did participate, she found that they were not as attentive as usual and she had to coax words out of them. She realized that they were not as interested in the topic because they had not selected it. The children seemed to be losing interest, so Judy came up with the idea of making a Semantic Map of the food words by mapping out a grocery store. The children then enthusiastically began categorizing the words. In the end, their supermarket map contained the following sections: *fruit, vegetables, school supplies, toys, meat, dairy, frozen*, and *cereal*.

Judy tried to tie the lessons she was giving the children at home to what they were studying in school. Nancy told Judy that she was studying geography, so during one of the sessions the children worked on geographic terms. By that time, the children had definitely established quite an efficient routine for working on the maps. They began by directly organizing the words into categories. Pedro preferred providing the ideas and letting Nancy make the map. David was also becoming more involved in all aspects of the process. The children were able to categorize words into countries, mountains, canals, volcanoes, oceans, and capitals. As a follow-up reading activity to this session, the children looked at an atlas. The atlas provoked a lot of discussion. Nancy became very excited when they turned to a map of Chile. She spoke excitedly in Spanish about the map, and even emphatically refused to speak in English when it was suggested.

The last semantic map done with the children involved words dealing with the seasons. Having completed the map, they read the book *Chicken Soup with Rice* by Maurice Sendak. David asked to read for the first time. He usually just listened to his brother and sister read and then made comments. This time, however, he wanted to actively participate in the reading. Judy read a line and he repeated it. He was quite excited that he was "reading." Although clearly still at a preliterate stage, Judy noticed over time that David did recognize certain words that they had used during the mapping activities, and was able to write some of the words they had learned.

While Judy believed that the Semantic Mapping exercises done by her tutees helped increase vocabulary and conversation in English, she came to realize that Semantic Mapping could be used for many pre- and post-reading activities.

COOPERATIVE LEARNING: JIGSAW

Purpose

The Jigsaw approach is a way for students to work cooperatively and help each other to learn new material. Students take an active role in their learning as they teach other students what they have learned. In a bilingual setting, students have the opportunity to learn appropriate vocabulary in both languages. For second language learners, this approach helps lessen the burden of trying to understand a large amount of expository text in a short amount of time.[11]

Procedure

To execute the Jigsaw approach:

1. Divide material into sections. (For example, divide a reading into four sections).
2. Have students form groups with as many students per group as sections of material. (For example, for a reading selection divided into four sections, there will be four students in each group.)
3. Ask each group to send one member to an "expert" group where one section of the material will be read, discussed, and learned. Each group should know where in the whole material their section fits. (In the example, there will be four expert groups with one student from each of the original groups.)
4. Once the students have learned the material, have them return to their original group and report to those students what they have learned.
5. After all students have taught the other members of their original group the material in which they are expert, have students do an activity individually in which they show how much of the material they have learned. (For example, write individually a summary of the *whole* reading.)

The Approach in Practice: All the Pieces of the Puzzle Fit Together!

The Jigsaw approach proved to be an effective way for Peggy Harrington's third- and fourth-grade Spanish bilingual students to learn about

---

[11]See Kagan (1992) and Pardon (1992) for further information about this approach and other cooperative learning approaches.

the events leading to the American Revolution. The class is comprised of 16 third-grade and 11 fourth-grade students in a transitional bilingual classroom with myriad levels of language proficiency and literacy development. Spanish is the first language of all the students. The English language proficiency, however, varies from very low oral language proficiency in English to near mastery. Many students are at or near grade level in reading (both in English and Spanish), whereas others are still developing their literacy skills in Spanish. Others are beginning to adapt and transfer skills learned in Spanish to English reading. Although many of the students are recent immigrants to the United States and began their literacy development in their native country, quite a few students were born in the United States and have learned how to read and write in bilingual programs in this country.

Peggy began working on the approach by discussing with the whole class the relationship between the colonists and the king of England. She wanted the students to understand that although the colonists expressed loyalty to the king of England, they also felt that their way of living was very different from the way people lived in England, and that they should have more of a voice in how America would be governed. She asked individual students who were born in the United States to identify their national heritage. Justina claimed she was Dominican, and Marcos said he was American. Julie then agreed that she, too, was American, but also Dominican. This led to a discussion of how different people feel about their allegiances to countries, and whether people could be loyal to two countries at the same time. The students also discussed the differences in lifestyle between their native country and the United States, and how it was often difficult for people living in one country to understand the way life was in another.

The students were placed heterogeneously into five groups, five students to a group. Because there were two more students than places needed, Peggy paired the two least-strong readers with another person and asked them to work together.

She then explained the Jigsaw method to the students. They were told that the Jigsaw method was a way for the students to work together and teach each other new material. She discussed the logistics of the Jigsaw. She wrote five major themes on the board (in both English and Spanish): Taxes, Laws, Boston, Continental Congress, and Declaration of Independence. One student from each group chose a theme. They were told that they would become the "expert" on the theme they had chosen; that they would read about it and discuss it with students from the other groups, and then report what they had learned to their original group. It took a few minutes for the students to completely understand the concept. Even after they had been working in the "expert" groups for a few minutes, some students were still confused. Eventually, all understood and the pieces of the jigsaw puzzle were fitting together.

For resources, the students were provided with materials in both English and Spanish, including social studies textbooks, copies of short essays about the particular themes, and other books. Unfortunately, there were many more materials in English than in Spanish. The social studies book in Spanish, however, did have a lot of good information for the students. They were given all the materials and could choose to read in Spanish or English, or both. The students then began reading their information. They were allowed to read either alone, or with one or two other students. Most chose to partner with someone else. Clara chose to read the material in English, but when she wanted to comment on what was read, she usually did so in Spanish. Her explanations in Spanish were a lot more detailed and descriptive.

When all the students had finished reading the materials, they were called back to their expert groups to discuss what they had read. Peggy walked from group to group during the discussions to assure that the students understood the material and to clarify any misunderstandings.

The students' individual styles of learning were evident during the discussion. Some students had written down important facts in order to remember them, other students had underlined important paragraphs in the materials they had read and referred to them during the discussion.

The discussions were lively with lots of switching back and forth from English to Spanish. Juana had read her material in English, but spoke both English and Spanish in the group, because she knew that some of the members of her group would understand better if she explained what she had learned in Spanish. Francisco, a dominant Spanish-speaker, intensely read the material in Spanish, but also read the other information in English and referred to it during the discussion. The students worked in their expert groups until they determined that they knew their material well and were ready to teach what they had learned to their original groups. For homework that night the students were told to write a summary of their theme, which they then read, or used as a reference, when teaching to their group the next day.

The students were reminded that although they had learned about only one aspect of the topic being studied, they were responsible for knowing all the material, and that they as a group needed to ensure that all members explained their themes well enough for all to understand. The student experts then returned to their original groups to report on what they had learned. Most students had prepared their summaries for homework the night before and chose to read what they had written.

The students read their summaries. While Mercedes was reading hers, students in the group noted some errors in what she was saying about the taxes imposed on the colonists, which led to the students referring to the material to verify the information. After Francisco had read his summary, he questioned the students in his group about what he had just read to make sure they understood what he was explaining. When he felt that they had not understood well enough, he elaborated on the point.

For some students, it was very difficult to either write a summary or read it out loud. Leslie, who has difficulty reading, did not come prepared with a written summary. The students called Peggy over to complain about her not being prepared. Peggy suggested to the group that they ask Leslie what she could tell them about her theme (taxes). Once Leslie began talking, she was able to explain a little of what she had read. Because Leslie had been partnered with another student, the students learned additional information about the theme from Gloria. Sandra, who is extremely shy, did not want to speak at all when it was her turn to read her summary. It took some convincing from the other students before she felt comfortable enough to read her summary. Once she felt comfortable with her group though, she did an excellent job of explaining her theme, and the other members of her group let her know that. The students in Juan's group complained about the lack of information in his summary. Juan knew he had let his group down and promised to work on a better summary that night for homework.

Often during the presentation of someone's theme, other students in the group commented to the presenter, adding information or clarifying a point. While Ana was explaining about the Stamp Act, Mercedes added her explanation of taxes to help the group understand better. At other times, students intervened to help if the student could not think of a good way to explain something. The students in the groups also began to see connections between what they had read about and what the other students in the group had explained. Clara, who had studied about the occurrences in Boston, began to see the relationship between what happened there to the laws imposed on the colonists. She said she now understood why the people in Boston were so angry.

Although there was no assigned leader to any group, it seemed that one person in most of the groups took over that role. Patricia easily took on the role as facilitator, making sure all had the opportunity to read their summaries and respond to comments. Clara saw to it that everyone was listening to the speaker in her group. During the summary readings in his group, Francisco often stopped and asked someone a question to see if they had been listening.

Because the groups did not all finish their summary readings at the same time, it was suggested to those that had finished that they either ask each other questions about their themes, or try to work on some of the questions found in the social studies textbooks as a way of reviewing the information learned.

In order to give the students an opportunity to tie all five themes together, Peggy assigned for homework a quick reading of the chapter. The students were told just to read through the chapter once, not worrying so much about detail, as much as seeing how one event affected the other.

To assess the students' individual understanding of the material, Peggy created a scenario in which the students were to imagine that they were living in Boston in the 1770s and had just received a letter from their grandfather or grandmother who was living in England. The grandparent had sent the letter in order to find out why the colonists would ever disobey their king. Each student was to respond to his or her grandparent's letter, explaining why the colonists were rebelling against the king. The students were given the option of being for or against the colonists' cause, but in their letter they had to explain in detail the five points covered during their Jigsaw method. They were allowed to use their books and other materials as points of reference when writing their letter.

Patricia dated her letter about a week after the Declaration of Independence had been signed (the English translation follows):

7/10/76

Querida Abuela,

Aqui en Boston esta matando personas y ahi muchos problemas. Yo se que tu quiere a tu rey pero haora el esta muy malo y tenemos que pagar Impuestos. En inglatera no esta pasando nada pero haqui esta pasando muchas cosa mala el. rey esta muy malo. Paraca casi no hay comida y todos los soldados esta cojiendo la comida y las camas aqui mataro cinco hombres y despues dos. Por que tiraron el te en el agua hay muchos problemas. Le estan mandando cartas al rey pero el no la contesta. Aya en inglatera viviendo bien poro paraca no. El 4 de julio mandaron una carta de Independencia pero el rey no le iso caso como las otras cartas.

En el comienso estaba fasil pero haora esta duro no hay comida ni hay camas y esta una gera como bamos a vivir aqui. El rey sepuso bien brabo cuado le tiraron 351 caja de te. Haqui todas la jentes se esta muriendo. aqui no esta fasil.

Sinceramente,

Dear Grandmother,

Here in Boston they are killing people and that are a lot of problems. I know that you love your king, but now he is bad and we have to pay taxes. In England nothing is happening, but here a lot of bad things are happening. The king is very mean. Here there is no food and all the soldiers are taking our food and beds. Here they killed five men and later two. Because they threw tea in the water they are many problems. They are sending letters to the king, but he doesn't answer them. There in England they are living well, but here no. On July 4 they sent a letter to the king, but he paid no attention, just like the other letters.

In the beginning it was easy, but now it is hard. There is no food, no beds, and we are going to be living in a war here. The king was very angry when they threw the 351 boxes of tea overboard. Everyone here is dying. It is not easy.

Sincerely,

By reading the letters, Peggy was able to tell which students understood most of the material, those that were confused on some issues, and the others who did not seem to understand the basic ideas of the themes. Although the majority of students did grasp the main ideas of the unit, some students did not. Sandra, for example, seemed confused about where the colonists lived. She kept referring to how difficult life and the laws were in England. Ana did not seem to understand that she was writing a realistic letter about historical events. She wrote a story as if it were a fairy tale.

Peggy asked the students how they liked learning social studies using the Jigsaw method. Clara said that she liked it because she got to work with other students, and did not have to read the material alone. Francisco liked the idea of learning from his fellow students. Justina felt that it helped her learn better, because she could learn a lot of material without having to read so much.

SITUATIONAL CONTEXT (SC) LESSONS

Purpose

Students and teachers have no control over situational factors, but they can objectively analyze them. In the SC lessons students research such factors and reflect on how they affect them as language and literacy learners, as students, and as members of our society. Objective analysis of these factors helps students understand their present circumstances and react in a constructive way. Carefully planned lessons allow students to objectively analyze external factors influencing their lives as learners. The instructional activities include: reading literature with pertinent themes, discussing and writing responses to this literature, using the library and internet as resources, conducting interviews, observations, and surveys, and writing reflections to connect the themes of the lesson with their own lives. Many of the other approaches recommended in this book can be used in the exploration of situational context factors. Bilingual and immigrant students often blame themselves, their language, and their culture for what happens to them. Study of the situational context turns these problematic circumstances into an opportunity for learning.[12]

Procedure

1. Establish the lesson objective based on a topic that is affecting the lives of your students due to circumstances in the environment.
2. Choose materials that will help you explore the topic. Literature that addresses the topic within a story help students voice their own ideas.
3. Prepare activities to address concepts and relationship between concepts (for example language use affects language proficiency. Students explore how much they use each language, how proficient they are in each, and then make connections between the two). As the lesson evolves, if there are current events related to the theme, incorporate them.
4. Connections to Self: Have students reflect on what they have found and how they are affected personally.
5. Discuss possible solutions. Arriving at solutions is difficult for young learners. Often the teacher proposes some ideas.

The Approach in Practice: The Impact of Violence on Immigrant Students Living in Unsafe Neighborhoods

To help her students better understand the violence they either observed or experienced in their lives, Meredith Dadigan implemented the situational context approach. She began the unit on violence by passing out three different colored (yellow, pink, and orange) self-stick papers to each

---

[12]Brisk, Burgos, and Hamerla 2004 explores in depth external factors affecting bilinguals, provides numerous sample lessons, and includes an annotated bibliography of books for elementary and secondary students.

student. On the yellow paper they wrote their definition of violence, on the pink, they wrote how violence affected them, and on the orange they wrote what they wanted to learn about violence. The students then placed their papers on the chalkboard in the appropriate section.

Meredith read all the students' responses to the class since all were eager to hear what others had written. The students' definitions of violence included: Violence kills . . . Violence is when people hurt others. . . . To use a weapon to hurt something or someone. . . . When you kill someone. . . . Killing, bad things happening, hurting something. . . . use their hands or weapons to fight people. . . . Punching, kicking, crude language, and hurting someone pyscialy [physically]. When she had finished reading the students' definitions, Meredith read the definition of violence from a dictionary. The students saw that what they had written was very close to the dictionary's definition of violence.

As the class reviewed the answers to the second question (How had violence affected them), Meredith realized that the students had written about violence in general terms, and not how it had personally touched their lives. So, she asked the students to think about how they had been personally affected by violence. The students provided vivid, personal, and touching stories of their own experiences with violence.

As to what the students wanted to know about violence, a few asked how did it start, while others wanted to know why people turned to violence or why people thought violence was the only way to solve problems. Some students also showed interest in weapons used in violent acts, such as guns.

When all the students' responses were read, they were read the following quote from Martin Luther King, Jr.: "Violence is anything that denies human integrity, and leads to hopelessness and helplessness." Meredith then had the students write down any act of violence that would fit Dr. King's description. When the students seemed to have difficulty with that assignment, Meredith suggested that they write down any acts of violence.

To end the lesson for the day, the students discussed how they learn about violence. They listed the news, websites, commercials, television, experience, CNN, games, wrestling, movies, parents, and friends. Meredith wrote all the suggestions on the board and then added newspapers, radio, magazines and song lyrics. She then assigned homework: the students were to look in the newspaper or watch the news and record what violent events took place in their metropolitan area where they lived and to indicate the neighborhoods in which they events took place.

When the students met the next week, they had information that they had obtained from the newspaper and television about violent acts that had taken place in the area. They noted the areas in which much of the violence was happening and discussed the different occurrences. Meredith then explained to them that the following week a police officer would be visiting the class to speak with them about violence. She reviewed the types of questions that the students might want to ask the police officer. She talked about how they should ask open-ended questions, rather than just questions with yes/no responses. She also discussed asking questions that began with *who, what, when, where, why,* and *how.* The students spent the rest of the class writing their questions for next week's visit from the police officer.

Meredith was pleased with the interview session with the police officer. The fact that he was Haitian, like most of her students, and was even related to one of the students, made the interview very successful. First, the police officer told the students who he was, what his job was, and then gave them a speech about violence. He explained to them that violence starts with conflicts and the bad choices that are made at the time of the conflict. He spoke further about choices and how making good choices begins in school.

When he had finished his talk, the students then asked him the questions they had prepared. They got information on when violence is likely to happen and what to do if they find themselves in a dangerous situation. After the police officer had left, Meredith and the students discussed what they had learned that day.

The students continued their unit on violence in art class. They each made a violence-free poster. Meredith talked to them about how posters and advertisements try to convince people to do or not do something. The students were enthusiastic and very engaged in the poster project. They diligently worked on finding creative ways to present the advantages of being violence free.

Meredith also read to the students about violence. She chose the book, *The House That Crack Built,* by Clark Taylor because she felt that it poignantly illustrated how the choices people make have a powerful effect on others. The students discussed the book and then responded to it in some way, either by writing about what they were thinking, writing a poem, or writing about ways they could make their country less violent.

During the next class, Meredith showed students statistics of crime indexes and the neighborhoods in which most of the violent crimes were taking place. They looked at a map of the city and color-coded the map for violence levels.

To end the unit, Meredith brought in an article from the newspaper that talked about a meeting the mayor had with community members and religious leaders about the increased violence in the neighborhood and what they could do to stop the violence. Meredith discussed this idea with the class and together they decided that to present what they had learned about violence during their unit of study to the school student council. The class planned the presentation based on all they had learned and two Haitian students delivered the message. They were very proud of themselves for doing such a public presentation. The student council brainstormed ideas of what they as a school could do to prevent violence.

While engaged in the topic of violence students practiced language through oral discussion, reading, and writing. The activity encouraged research, analysis, and other types of academic skills. This unit allowed students to objectively analyze a pressing issue in their lives, connect it with themselves, as well as seek some solution. The activity gave the students a sense of purpose and hope. They were able to voice openly their concerns and experiences with violence and realize that efforts can be made to improve their condition.

8

Individualized and Small Group Instruction with Support of Tutors

Literacy development requires individualized attention. One-to-one or small group interaction with an adult can assist students with misunderstandings or decoding of unknown words, vocabulary development, comprehension of details, choice of the right word to express an idea, improvement of grammar and expression, and other necessary crossroads for comprehending reading and composing text. Great differences in level of proficiency of students in a classroom make it close to impossible for a single teacher to efficiently help students develop literacy in an individualized or small group setting.

A productive resource is tutors from neighboring colleges, especially those who are in teacher preparation programs specifically geared to bilingual learners. These tutors are supervised and have developed useful background on how to work with bilingual students. Tutors' work needs to be closely coordinated with classroom teachers. Sylvia, an ESL major, was in charge of helping a seventh-grade Russian student in a mainstream classroom. She consulted with his teacher and found out that he needed particular help with summaries of his readings. One reading assignment was about Thomas Edison. Drawing from the Reader-Generated Questions approach (see chap. 4), she asked Steve to imagine what his friends would like to know about Edison and formulate some questions. Steve asked: When did Edison invent the phonograph? How did he get the idea? How did he make it? How does it work? Why did he invent it? What other things did he invent? Sylvia copied down the questions and put them aside while Steve read the excerpt on Edison. Then she asked

Steve to write down answers to his questions based on the reading. Using a process approach to writing, they turned the list of answers into a summary of the reading. This was an elaborate process that required a one-on-one approach quite appropriate for a tutor and extremely helpful for Steve's participation in his class.

Often college students speak the native languages of the children in the classroom and can prove invaluable to teachers who do not. For example, Toshiko, a preservice teacher fluent in Japanese, helped Yuri with her English literacy while completing her field practice at an English-speaking teacher's classroom. Yuri, a 9-year-old recent arrival from Japan, withdrew when demanded to read and write in English. Toshiko decided to try a dialogue journal (chap. 3). Initially Yuri wrote in Japanese while Toshiko responded in English, followed by paraphrased version in Japanese. For example, in the first entry Yuri wrote in Japanese about the cold weather and the need to use heavy coats. Toshiko responded: "It is really cold. Please take care of your health." Followed by a sentence in Japanese: "It is really cold, isn't it? Please do not catch a cold." By the fifth week, Yuri attempted a few English words in her Japanese writing and the teacher responded mostly in English. In week 7, she wrote a full sentence in English, and in week 10, she wrote a full story in English as a class assignment apart from her dialogue journal. Allowing the use of the native language was an effective strategy to change Yuri's attitude toward reading and writing in English.

Some school districts offer pull-out ESL services. These are most helpful when they help students participate in their classroom activities. For example, a tutor helped a group of 5 students produce books that they then shared during their whole class sharing time. These students would not have been able to produce these books with a teacher attending the other 15 native speakers of English in the room. Monica, a third grade teacher, was concerned about a native Spanish-speaker who was afraid to participate in class. She instructed the ESL tutor to read books in English with him appropriate to his English proficiency level. The books were carefully chosen to address topics that the class would cover the following week. Having acquired the knowledge and vocabulary, allowed Cesar to join the class in discussions with more confidence.

Tutors can also help teachers get to know their students in greater depth. Eileen, a pre-service teacher, and Abdul, a newcomer to 5th grade, developed story maps (using drawings) about their own lives and shared them. This activity allowed Eileen to understand the personal and cultural story of her student and gave her a better sense of his strengths and

challenges. In turn, she shared her findings with the teacher.[1] Knowing
the students includes awareness of their level of literacy ability and background. This knowledge should guide tutoring activities. Rich language
development should precede any detailed teaching of language and literacy skills. This does not mean avoiding teaching literacy until the student
is fluent in English. Rather through oral activities, reading, and writing
the students gain knowledge of the language in general first and in particular later. For example, Afra (see Reformulation approach below) had
to work with the students on making sense of the message in their writing before she could use the Reformulation Approach to work on the accuracy of their grammar and spelling.

An important consideration for tutors working with older students is
to make clear the purpose of the tutoring. Tutors and students need to
make clear what are the expectations of the tutoring activities to avoid
frustration and to ensure participation. Reynolds[2] reports on tensions created by contradictory expectations. The tutors wanted to elicit language
from their students, the students expected the tutors to "teach" by initiating the conversations themselves, choosing the topics, and modeling talk.
Tutors need to be aware that their students bring different schooling experiences and notions of what teachers and students' roles are.

This chapter reports on two approaches, Reformulation and Read
Aloud that were used effectively to help students acquire second language, reading, and writing. In the Reformulation Approach the teacher
rewrites a student's piece the way a native speaker of the language would
and has the students compare the two versions. This approach draws
on second language acquisition theory that maintains that second language is learned by both talking about language and noticing how the
language works.[3] Teachers need to draw attention to inaccuracies in the
language, be it spelling, grammar, incorrect use of words, and so on.
Otherwise second language learners may not notice. Those inaccuracies
could become part of their dialect.[4] The timing for using Reformulation is
important. Students need to have had practice with writing and must have
developed confidence in writing so that the more thorough scrutiny of

---

[1] Alexandrowicz (2002).
[2] Reynolds (2000).
[3] Swain, Brooks, and Tocalli-Beller (2002).
[4] Reyes, (1992).

their writing does not inhibit them. In addition, it is difficult to reformulate an unclear piece because the teacher might change the message in the process. Afra used semantic mapping to clarify the piece. Once the students developed a more organized piece she applied the Reformulation Approach. Because of the attention to detail and time needed to implement, it lends itself to be carried out in small group instruction. For example Liz used it in a before school program working with 5 bilingual students from her class. Each day of the week they would apply it to one of the students' writings. The students were supposed to bring something that they had done in class to work during this time.

To support the teachers and pre-service students who visit classrooms once a week, a college developed a Read Aloud project. The purpose of the project was for pre-service students to read aloud with a second language learner during their weekly visits to the classroom. This provided help for a student and provided the pre-service students with a structured activity so that the cooperating teacher did not have to plan for them. (Cooperating teachers find it easier to plan with full-time practicum students than with those who are there only once a week.) The students received preparation on how to use the Read Aloud approach as well as some basic information on second language acquisition and the role of culture in working with students who are learning English as a second language.

Full time student teachers can play an important role in helping bilingual students who are developing English and need more individualized attention. While he was completing his semester of student teaching, Andrew Mahoney worked after school with some of his bilingual students tutoring them in History. In one case Andrew taught Cassandra how to structure her term paper. Together they developed an outline on what to include in her essay. He also went through her class notes and reviewed difficult vocabulary with her. Through Andrew's efforts Cassandra improved in her overall History grade. For another student, Brayan, Andrew worked in partnership with Brayan's parents to help him prepare for history tests. He met with Brayan after school and went over the most important information to study for the test. Brayan would then go home and work with his mother who helped modify the English content for him as he studied. As a result of this collaborative tutorial effort, Brayan finished the term with an overall average of 80 percent. Andrew believed that his efforts to modify content for the ELLs in his class and his tutorial work with them had a positive impact on their learning.

REFORMULATION STRATEGY

Purpose

Reformulation is having a native writer rewrite a learner's piece, preserving all the learner's ideas, but making it sound as native-like as possible. It is best to apply this approach to pieces that are organized and have a message that is clear. This approach helps second language development by calling attention to issues of vocabulary, grammatical structure, and spelling. It lends itself to small group work or during conferencing time. The most important aspect is the discussion about language. Teachers can create a rubric for the aspects of language they want the students to focus. It is important to also consider the developmental stage of the students, both with respect to age and level of second language. For example for a second grader overusing *and* to connect sentences, the teacher may simply eliminate some of the *ands* by separating the sentences with a period. While this sentence, produced by a fourth grader, "Sence we met eachother he's never misted my birthday parties and I never misted his . . ." could be further reformulated to something like "Since we met we haven't missed each other's birthday parties." Two case studies using the Reformulation Approach illustrate the use with students at the elementary and at the secondary levels.[5]

Procedure

1. Using the writing of a student, rewrite it on a separate piece of paper as a native speaker would.
2. Working with the whole class, a group of students, or a pair of students, have them compare the original and reformulated version with respect to vocabulary, grammar, spelling, cohesion, and rhetorical functions.
3. To help students notice, you may provide them with a rubric that includes the various aspects of writing and the language that you want them to notice.
4. Have students rewrite their original piece. (Even students whose piece was not reformulated can revise their piece based on what they learned from the discussion.)

---

[5] Allwright, J. (1986); Cohen, A. (1983); Lapkin, Swain, and Smith (2002).

Additional Activities:

* From the issues that are discussed, design one or two mini-lessons.
* Create a checklist where you add the points discussed and taught. Students must consult this checklist before handing in their writing. They should have taken care of aspects of language already discussed.

The Approach in Practice at an Elementary Grade

By implementing the Reformulation Approach with two fourth grade bilingual students with whom she was working, Afra Ahmed Hersi hoped to improve the students' grammatical understanding of English. One of the students, Marcus, was born in the United States of Ethiopian parents. Although both parents and an older sibling spoke Amharic, a language spoken in Ethiopia, Marcus denied speaking that language. He stressed that he spoke only English. Likewise, the other student, James, stated that although the adults in his family spoke Spanish, he did not. Afra sadly noted that both students seemed to be uncomfortable acknowledging their bilingualism.

Their teacher recommended the students to Afra since their reading and writing ability were evaluated as second grade level. The teacher provided Afra with writing samples that were previously written by Marcus and James. The samples were the result of an in-class writing prompt that had students write about the greatest day in their life.

Afra knew that as she reformulated the student's original text, she had to be sure that she maintained the student's original meaning and voice. For example, in James' essay, she had difficulty determining if James was writing about one incident or several. Therefore, before she began reformulating the essays for the two boys, she held a brainstorming session with them to clarify any misunderstandings. The boys redrafted the papers to make their content clear. Afra used this version to reformulate.

The first stage of the activity was the discussion phase. The students read both of their original essays and then the reformulated versions. When they had finished reading the essays, they discussed them. In order to make it easier to discuss individual sentences, Afra gave Marcus and James a handout containing both the original and the reformulated essays written out as numbered sentences. Each original sentence was followed by its reformulation in bold. Afra encouraged examination of the two sentences, making sure the students highlighted and discussed the changes. The students had to decide whether to maintain the original sentence or change it as suggested by the reformulated sentence.

Afra noted that in many instances the students were not able to elaborate why they chose one sentence over another. They just felt it didn't sound right or didn't make sense. They lacked specific grammatical or linguistic knowledge to explain their thinking. The following dialogue illustrates the point:

Original: One of the greast day is when I went to water contry.

Reformulation: The day I went to Water Country Park was the greatest day in my life.

Excerpt: 1.A: Marcus' Essay

Marcus: The first (One of the greast day is when I went to water contry) makes more sense.

James: Yes, the first one makes more sense . . .

Afra: Can you explain why?

James: Re-reading the reformulated sentence. (The day I went to Water Country Park was the greatest day in my life) . . . because it doesn't sound right.

James: one of the greatest days of my life is . . . (trails off)

Marcus: Yeah . . . one of the greatest day is . . . sounds much better

Afra: Why don't you like that sentence? What don't you like about it? (Both students repeat that it doesn't sound right.)

James: Yes, (one of the greatest) . . . makes more sense.

During the second stage of the approach, the students re-wrote their essays incorporating the reformulated sentences they agreed to include from their discussion. It was during this activity, as the two boys collaboratively wrote the essays, that grammatical and mechanical errors were noticed. For example, James realized that they needed an "s" on the word *days* in the sentence: *One of the greatest days is when I went to Water Country.* But Mark was confused because while the construction <u>one of</u> requires a plural noun, they still were talking about one day. The following discussion ensued:

> **Mark:** *One of the greatest day is* . . .
> **James:** He forgot the *s* on days.

Mark: It's a *day* . . . one day that was really fun.

James: Yeah, but you have more days right . . .

Mark: No. Only one day at Water Country . . . she [the teacher] said you can only do one day.

James: I know . . .

Mark: Yes, so its Water Country . . . I'm not going to have two days . . . only one day.

Researcher: James, can you explain why you think there should be an *s* after *day*.

James: Hmh . . . because it says *one of the greatest days* . . . he must have some more days because he said *one of* . . .

Mark: I just have one day . . .

Researcher: Marcus, do you understand what he was saying?

Mark: Yeah, a little . . . he probably things that . . . since it *says one of the* . . . there is more than one day.

James: I think it would make more sense if . . . it said *days* . . .

Although in many instances (perhaps because of their limited linguistic and grammatical proficiency in English), the students chose to keep their original sentence instead of the reformulated one, when they rewrote their story they incorporated parts of the reformulated sentences into the essays. For example:

Original: *I swam, and I played with friends and we went boating.*

Reformulation: *During that day, I swam, played with my friends and went boating.*

Revised essay: *During that day I swam, played with my friends and we went boating.*

Afra believed that this approach helped Marcus and James discuss their writing at a deeper level. It is easier for a teacher to explain why the noun after "One of the . . ." has to be plural after such an intense discussion. Moreover, the students are more likely to remember next time because they remember their discussion. As the students worked on the essays, they seemed to be less concerned about finding the "correct" answer and more attentive to finding a way to express what they wanted to say. They focused more on meaning. However, when they attempted to rewrite their original looking at it and the reformulated version is when they noticed language issues. They worked on being explicit and solving grammar and spelling problems.

The Approach in Practice at the Secondary Level

When Carolina, a 15 year-old student from the Dominican Republic, first met her tutor, Anthony Jacobs, she expressed a desire to improve her skills in written English. She was having difficulty in both the poetic and essay forms of writing. As she stated: "I don't know how to write like this [formal essay]. It's too hard for me." When Anthony asked her about the process she used for writing, her reply was: "I just sit down and it takes me fifteen minutes." Anthony decided on two ways of helping Carolina: (1) introduce her to a more organized writing process approach; and (2) use the Reformulation Approach to help Carolina improve her written English and notice the difference between formal and informal language.

Anthony met with Carolina once a week for 45 minutes. Initially, he explained the difference between academic writing and less formal styles of writing. He then gave her a list of topics from which she was to write a persuasive essay. She chose "Why Music is Essential to Life."

An important component of the Reformulation Approach is the development of a rubric for the writing sample. During his conversations with Carolina, Anthony learned that she wished to become a lawyer. So, instead of developing a rubric with a generic scale of 0–5, he created an analytic rubric that measured the writing with respect to style and voice, content, organization, and grammar and mechanics on a scale pre-law (0) to Supreme Court (5).

After they had met for five weeks, two other students (Elijah, a bilingual learner from Trinidad, and Alessia, a U.S. born Spanish bilingual) joined Carolina for the sessions. Anthony had read that an important part of the reformulation approach was the discussion. He felt it would be helpful for Carolina to discuss her writing with other students.

Anthony shared the rubric with all three students and discussed the differences in the rating and measurement. At the next meeting, the students assessed Carolina's essay using the rubric. The two new students assessed her writing in the different categories of the rubric and scored Carolina's writing as a one or at the Law School level. In this meeting what dominated the discussion was not the assessment, but the two students offering improvements to Carolina's writing piece. The two other students didn't have the meta-cognitive knowledge to describe why things should change. They used sentences like, "Write it like this . . . it sounds better." Or, "Let's change this. It's supposed to sound like this." The two students didn't use the language from the rubric to describe the very appropriate changes they recommended to Carolina's writing. They used their knowledge of how Standard English was supposed to look and sound and helped Carolina. They knew what she wanted to say (in many ways better than Anthony did) and the one student, Alessia, took owner-ship over Carolina's writing and started making changes to it. Carolina took notes and began to revise her piece during this meeting. At the fol-lowing session, they read Anthony's reformulated version of Carolina's essay and discussed possible reasons for the changes and how the changes affected the essay. Additionally, they rated the reformulated essay. They remarked that the conclusion caught their attention; it offered good ex-amples in each paragraph, and that it just sounded and looked right. Anthony felt that there were so many changes they were unable to ver-balize all of them. The students rated the reformulated piece at the Supreme Court Justice level.

Interestingly, as the students read the reformulated version of the es-say, they expressed discomfort in writing that way, feeling that it was "rich people's language." Carolina even read her reformulated essays using a high-pitched tone, or in her words a "rich person's" voice. This interaction alerted Anthony to the realization that at this point in her aca-demic career, since Carolina did not identify with those who use formal academic English, it would be more challenging for her to master it. How-ever, he also recognized that she had strong personal and situational fac-tors (high motivation, good oral language proficiency, and family encour-agement) that could support her in her academic goals.

Carolina then rewrote her essay consulting individually with An-thony. At the final meeting, the group met and discussed Carolina's revi-sion and writing process. They thought her revision improved. Anthony asked Carolina to describe the changes she made. The other students spoke positively and didn't recommend any further changes. They rated the piece a step higher at the Rookie level. What follows is an excerpt from Carolina's first draft, the section reformulated, and then the final revi-sions Carolina made:

> 4th paragraph original: Music! There's different tunes, sounds and meanings. There's every type of music for many individuals. There's Bachata, Merengue, salsa, Reggae, caribbean reggae, hip hop, R & B, Rock & Roll, Metallic, and Romantic music, My favorite. So there you go any type of music you wanna listen too, you would have a great selec-tion. (All errors included)
>
> 4th paragraph teacher's reformulation: There are many kinds of mu-sic i.. the world with different, rhythms, styles, and sounds. Whether it is dance music or romantic music there is a style of music essential for everyone's life. People from the Caribbean might prefer listening to bachata, merengue, or salsa. Individuals from the United States might prefer hip hop, heavy metal, or rock and roll. With so many different kinds of music, anyone can select a style essential to their life.

4th paragraph student's revision: There are many ways music has been created such as tunes, sounds, styles, and different meanings to each one of them. Imagine there would be no music how would people enjoy their life? People from the Caribbean like bachata, merengue, reggae, and salsa. People from the United States like hip hop, heavy metal, and rock and roll. In other words any type of music you want to listen too, you would have a great selection.

It is evident that the Reformulation approach helps students but does not take away their ownership of the piece. Carolina's revision shows that she changed only those things that she had internalized. For example, the very last sentence changed to look more like written language but she could not yet depersonalize it as Anthony showed in his reformulated version. Carolina changed back to second person.

Since working with Carolina, Anthony has used the Reformulation Approach with other students. He subsequently made a chart for his students in an effort to help them better understand why sentences were changed:

Original Text	Reformulated Text	What are the reasons it was changed?	What are the effects of the change:

He used this chart when working with high school seniors who were writing essays for college entrance applications. It has been successful. After reading a reformulation he breaks the class into groups of three or four and with both essays in front of them they examine them for changes. The students/groups at times became a little competitive to see who could find the most changes. The charts were then used to guide a class discussion on the changes. The charts increased participation and clarity in the class discussion. He collected the charts and synthesized them into one sheet documenting all the changes. He shared the results with the students the next day.

READ ALOUD INTERVENTION

Purpose

The purpose of the Read Aloud approach when done on a one-on-one basis is to facilitate reading a text that it is too hard for a student to read independently. As the tutor reads with the student, meaning is made clear by the intonation of the voice, facial expressions, and even body movements. The student or the tutor can stop for clarification or teaching vocabulary. If the tutors know the students' heritage language they can use it or allow the student to use it to facilitate further understanding of the text. It is important not to interrupt the reading too often or the thread of the text will be lost. Alternatively, the text can be read more than once, making the reading uninterrupted one time.

Distinction Between Individual and Whole Class Read Aloud

It is important to distinguish this type of Read Alouds and reading aloud to a whole class. When a tutor reads aloud to one student they are both looking at the text together. The oral and written language are being connected and support each other much in the same way that happened with Shared Reading (chap. 4). When a teacher reads aloud to a whole class, only the teacher is looking at the text. This activity becomes more a listening comprehension activity, much harder for second language learners. Thus, the purpose of reading aloud to a whole class is different. It helps promote listening comprehension for those with a certain level of proficiency. For newcomers, reading aloud gives them a sense of the sounds and rhythm of the language. These students should not be pressed to respond to comprehension questions. Teachers can invite the newcomers to sit next to them while reading aloud so that they can follow the text.[6]

Procedure

Have a reading corner where you can seat comfortably on a round, with the classroom library nearby.

1. Choose a story that you and children like or let the children choose. It is better if it is a short traditional children's literature. You should be able to read it in one sitting.
2. Give students a general sense of what the story is about either by introducing the main character, or talking generally about the story (let them use native language to clarify among themselves). Do not spend too much time at this. If they have read this story before you may want to skip this step.

---

[6]Lester Laminack (2006); Trelease, J. (1982).

3. Read with expression, not too fast but flowing. Let the children join in, make comments, ask questions. Eventually they will learn to listen to the whole story. Be patient, do not discipline them—you want to make it a fun activity.

4. After it is finished, let children make comments on their own. Do not question them.

5. Leave books handy so that children can read on their own these same books

6. Teaching vocabulary. You may choose to teach a few key words before reading the story. These words should be related to the main message of the story. You can teach a few additional words as you are reading, if the students seem to have difficulty with them or ask for the meaning.

The Approach in Practice

Nicole Gunderson was searching for an approach that would help Juan, her tutee, with his reading comprehension. She had done extensive reading on the Read Aloud approach and felt that with a few adaptations, she could help Juan better understand what he was reading.

Juan was a nine-year old boy of Puerto Rican descent, enrolled in the fourth grade at the time of this intervention. Juan spoke both English and Spanish in his daily interactions; he was residing with his Mother, an older sister and two younger brothers. Juan received all formal schooling up to this point in English, which greatly affected his Spanish language development, as he was able to speak and understand Spanish, but was not able to read or write it. He seemed to be very proud of his heritage, but it appeared that connections to his homeland were minimal.

Before initiating the project, Nicole talked with Juan about the types of books he enjoyed reading, since she wanted to find material that would be of interest to Juan. He told her that he enjoyed "The Bailey School Kids" series. Nicole began the project by reading from one of the books of that series; however, she determined that they didn't seem challenging enough for the purposes of the Read Aloud. She suggested that they try one of the books from the Magic Tree House series. Juan was familiar with the series, having read one of them, and agreed to use one of those books for the Read Aloud.

At the beginning of each session, Nicole presented three vocabulary words from the story to Juan. She reviewed the words and their meanings with him before reading the story. Juan enjoyed learning the new words and their meanings so much so, that at the beginning of each session he excitedly demonstrated his ability to recall the pronunciations and definitions of the vocabulary words from the previous sessions. Nicole encouraged Juan's interest in learning new vocabulary by making him a "vocabulary ring." She wrote all the words he had learned on index cards which she then laminated, hole-punched, and placed on a ring. During one session, Juan asked that three more words (words that he did not understand when he was reading) be added to his ring. He told Nicole that he liked having the "vocabulary ring" because it helped him recall the new words he had learned, and that he liked taking it home to study and also to show his mother the new words he had learned. Nicole felt that this part of the Read Aloud approach was very helpful for Juan. She noticed that his vocabulary recognition was improving and that he was using the new words in his retellings.

During the first session, Juan asked Nicole if he could read part of the chapter to her. She agreed. As he was reading, Nicole took note of Juan's fluency. She noticed that he did not stop at punctuation signals and that when he read on his own, his retellings were less descriptive and he relied more on picture clues than on text. She decided to work with him on his fluency, so from the first session on, Juan read some of the material aloud. When he was reading, Nicole taught him specific strategies to use when reading, such as taking a breath after a period and thinking about what a question sounds like before reading it. She also modeled appropriate intonation for him. These strategies helped Juan somewhat when reading, but he had to be constantly reminded of them.

Nicole also decided to adapt another approach into her work with Juan. She had read about the Reader-Generated Questions approach (see Chapter 4) and thought that having Juan pose questions about the story before reading it might help his comprehension. As they read the chapter, they stopped if one of his questions had been answered and discussed it. Nicole believed that this approach significantly improved Juan's comprehension. Juan himself acknowledged that he was able to focus more when he had "questions in his head."

Nicole met with Juan for eight sessions. She felt that combining the Read Aloud approach with several other approaches was a successful way to tutor Juan and help him improve his own reading fluency and comprehension.

9

Learning from Students' Performance

Teachers can learn from students' performance through assessments or through research. Assessments can become part of the data collection of their research project. This chapter includes two sections. The first one gives suggestions of how teachers can assess students and how assessment can be embedded in instruction. The second section outlines how a teacher can carry out a research project while implementing a teaching approach. An example of a teacher research project with one of the approaches featured in this volume is also included.

ASSESSMENT

Assessment is a vital component of every classroom. It can inform teacher-research as well as general progress of the students in the class. Teachers assess their students by collecting data in order to aid in the planning, carrying out, and altering of classroom instruction for one, some, or all the students. Teachers constantly monitor their students' learning to assure that the intended instructional goals are being met. When assessment in the classroom is coordinated with instruction, it provides a productive, meaningful, and fair way of improving teaching and enhancing learning.[1]

Assessment procedures should become an integral part of teachers' lesson planning. In this way, instruction informs assessment, and vice

---

[1]See Brisk (2006) for a discussion of the benefits of planning instruction in conjunction with assessment and Stefanakis (1998) for examples of teachers carrying out this practice.

versa. Instead of waiting until the end of a unit to assess what and how much was learned by the students, ongoing, integrated assessment provides immediate feedback to both students and teachers. Any needed changes in instruction and direction can occur at the most opportune time, during the learning itself.

The act of becoming literate is both ongoing and developmental. Therefore, assessments for bilingual students should focus on the process as well as the product. It is often during the process of reading and writing that one observes students using, improving, and eventually mastering literacy skills and techniques.[2]

The process of literacy assessment in the classroom is multidimensional, and includes assessing knowledge of content, knowledge of text structure, vocabulary, grammar, orthography, phonemic awareness, and sound—symbol correspondence. It is important for teachers to determine the processes and skills the students have mastered, those that need reinforcement, and those that need to be taught, or retaught.

For bilingual students, assessment should be performed in both the first and second language, because many literacy skills are not language specific. Students demonstrate literacy knowledge through either language, whereas they demonstrate ability to read and write in a particular language through that specific language. Students can demonstrate the ability to encode words through either their first or second language; however, demonstrating the correct spelling of a word is done in the language in question.

By assessing in either language, teachers can ascertain the students' ability to read and write various genre, how well students manipulate aspects of language in context, as well as how students understand content-specific material. Assessing in both languages will also provide the teacher better information as to the developmental level of literacy of the students. Students can best demonstrate what they know and what they have learned when they are given the opportunity to relate it to prior knowledge and experience. For bilinguals, that prior knowledge and experience may be in the first language.

Teachers who are not speakers of the students' other language should find ways to evaluate students' performance in that other language. Alicia, a monolingual English teacher, asked Angela, a bilingual colleague, to assess José's reading ability in Spanish. Angela heard José read aloud and checked for comprehension while Alicia watched. They were both able to see that José had limited Spanish reading skills. Further talks with the mother confirmed that she did not encourage José's Spanish development.

---

[2]Cappellini (2005) provides many examples of informal assessment during the process of reading and writing.

There are also occasions when both languages can be utilized for one assessment. Students, who may be able to read and understand a passage in the second language, but cannot produce a written summary in the second language, would better demonstrate understanding of what was read if given the opportunity to write the summary in their native language. Again, translation assistance can be asked of teachers, paraprofessionals, other students, and parents if the teacher is not proficient in the first language of the student.

When assessing a bilingual student's performance, teachers must also be aware of the effect culture and background knowledge have on student responses and reactions. A more complete picture of students' literacy experience and knowledge is obtained when teachers have an understanding of how much students' answers are dependent on their first language and culture. When asked for the identity of the character, as the teacher pointed to the hen (in *The Little Red Hen* story), one girl exclaimed: "The mother." In her culture, a female wearing an apron always represents the mother. Teachers need to investigate further when students give a seemingly incorrect answer.

Assessment Practices

Teachers need to decide exactly what will be assessed, how, and when they will assess students, how the information will be recorded, and how feedback will be given to the students and, when appropriate, to the parents or other members of the school community.

The decision on what will be assessed should be made during the planning stages of the lesson, so that instruction and assessment complement each other. Once teachers determine which aspects of literacy development will be assessed, they will need to select a method of assessment. There are a number of highly recommended assessment practices such as oral interviews, read alouds, retellings, writing samples, experiments and demonstrations, projects and exhibitions, response journals, learning logs, constructed responses, and conferences. (See Appendix E for description of these practices.)[3] Many of these assessment practices are embedded in the approaches recommended in this book (see Table 9–1).

Patricia, a mainstream computer teacher, experimented with Process Writing with her class of fifth graders. She used read aloud during revision, collected writing samples, and carried out conferences with individual students. All these activities provided rich information regarding her students' writing ability with respect to both process and product. She

---

[3]Genesee and Hamayan (1994) and O'Malley and Valdez-Pierce (1996) explain in detail these practices.

TABLE 9–1

Assessment Practices That Can Be Used with the Approaches

	Oral Interviews	Read Alouds	Retellings	Writing Samples	Projects Exhibitions	Experiments	Response Journals	Learning Logs	Constructed Responses	Conferences
1. Anticipation Guide	X		X				X		X	X
2. Coop Learning–Jigsaw	X		X		X	X		X	X	X
3. Cross-age Project	X	X		X	X				X	
4. Dialogue Journal	X		X				X	X	X	
5. Dictogloss			X	X					X	
6. Drawing as Prewriting	X			X						
7. Graphic Org–Semantic Mapping	X									X
8. Language Experience Approach	X	X		X						X
9. Mailbox Game	X			X						
10. Process Writing with Computers	X	X		X					X	X
11. Read Aloud	X	X	X	X			X		X	X
12. Reader-Generated Questions	X	X	X			X	X		X	X
13. Reformulation	X	X	X	X						X
14. Response to Literature	X		X	X	X		X		X	X
15. Rhetorical Approach	X			X	X					X
16. Shared Reading	X	X		X					X	
17. Show Not Tell	X			X						X
18. Situational Context	X			X	X				X	
19. Student Directed Sharing Time/Group Discussion	X			X	X	X	X	X	X	
20. Talk-Write				X						X
21. Vocabulary Connections	X			X			X	X	X	X
22. Word Cards	X	X								X

191

that several Spanish speakers' first drafts lacked some articles. One student wrote: "When I was baby . . ." Another wrote: "What I think of me being Scorpio is . . ." When the students read aloud, however, they included the missing article and later corrected the error while producing their final version.

Teachers must plan assessment of both process and product. By observing, talking to the students, and taking notes during a lesson or activity teachers are able to see more clearly how well students are progressing, or if parts of a lesson or concept have been misunderstood or forgotten by the students. Observations and questioning of the students during a lesson or activity may help prevent an incorrect assessment of students' ability.[4] Tests, as well as demonstrations, exhibitions, projects, experiments, running records, and writing samples, are means of assessing a product. Bilingual students do need to learn the traditional method of question and answer, multiple choice, and true–false type evaluations, because it does assess declarative knowledge of a subject,[5] and it is the more common type of assessment in many classrooms, not to mention the more formal standardized tests. However, assessments involving exhibitions, projects, or demonstrations can give teachers a broader perspective both on what the students learned as well as how the student was able to apply what was learned. Students in a bilingual third-grade class were studying about different communities (i.e., urban, suburban, and rural). As a culminating project, the students worked in cooperative groups and designed the type of community they would like to live in. Students worked together to decide the types of buildings and services their community would have. When the projects were finished, mainstream teachers were invited into the classroom to question individual students on components of their project. It was each student's responsibility to know the community well enough to answer any question asked. Gene, the classroom teacher, observed while the students were being questioned and made notes of how well each student was able to explain the project. He was pleasantly surprised to hear Miguel, a student who always seemed to have trouble demonstrating his knowledge in writing, talk at length about his community.

Information emerging from the assessment activities can be recorded with the assistance of checklists; narrative and anecdotal record; miscue analysis; video and audio recordings; and portfolios. These descriptive records enable teachers to show in some detail the progress a student is making. Bilingual and ESL teachers, for example, can use this type of assessment and recording when consulting with other teachers or admin-

---

[4]See Farr and Trumbull (1997) for a more detailed explanation of process assessment.

[5]See Marzano, Pickering, and McTighe (1993) for assessment standards for declarative and procedural knowledge.

istrators to decide whether a student is ready to be mainstreamed into an all English curriculum. On the other hand, a portfolio, containing selected samples of students' work in all subject areas, gives parents a comprehensive overview of what their child is learning and how their child is performing in the classroom.

Putting It All Together: Approaches As Assessment Tools

There are innumerable opportunities during the implementation of the approaches recommended in this handbook for teachers to assess the literacy development and specific skills acquisition of their students. One approach can be used in several ways to evaluate literacy development and skills. As mentioned previously, teachers should have a clear understanding of what, why, and how they are assessing before proceeding (i.e., which literacy skills do they want to assess and for what purposes).

Table 9–2 shows examples of skills that can be taught and assessed through the Reader-Generated Question approach and where in the process of the approach the skill is demonstrated.[6]

Renate (see the Reader-Generated Question approach) was able to assess many of the skills listed previously for the children with whom she was working. Often during the Generation of Questions and Responding to Questions steps of the process, the children self-corrected their remarks. For example, George had begun a response to a question about plants by saying, "Cause . . .", but corrected it to *because* as Renate was beginning to write it down. Angel also rephrased a question he had about plants and energy to make it more explicit. He had first asked: "Why do plants like energy, energy?," but then changed it to: "Why do trees need the light energy?" Renate was also able to determine which students needed reinforcement in the formation of questions in English. In addition, she noticed during the Checking Out Responses step, that the students seemed more comfortable writing the answers directly from the text instead of rephrasing. From this observation, she realized that the students needed to practice extracting information from text and writing it in their own words. During the reading of the text, in an effort to find answers to their questions about plants, students reread paragraphs and discussed the main points of them. At other times, when the information was not available in the textbooks, the students had to use other sources of information to find answers to their questions. Renate was able to see which students knew how to use sources such as other science texts, science information books, and encyclopedias.

---

[6]Many of these skills are listed in literacy record folders used by many public school systems.

TABLE 9–2
Literacy Skills Assessed Through Reader-Generated Question Approach

Reading Skills Assessed	Where in the Approach
Uses context cues	Step 4: Presentation of Text Step 5: Checking Out Responses
Uses knowledge of language structure	Step 2: Generation of Questions Step 3: Responding to Questions
Predicts	Step 1: Stimuli Step 4: Presentation of Text
Rereads to establish meaning	Step 4: Presentation of Text Step 5: Checking Out Responses
Reads further to gain more information	Step 5: Checking Out Responses
Self-corrects	Step 2: Generation of Questions Step 3: Responding to Questions Step 4: Presentation of Text
Uses picture cues to establish meaning	Step 1: Stimuli Step 4: Presentation of Text
States main idea of paragraph	Step 6: Final Activity
Gives details to support main idea	Step 6: Final Activity
Infers meaning from text	Step 5: Checking Out Responses Step 6: Final Activity
Expresses and supports an opinion	Step 3: Responding to Questions Step 6: Final Activity
Uses a range of books and other materials to locate information	Step 5: Checking Out Responses
Interprets maps, graphs and tables in context	Step 4: Presentation of Text Step 5: Checking Out Responses
Skims a paragraph to find relevant information	Step 4: Presentation of Text Step 5: Checking Out Responses
Compares and contrasts information	Step 4: Presentation of Text Step 5: Checking out Responses Step 6: Final Activity
Draws conclusions	Step 6: Final Activity

Writing Skills Assessed	Where in the Approach
Writes comprehensible sentences	Step 2: Generation of Questions Step 3: Responding to Questions Step 6: Final Activity
Stays on topic when writing	Step 6: Final Activity

(continued)

TABLE 9-2 (*Continued*)

Reading Skills Assessed	Where in the Approach
Connects ideas	Step 2: Generation of Questions Step 3: Responding to Questions Step 5: Checking Out Responses Step 6: Final Activity
Is aware of audience	Step 6: Final Activity
Uses compound sentences	Step 3: Responding to Questions Step 6: Final Activity
Uses content specific vocabulary	Step 2: Generation of Questions Step 3: Responding to Questions Step 6: Final Activity
Uses correct punctuation	Step 2: Generation of Questions Step 3: Responding to Questions Step 6: Final Activity
Uses invented spelling	Step 2: Generation of Questions Step 3: Responding to Questions Step 6: Final Activity
Uses conventional spelling	Step 2: Generation of Questions Step 3: Responding to Questions Step 6: Final Activity
Revises work	Step 6: Final Activity
Edits work	Step 6: Final Activity
Uses dictionary, thesaurus and so forth to increase vocabulary and understanding	Step 5: Checking Out Responses Step 6: Final Activity
Uses standard grammar	Step 2: Generation of Questions Step 3: Responding to Questions Step 6: Final Activity

Clearly, a teacher would not want to assess all the skills a particular approach allows. The purpose of the checklist is to show the numerous skills that can be assessed by using one of the approaches. Teachers can adapt the list depending on what they have decided to assess. When using a checklist, teachers should indicate whether students were able to complete the skill independently, with assistance, or not at all.

For example, a teacher might want to create a checklist similar to the one shown in Table 9–3. Teachers should indicate how well the student could perform a task by circling the appropriate letter. Write the date of the observation on the line next to the letter. Indicate the language in which the skill is observed.

TABLE 9-3
Sample Checklist

1. Indicate how well student can perform task by circling appropriate letter.
Write the date of the observation on the line next to the letter.
2. Indicate the language in which skill is observed.

Student Name	Uses Context Cues	Predicts	Infers Meaning
	I __ H __ N __*	I __ H __ N __	I __ H __ N __
	I __ H __ N __	I __ H __ N __	I __ H __ N __
	I __ H __ N __	I __ H __ N __	I __ H __ N __
	I __ H __ N __	I __ H __ N __	I __ H __ N __

*I = Can do Independently; H = Can do with Help; N = Cannot do at all

Observations and anecdotal records are helpful when teachers want to track the development of certain skills of the students. Susan (see Drawing as Prewriting approach) was able to observe developmental changes in Alex's ability to decode the words he had written. In the beginning of her study, Susan had noted that Alex demonstrated great difficulty in reading the stories he had written. Later on, she observed that he was able to read some of the sentences he had written, but not many. Eventually, Susan observed that Alex was able to completely read his story aloud to his classmates. An example of her anecdotal record follows:

February 12, 1993

When I had Alex read me his story, he couldn't remember what it said. We went through it very slowly together and tried sounding out the words. Alex did not know the sounds of most of the letters and when I gave them to him, he had difficulty putting them together. We read the story three times together, and by the third time it was better, but he still did not know all of the words. When he showed his teacher, he made no attempt to read it and she read it to him.

Later on, Susan observed that Alex was able to read more of the sentences he had written:

February 26, 1993

. . . Alex was able to read aloud what he had dictated to me, which he could not do last week.

During the course of her time with Alex, Susan noticed that he was remembering the sound—symbol correspondence of many consonants:

March 4, 1993

Alex recognized graphophonemic correspondences for *s, d, f, l, t,* and *v.* He had some difficulty with vowel sounds, but even then he knew they were vowel sounds. He also knew that the letters *k* and *c* can sound alike.

Eventually, Susan observed that Alex was able to confidently read his story aloud to his classmates:

April 6, 1993

Alex read last. Saroeut and Elvin had stood up and were talking and Alex hit Saroeut in the knee with his paper. "Sit down!" he said and they did. When Alex read, all of the students moved in very close so that they could hear him better. While some of the other students read, there were people kind of shuffling around and looking around. When Alex read, they all practically sat on top of him and everyone wanted to help him read. He read his story very well and the few places he got stuck, Saroeut helped him with the words.

While using the LEA with Teddy, Laurie was able to observe the progress he made decoding words in a story. She writes:

March 21, 1996

I told Teddy to read one sentence at a time and I would write it on the sentence strip. Teddy read the first four sentences with accuracy and fluency. He had difficulty with the word *figured* in his next sentence. He identified the initial sound and used the long i vowel sound. He then made a guess *fired*, based on these first two sounds and looked at me. I said, "Let's skip over that word and read the rest of the sentence. This may remind you of what you said." He was able to read the rest of the sentence and then exclaimed, "Oh, yah! Figured." as he went back to the beginning of the sentence. In the next sentence he struggled with the word *friends.* Again he identified the two initial sounds and made an attempt at the word, coming up with freed. With a single cue to recall his story he readily came to the conclusion that the word was friends. When *friend*s reappeared in the next sentence he had no difficulty recalling it.

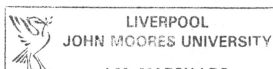

March 26, 1996

At the beginning of our third session I asked Teddy to continue to read his dictated text, . . . He was able to read "Please ostrich play with me." He self-corrected when he began to read *play* as *please* . . . Teddy at times will confuse *b* and *d* as he did in the next sentence, as he attempted to decode *didn't* with the /b/ sound. He realized his own error because he self-corrected without any cues.

April 29, 1996

. . . Teddy was able to read the first twelve pages of the original *Milton the Early Riser*. His reading was quite fluent, in that he was able to recognize many of the words by sight. He read seven of the twelve pages without any errors . . . Teddy applied his decoding skills when he reached *trembled*. He omitted the /r/ sound in his initial attempt, on the second attempt he went back over the sounds and said all of them. However, he guessed the word to be troubled. I cued him to try it again. I assisted him by covering up some of the phonemes as he proceeded. He then arrived at the correct response.

By having her students act out *The Little Red Hen,* Marta was able to assess how well her deaf kindergartners understood the story. After having been read the story in ASL[7] the children dramatized it.

Throughout the dramatization, Marta was able to observe and note how well Nancy, playing the main character, sequenced the story. She assessed other students' ability to understand the characters in the story as they acted out their parts in the play:

Nancy has all the appropriate props and proceeds to busy herself with the hen's work trying to follow the sequence set forth in the story. Tommy is playing an excellent dog staying in character by improvising and going to the refrigerator for some imaginary food, he then goes back to sleep. Mike, Sara, and Donnie are having a more difficult time creating spontaneous language about other characters (gossiping). We did model the character for him, but sustaining conversation with Donnie and Sara, whose expressive language is limited, was a difficult task for him. Mike improvised by inviting his guest into the kitchen for food. The surroundings and food props were familiar to Donnie and Sara, and this enabled them to converse in a comfortable setting at their own level.

---

[7]Children look at English text while teacher interprets using ASL.

The Home–School Connection

An often-underutilized source for assessing the complete literacy development of bilingual students is information on home literacy activities.[8]

Many bilingual students are often the more proficient second-language speakers in the home, and may be the only first language literate members of their family, or they are frequently relied on to read important information sent to the home in the second language, fill out necessary applications and other forms, interpret bills and legal documents, and so forth.

Logs could be kept by either by the students or their parents, in which literacy activities are recorded, indicating the languages used, the types of activities, the purpose, and any other pertinent information. These activities should not be prescribed by the teacher, bur rather should be naturally occurring and could include writing journals; reading books or manuals; reading and writing notes to parents/children; reading and writing letters to relatives; reading newspapers and magazines; writing shopping lists; or filling out forms and applications.

TEACHER RESEARCH

"Teachers are seen—and principally see themselves—as consumers rather than producers of knowledge."[9] Yet closely observing students offers natural opportunities to reflect on teaching and learning. By observing students as they are participating in class, teachers determine the effectiveness of a lesson or approach to learning; and decide if, when, and how to change the lesson or approach to ensure that all students learn. By analyzing their experiences in the classroom, good teachers enhance their skills. By further disseminating what they have learned, such teachers can become significant producers of knowledge. Good schools support teacher research,[10] provide opportunities for teachers to share their findings with other educators, and incorporate teacher research into the agenda of school improvement.

---

[8]Paratore, Homza, Krol-Sinclair, Lewis-Barrow, Melzi, Stergis, and Haynes (1995) describe a home-school literacy project in which parents share students' literacy activities with teachers through a home portfolio.

[9]Freeman (1998, p. 10).

[10]Teacher research is "systematic and intentional inquiry carried out by teachers" (Cochran-Smith & Lytle, 1993, p. 7).

Relating instruction and assessment, even informally, to research improves classroom practices. By conducting research, teachers (a) systematize teaching and assessment, (b) evaluate their own teaching, (c) relate their practices to other research, (d) use innovative instructional practices other than talking and lecturing, and (e) collaborate and share ideas with colleagues. Extending data collection to documentation of learning in the home enhances communication between teachers and families.

Teachers routinely collect data by observing, making mental notes, writing anecdotal notes, formally assessing students, and saving student products. When teachers add careful analysis and reflection to this process, they contribute to the body of knowledge about teaching and learning. Because time is a barrier to conducting research, teachers should limit the scope of the research, turn instruction and assessment into data collection opportunities, and contribute to building a culture in schools that supports research and values teachers' findings. Teachers can limit their questions or goals, the amount of time they dedicate to data collection and reflection, and the number of students involved.

This section describes how to conduct research while implementing literacy practices recommended in this handbook.[11]

The process includes:

Planning and preparation.

Implementation and data collection.

Analysis, reflection, and dissemination.

The process is illustrated through a project carried out by a teacher over the period of 12 weeks.

Planning and Preparation

In planning research within the context of their teaching and assessment, teacher—researchers follow these steps:

Describe students

Assess reading and writing in both languages

Review approaches and choose one or more

---

[11]This research can be done individually by a teacher or as part of the work required of professional development or university courses.

Set goals for research by concentrating on:
a) one aspect of students' development
b) chosen teaching approaches

Read research about:
a) specific aspect of student development
b) chosen approaches

Evaluate appropriateness of classroom layout

Design study

Information about the learners, an essential initial step for instruction and assessment, is also the first phase of research. Teachers must gauge students' needs and the particular literacy approaches to decide which approaches to use and in what combination. Students' literacy skills in both native and second languages are assessed through testing, observation, and interviewing other teachers, parents, and the students themselves. Other information collected about the students (see Appendix A) determines strengths, needs, and interests, as well as students' linguistic, educational, and cultural backgrounds.

An overview of the approaches, as well as reading more in depth about those that appear suitable, helps teachers make and justify decisions on the approach or approaches to use. By reviewing relevant research, teachers can understand better why they are following particular steps or procedures. Familiarity with the theoretical foundation of each approach allows for modifying approaches to suit particular students.

Next, questions are formulated or goals are set based on the knowledge of both students and the chosen approaches. Goals or questions relate to specific skills teachers hope their students will develop and to the effectiveness of the approach chosen.

By outlining a study design, teachers collect data while instructing and assessing. Implementation of the literacy approach and assessment can be done for all students in the class and the research component can focus on a few students. Although the whole class is engaged in writing, the teacher might collect data on a small group of students.

An alternative is to do both implementation and research with only a group of students. Katherine, for example, wanted to study higher order thinking skills in students' oral discussions and response journals. She chose ten students with whom she worked during nine 45-minute sessions, videotaping their sessions and collecting their journals. The rest of her students completed assignments supervised by a classroom paraprofessional. The experience taught her how to better facilitate the process of reading comprehension and how to encourage thinking skills. After the study, she then used these approaches with her whole class. The students who had participated in the small group project assisted the rest of the class making elaborations, inferences, and syntheses of their readings.

Steps in a research design include initial assessment of students, data collection, analysis, and reflection. For example, a teacher choosing the Reader-Generated Questions approach with the goal of developing ability to make predictions might follow closely students reading four selections over a period of four weeks. Each week a different group would be studied. After introducing the reading selection, students in each group write questions they think the selection will answer and guess answers for their questions. Students then read the passage, check their responses, and write summaries. The teacher observes and takes notes on the focus group of the week. The students' ability to predict independently, with help from classmates, or not at all, is gleaned from sheets with students' questions and answers and from teacher's notes. The teacher assesses the summaries for the main idea and number of details to obtain data on reading comprehension. These results are not only used for the research project, but also become part of the assessment records of the students. As with all research, original plans may need modification once instruction takes place.

Teachers analyze the setting to determine if it facilitates the implementation of the particular approach. For example, Reader-Generated Questions requires whole class, group, and individual work arrangements.

Implementation and Data Collection

Teachers try the chosen approach with their class in the context of their regular instructional and assessment agenda. Teachers implement the chosen approach and gather data following the plan in their study design. The following activities occur simultaneously:

Implementation of the approach

Collection of data, including assessments

Discussing data and assessment results with colleagues (and course instructor if done as part of professional development)

As teachers implement the teaching approach they carry out assessments and data collection. There are a number of ways to collect data while teaching. Teachers can write notes on copies of students' products to detail students' performance around these products. In personal files, teachers keep classroom observations, self-memoranda, and audio and video recordings. Classroom observations include factual descriptions and verbatim quotes. Any thoughts that come to mind should be noted by clearly marking with parenthesis or by adding o.c. (occasional comment) to distinguish from the facts. For example, as Laura was observing her students during Dialogue Journal she notes:

> Eduardo brought stickers to personalize his journal [o.c.: this indicates to me that he is interested in his piece].

Teachers write such notes while the students pursue group or individual work. Some teachers use sticky pads or address labels to write quick reminder notes or a student quote. They can write memoranda at the end of the day. These should be free-flowing descriptions of facts, ideas, reflections, or a synthesis of events over time. Using chart paper, rather than a board, they compile and save ideas produced by the whole class. Audiotape or video recordings are very helpful in collecting accurate information.[12] Any formal or informal assessment becomes part of the data sources.

Teachers organize their data, including assessments, in students' portfolios and personal files. Teachers create a portfolio for each focus student. The portfolio includes the protocol with general information about the student (Appendix A), instructional goals, assessment results, and student products. The systematic collection of samples of students' performance required for research purposes provides authentic data on students' abilities over time and without the distortions of stress typical of one time formal tests situations. As shown in the assessment section, Laurie's observations of Teddy's performance while reading provided a clear picture of his reading difficulties and his improvement over time.

Discussing with colleagues the implementation and data helps teachers reflect on the process. The length of time dedicated to data collection depends on the frequency and nature of the project and goals. Five weeks of daily observations may provide adequate data as can bi-weekly collection over 6 to 10 weeks. Carrying the approach through a full cycle is essential to answer questions about the approach.

Analysis, Reflection, and Dissemination

Much learning occurs in this last phase where teachers:

Analyze results.

Discuss results with colleagues.

---

[12]See Freeman (1998) for detailed suggestions on data collection strategies.

Draw conclusions and relate to existing research.

Make recommendations.

Disseminate their findings.

Teachers analyze and reflect on data collected, at times leading to changes while implementing the approach. They also analyze their data collected over a few weeks chronologically, thematically, or both. They either focus on all students together or on individual students. Much depends on the particular nature of the project and the variability on student performance. This analysis encourages teachers to reflect on their students' performance over time. It gives teachers a clearer picture of their students' development than impressions formed from one day to the next. It also illustrates the impact of a particular approach on students. Often teachers are surprised at how much students have developed and how different ways of implementing the various stages of the approach helped or hindered the process. For example, going back to our example of developing and studying the ability to predict doing the Reader-Generated Questions approach, the teacher analyzes each student's questions to see if the questions are connected to the topic of the reading. The teacher also reviews classroom notes on group discussions for evidence of improved performance with the help of classmates. These notes can shed light on students' interpretation of the topic, misunderstandings, and cultural differences.

Careful analysis of data reveals goals attained, questions answered, or even unexpected findings about the literacy approaches and their students' development. Teachers arrive at a concrete realization of their students' learning and their own teaching through reflection on the results, comparison with other studies, and discussions with colleagues. They also decide which approaches merit implementation and how best to modify them. This process enlightens teachers as to the way bilingual students function.

Collaboration is essential for this type of research. All projects described in this handbook were carried out within literacy courses offered either on campus or at the school districts. Course participants worked in groups discussing and critiquing each other's plans, goals, assessment strategies, implementation, data collection, and analysis. Such experiences might be replicated in teacher-led study groups.[13]

Disseminating findings is valuable both to teacher-researchers and their colleagues. A poster session is a good initial way to disseminate

---

[13]See Clair (1998) for research on teacher study groups.

findings. Teachers present, in a clear and didactic fashion, the key results and conclusions of their research on a poster board. Four or five participants present simultaneously in their own stations while the audience walks around looking at their posters and asking questions. This format is less threatening than a conference presentation and provides a rehearsal for presentations at conferences or school workshops.

Teachers can use these research strategies to try new approaches not included in this volume. Through this systematic observation of students' performance, they can evaluate the effectiveness of any approach, what aspects of literacy the approach helps develop, how the students react, and what modifications can be introduced to improve bilingual learning.

A Teacher-Researcher In Action

Ivelisse Nelson, a middle school bilingual teacher, works in a bilingual special education resource room where some students stay all day and others come for special help. She received a tuition voucher to attend a graduate course in literacy. She carried out her research as a class project, sharing her work throughout the semester with the course instructor and classmates.

After reading about various approaches described in chapters 2, 3, and 4, class participants discussed the approaches and their students in order to find the best match. Ivelisse described her students' reading comprehension difficulties. She was particularly interested in María, a 14-year-old Puerto Rican student with a history of language and literacy difficulties. She decided to look into the use of Graphic Organizers.

For the first four weeks Ivelisse gathered information on María using the Protocol provided to class participants as a guide (see Appendix A). Conversations with María, her family, and other teachers provided valuable information on María's background. Observations and testing of María's reading and writing skills in Spanish and English revealed, among other things, that she became easily frustrated when making mistakes and had a low opinion of her academic abilities. She had difficulty with story elements, predictions, and oral retellings in Spanish. She had little knowledge of English. To assess María's reading comprehension, Ivelisse read her a first-grade level book, *Ricitos de Oro y los Tres Ositos* (*Goldilocks and the Three Bears*). Her comprehension of the story was extremely limited and confused. Of eight comprehension questions Ivelisse asked, María could only answer two accurately. She shrugged her shoulders or answered "I don't know" to four. The other two were completely or partially incorrect.

Ivelisse had some experience using story maps as a postreading activity. She decided to use Graphic Organizers as a prereading as well as postreading activity after becoming familiar with the variety of uses of this approach and concluding that they would be especially useful to María as a concrete learner. Spanish, María's dominant language, was chosen as the language of instruction. Ivelisse set as a goal for the project the improvement of María's reading comprehension of first-grade level Spanish books. She wanted to investigate if using Graphic Organizers would assist María in identifying accurately the various story elements.

The classroom where Ivelisse worked had several tables appropriate for group work. They had resources in English and Spanish as well as computer facilities and access to the Internet. Ivelisse worked with the focus group at one of the tables while the other resource teacher taught students at a separate table. The conditions of the room were well suited for the implementation of the project.

Ivelisse used Graphic Organizers with a small group of students everyday for 5 weeks during her 55-minute literacy period. The first story was *Coco Ya No Espera Más* about a girl and her grandmother who kept missing each other when visiting. Ivelisse introduced the theme with the poem *Abuelita (Grandmother)* by Tomás Allende Iragorri. Students then created a variety of semantic maps (as a group and individually) with ideas on what they liked to do with their grandmothers, how they travel to visit their grandmothers, and their family tree. These maps provided a good opportunity to develop vocabulary. Students drew a picture illustrating a visit to their own grandmother.

Ivelisse then showed the cover of the book and wrote predictions from students about the content of the story. Ivelisse read the story aloud, given her students' difficulty reading. She frequently stopped to discuss what was happening, to discuss illustrations, and to make further predictions. After reading, they reviewed the prediction chart. Then students individually filled in story elements in individual story charts and illustrated a sequence map, annotating their drawings. For the final activity, students received a sheet with a square and lines below where they were to draw and write about their favorite story part.

Ivelisse kept notes on what happened during her lessons with special emphasis on what María was doing. She wrote:

I invited my students to share something about their grandmother and to say what kind of things they like to do with her. María started hugging herself, while answering "gusta cuando me acaricia" (I like being hugged), "gusta hablar" (I like to talk to her), "ir a la tienda" (go to the store). María continued to answer, while I wrote on the board. After giving several answers she copied from the board what she likes to do with her grandmother on a personal web. [o.c. It seems easier for María to read what she copies on her own paper] (Ivelisse's field notes 2/9/98).

Ivelisse typed her daily observations, filing them on her classroom computer. She also created a portfolio with copies of María's various individual semantic maps and story drawings. Ivelisse brought copies of her observations and students' products every week to her class at the university. Working in pairs, course participants exchanged observations, read them, and then asked each other questions for clarification. Special emphasis was placed on objective and descriptive information.[14]

For example, Ivelisse had written: ". . . students were asked to draw themselves visiting one of their grandmothers. María seemed confused . . ." (Ivelisse's field notes, 2/12/98). Cristina, Ivelisse's colleague, asked her what María had done to appear confused. After checking her handwritten notes, Ivelisse added to her observation:

María's first reaction was "Cómo? Yo no sé" (How? I don't know.).

Ivelisse handed her observations to the course instructor for further reaction to both her teaching and her data collection strategies.

Ivelisse used data in her computer files and portfolio for periodic assessment of and reporting on María's progress as well as for her research project. To analyze data, Ivelisse grouped observations and María's products into three stages: prereading, reading, and postreading activities. For each period she analyzed the strategies used as well as María's performance, looking at everything María said and produced.

Ivelisse analyzed her notes, looking for evidence of what María did and what she said during each of the activities looking for evidence of development. María, helped by this particular approach, began using strategies (prior knowledge and prediction) in the reading process that are characteristic of good readers. Her requests for help were mostly for spelling.

A comparison between María's story map and her initial reading comprehension assessment reveals María's comprehension of stories improved. In her initial assessment, María missed one main character, did not know the setting, the problem, or solution of the test story. She could only report one event correctly. Writing her story map after reading Coco's story, María was able to correctly fill in main characters and most additional characters, setting, problem, and solution. She filled in all the

---

[14]Course participants used the guidelines of the approach Show Not Tell (chap. 2) to critique each other's field notes.

sections of the story map, unlike her initial assessment, where half of the answers were a shrug of the shoulders.

Analysis of an earlier and later version of the sequence map shows that María could correctly sequence the story after additional reading. She included most events in her first attempt at a sequence map, although some of the order was not correct. She was able to complete it and sequence it correctly after an additional reading of the story. By using a sequence map, María was able to express her thoughts through drawings and labels. These maps show the student's drawing and writing abilities and corrections she made.

Throughout the process, Ivelisse met during her university class with three other students to discuss María's performance and progress in her research. Much of the discussion took place in Spanish, a language common to all members of that group. The course instructor was often called on to answer questions or provide clarification.

In discussing her results, Ivelisse concludes that the instructional approach had helped María achieve the main goal of identifying story parts and improving reading comprehension. María still had some difficulty with characters, spelling, and other aspects of language. Rereading the story after having established some comprehension filled in details.

Graphic Organizers helped prepare students for reading and allowed them to demonstrate understanding a story in concrete and manageable ways using drawings and single words. In María's case, this approach enhanced her classroom participation. After the first couple of sessions, María stopped saying "Yo no sé" (I don't know) or shrugging her shoulders, responses characteristic of this learner in the initial evaluations and observations.

Ivelisse states that she learned the importance of preparing students for reading as a result of this project. The concreteness and style of Graphic Organizers greatly help students who feel overwhelmed when looking at extended text.

At the final meeting of the course, Ivelisse presented a poster consisting of three panels. On the left side she illustrated prereading activities with copies of María's semantic maps and drawings, on the right side were postreading activities such as the story web and sequence map. In the middle Ivelisse stated what the project did for her student and recommendations about the use of Graphic Organizers. Discussion and questions during the poster session drew further reflection and ideas for future implementation.

Careful choice of a reading approach and analysis and reflection of its implementation helped Ivelisse realize that there are ways to improve her students' performance. Writing and sharing her research concretely demonstrated to Ivelisse her capacity for teaching and her students' ability to learn.

CONCLUSION

The need to prepare and retool teachers in literacy instruction for bilingual and second-language learners is great. The numbers of students entering American schools with languages other than English or in addition to English continue to increase. There is also growing interest in expanding second-language education for English speakers. Success for such students requires becoming truly functional in another language.

This handbook presents practical ideas as well as a process for preparing good literacy instructors. There is no question that knowledge of the students' native languages facilitates instruction in the second language, especially for beginners. However, the process documented in this handbook has been useful for many teachers who are not bilingual, helping them gain expertise and confidence to teach students in their second language. "I learned a great deal concerning many areas of bilingual education using this approach [Computers in Process Writing]" declared a computer teacher working for the first time with bilingual students. She adds, "These students were all strangers to me in September but I feel that I know them well now."

Theory, practice, and research, the three components in the process of teacher preparation (see Figure 9–1), are important and sustain each other. Teachers must be grounded in the theory of literacy and bilingualism as well as teaching approaches and assessment. This knowledge informs instruction and assessment. Teachers carry out instruction and

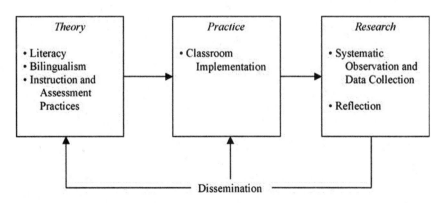

FIGURE 9–1 Content and process for preparing literacy teachers.

assessment while they test the value of content knowledge through their research. While observing students and trying to understand their strengths and weaknesses, teachers enhance their knowledge about bilingual learners, improve their teaching, and become more fair and accurate in their judgment of students. Their reflections and conclusions enhance theory and practice.

Although the focus of this handbook is to present useful approaches for teaching literacy to bilingual learners, preservice and in-service teachers benefit from experiencing the whole process of theory acquisition, practice, and research. By researching the implementation of these approaches, teachers gain a solid grounding on how to work with bilingual and second-language learners. What they learn in many cases greatly differs from their initial notions about bilingualism and second-language learning and how to teach literacy. Teachers acquire lasting knowledge about diverse populations through firsthand experience with these learners coupled with guided reflection and instruction.

Appendix A

Protocol to Gather Information about Learners

NAME:
External and family characteristics
Country or place of origin
Reasons for coming to the U.S. (learner or family)
Date of arrival _____ Born in the U.S._____ Intended length of stay in USA
Parents' occupation
Parents' education
Parents' language and literacy ability
Uses of literacy at home (specify languages)
Family attitudes toward native language and culture
Family attitudes toward English and American culture
Language(s) used at home for speaking
Language(s) used at home for reading/writing

Personal characteristics
Age
Oral language proficiency in L1
Oral language proficiency in L2
School experience
–Previous school experience (in the home country)
where
how long
language(s) used (specify subject if more than one language used)
student population (majority and minority status)
Current school experience
how long
language(s) used (specify subject if more than one language used)
student population (majority and minority status)
Attitudes toward L1 and L2
Personal goals for L2 and L2 literacy
Personality traits
Interests

Outside of class responsibilities (helping family)
Is s/he physically challenged?
Are there issues in regard to substance abuse or mental health?
Characteristics as reader and writer
Language(s) in which literacy was initiated
L1 literacy level (and how it was determined)
L2 literacy level (and how it was determined)
Attitude toward reading and writing
Language preference for reading and writing
Conception of literacy
–Motivation for reading and writing
–Preferred strategies for reading and writing
Other characteristics:

Appendix B

Books with Multicultural Themes

The following books present salient multiethnic themes and subject matter. Immigrant students also need to be introduced to American cultural traditions. A few books illustrate these themes. Recommended grade levels are specified.

OVERCOMING THE HARDSHIPS OF IMMIGRATION

Title: *Who Belongs Here?*
Author: Margy Burns Knight
Copyright: Tilbury House (1993)
Grade Levels: 1–6
Summary: This is the moving story of a Cambodian boy whose family flees the violence of their home country to begin a new life in America. While the boy's grandmother assures him the United States will be "better than heaven," he is actually met with great animosity, racism, and racial epithets at his new school. In witnessing the struggles of this boy and his family, readers are confronted by the horrors of human cruelty—and reminded of the beauty of human compassion. Based on a true story.

Title: *Esperanza Rising*
Author: Pam Muñoz Ryan
Copyright: Scholastic (2000)
Grade Levels: 4–12
Summary: Esperanza is a young girl growing up in Mexico on her family's beautiful *Rancho de las Rosas*. Despite their wealth and comforts, however, Esperanza and her parents are forced by tragedy to flee to the United

States and settle in a Mexican farm labor camp. Thus, the young Esperanza slowly learns to let go of her old way of life, and to realize the riches of her family and her new community.

Title: *Of Beetles and Angels*
Author: Mawi Asgedom
Copyright: Megadee Books (2001)
Grade Levels: 8–12
Summary: This memoir tells the true story of a young boy whose family fled a refugee camp in Sudan, and moved to America. Despite poverty, racial prejudice, and language barriers, the author received a full-tuition scholarship to Harvard University, and found success while retaining reserve and compassion, and never forgetting where he came from.

BIRACIAL/BICULTURAL IDENTITIES

Title: *What Are You?*
Author: Pearl Fuyo Gaskins
Copyright: Holt & Company (1999)
Grade Levels: 8–12
Summary: The author of this book (herself the daughter of a Japanese American mother and a European American father) conducted interviews with 80 mixed-race individuals, collected their testimonies, and brought them together with her own reflections, to create a compelling, real to life book. She includes an impressive spectrum of races, heritages, and perspectives about bicultural identity.

Title: *Jalapeño Bagels*
Author: Natasha Wing
Copyright: Atheneum (1996)
Grade Levels: K–3
Summary: Pablo, a boy with a Jewish father and a Mexican mother, must decide what food to bring to his school for the International Day celebration. Rather than bring a traditional dish from only one of his cultures, Pablo decides to invent a delicious combination of both.

Title: *I Love Saturdays Y Domingos*
Author: Alma Flor Ada
Copyright: Atheneum (2002)
Grade Levels: K–3
Summary: As its title suggests, the narrator of this book is a bilingual child who often spends Saturdays with her English-speaking grand-

parents, and Sundays with her Spanish-speaking ones. The book celebrates both cultural identities, and the young girl delights in having two
languages, two heritages, and two sets of loving grandparents.

PRESSURES TO ASSIMILATE

Title: *The Name Jar*
Author: Yangsook Choi
Copyright: Knopf (2001)
Grade Levels: K–3
Summary: A young Korean girl moves to the United States and worries
that no one at her school will be able to pronounce her name. She decides
to enlist her new classmates to help her select a more American name, but
they ultimately persuade her to keep the one she has. The book's final
message is that being different is a good thing, and that people should
take pride in what makes them unique.

OTHER FAMILY SITUATIONS: MIXED RACE
ADOPTION, INCARCERATED PARENTS

Title: *Lucy's Family Tree*
Author: Karen Halvorsen Schreck
Copyright: Tilbury House (2001)
Grade Levels: 3–6
Summary: Lucy, an adopted child of Mexican heritage, feels discouraged
when she has to create a family tree for a school project. She thinks there
is no way she can complete the assignment accurately, and feels bad that
she doesn't have a "normal" or "all-American" family structure. At her
parents' encouragement, however, Lucy decides to take a closer look at
the different family structures among her neighbors and friends. She
learns that some have stepparents, two mothers, or a stay-at-home father
and a working mother. Ultimately, Lucy comes to realize that every family
is in some way unique, and that her own that family tree can both accom-
modate and celebrate the different sides of her background.

Title: *Jin Woo*
Author: Eve Bunting
Copyright: Clarion (2001)
Grade Levels: 1–6
Summary: A boy named David becomes anxious when he learns that his
parents are adopting a baby, Jin Woo, from Korea. David, who is Cau-
casian but was also adopted, worries that his parents will spend less time

with him and love him less. After Jin Woo comes home, however, David realizes that he likes being a big brother, and that his parents love him just as much as they always have.

Title: *Visiting Day*
Author: Jacqueline Wodson
Copyright: Scholastic (2002)
Grade Levels: 1–6
Summary: A little girl goes with her grandmother to visit her father in prison. She is overjoyed to see him, sits on his lap and tells him everything that has happened since the last time they met. When their time together is over, the girl's grandmother tries to comfort her, saying "it's not forever going to be like this." At home, the little girl makes crayon drawings to mail to her father and talks with her grandmother about all the things they will do together when he comes home.

BOOKS RELATED TO A SPECIFIC HERITAGE

Title: *Going Home* (Hispanic American)
Author: Eve Bunting
Copyright: HarperTrophy (1998)
Grade Levels: K–4
Summary: This lavishly illustrated picture book tells the story of a Mexican American family going back home to reunite with their family for Christmas. The children of the family, who have grown up speaking English and surrounded by American culture, have mixed feelings about going "home." But they find that Mexico does feel like "home," in another sense, because their family and heritage are there.

Title: *Growing Up Black* (African American)
Copyright: Quill (1992)
Grade Levels: 8–12
Summary: This is a powerful collection of short autobiographical pieces describing the struggles and triumphs of growing up as African American. The anthology includes writings by Richard Wright, Maya Angelou, Booker T. Washington, Audre Lorde, and many more.

Title: *Lost in Translation* (Polish)
Author: Eva Hoffman
Copyright: Penguin (1990)
Grade Levels: 8–12
Summary: This is Eva Hoffman's autobiographical memoir of her childhood in war-ravaged Poland, her family's move to Vancouver, British

Columbia, and her own personal journey to come to terms with her bicultural identity and pursue her literary aspirations.

Title: *Mama Rocks, Papa Sings* (Haitian)
Author: Nancy Van Laan
Copyright: Knopf (1994)
Grade Levels: K–3
Summary: This book is set in Maissade, Haiti, and features Creole words and rhythmic storytelling. As the narrator's family gets larger and larger, she watches her mother and father rock and sing the babies to sleep. The book is illustrated in vibrant color, and includes an account of the Carnival celebration.

Title: *Join In: Multiethnic Short Stories by Outstanding Writers for Young Adults* (various cultures)
Editor: Donald Gallo
Copyright: Laurel Leaf (1995)
Grade Levels: 8–12
Summary: This is a collection of seventeen short stories about teenagers from a variety of cultural backgrounds and their personal accounts of universal experiences of American adolescents. The teenage protagonists fret about the SATs, their driver's tests, their parents' expectations, and their unrequited loves; and they rejoice in their friendships, their music, their sports teams, and their personal achievements. Despite their universal themes, these short stories present unique individual portraits of what it's like to grow up in America as a bicultural individual.

*   *   *

Multicultural learning also encompasses the study of American culture. Students from every background have much to gain from cultural lessons which outline and clarify some of the customs, traditions, routines and lifestyles shared by many people in the United States. American culture lessons can be made engaging and edifying for all students, whether they have lived in the country a year or all their lives. Such lessons can also serve a further objective: They can reinforce the notion that America is a place of extraordinary cultural diversity, and that everyone here may equally share in the holidays, traditions, and history which make the country unique.

The following books may be helpful for bilingual and recent immigrant students who are learning more about American culture and the English language.

AMERICAN HOLIDAYS

Title: *America Celebrates! A Patchwork of Weird & Wonderful Holiday Lore*
Author: Hennig Cohen and Tristram Potter Coffin
Copyright: Visible Ink Press (1991)
Grade Levels: 1–8
Summary: This teacher resource book views American culture as "an intricate quilt of distinct ethnic influences," and thus presents descriptions and historical vignettes about universal American holidays as well as holidays celebrated by a specific religion, heritage, or geographic region. The book is organized from January to December, and also incorporates recipes, games, songs, legends, and excerpts from news and human interest articles.

Title: *Rivka's First Thanksgiving*
Author: Elsa Okon Rael
Copyright: McElderry (2001)
Grade Levels: 1–6
Summary: Seven-year-old Rivka is a Jewish girl whose family emigrates to America from Poland in the early 1900s. When she learns about Thanksgiving at school, she is told that it is a holiday for *all* Americans; her parents and grandmother, however, having heard little about it, decide that they must go ask their rabbi to determine whether Thanksgiving is truly a holiday that Jews can celebrate. When the rabbi pronounces that it is not, Rivka writes him a letter explaining the meaning of Thanksgiving and why Jews have much reason to celebrate it and give thanks. Ultimately, the rabbi concedes to her reasoning, and Rivka's family celebrates their first Thanksgiving Day in America.

AMERICAN SPORTS

Title: *Champion: The Story of Muhammad Ali*
Author: Jim Haskins
Copyright: Walker Publishing (2002)
Grade Levels: 1–6
Summary: This illustrated autobiography begins with the birth of Cassius Clay in Louisville, Kentucky, and proceeds to relate the remarkable and controversial boxing career and life of Muhammad Ali. The book emphasizes how Ali's spirituality and pacifism were palpably ironic in light of his violent profession; it also describes Ali's membership in the

Nation of Islam, his evasion of the Vietnam draft, and the legacy of courage, strength, and honor he will inevitably leave behind.

Title: *A Picture Book of Jackie Robinson*
Author: David A. Adler
Copyright: Holiday House (1994)
Grade Levels: 1–6
Summary: This book chronicles Jackie Robinson's humble beginnings in rural Georgia, his baseball stardom in high school and college, his service in World War II and his unprecedented move from Negro League baseball to the all-white Major Leagues and the Brooklyn Dodgers. Throughout his career, Robinson was subjected to constant racial prejudice, verbal and physical attacks by other players, and demands that he quit the league and even anonymous death threats. In spite of all this, he was selected as Rookie of the Year in 1947 and Most Valuable Player in 1949, and was named to the Baseball Hall of Fame in 1962. His courageous struggle helped pave the way for professional baseball to become more racially diverse; it also stands as an important event in the advancement of liberty and equality in America.

FOR LANGUAGE AND GRAMMAR ENRICHMENT

Title: *Jazz Chants* and *Small Talk: More Jazz Chants* (sequel)
Author: Carolyn Graham
Copyright: Oxford (1978, 1986)
Grade Levels: 1–12
Summary: The rhythmic poems of *Jazz Chants* and *Small Talk* are designed to familiarize students with the rhythm and intonation patterns of Spoken American English. The chants and their accompanying cassette recordings are a fun and lively way for learners of all ages to improve their speaking skills and their listening comprehension.

Appendix C

Popular Books Taught in American English and Language Arts Classes

The following books are among the most commonly used in Beginning Reading and English Language Arts classrooms throughout the country. Because of their enduring popularity, these books, among others, account for a collective cultural literacy and a common knowledge base that is shared by generations of American students. Many of their themes, storylines, lessons, and questions reflect both implicitly and explicitly prevalent American values, ideas, and societal norms. Teachers of recent immigrant students can therefore call upon these and similar books to use as a gateway to critical discussions about prominent aspects of American culture.

Title: *The Berenstain Bears* series (over 50 books in all)
Author: Stan & Jan Berenstain
Copyright: Random House
Grade Levels: Preschool–Grade 2
Summary: The books of the Berenstain Bears series present many standard challenges and experiences of growing up: Brother Bear and Sister Bear confront bad habits, messy rooms, peer pressure, competition, and fears about the first day of school; they also embark on adventures through Bear Country, celebrate birthdays and holidays, and learn about family and community values. Mama Bear and Papa Bear are constantly a source of love and support for their cubs, helping them make good decisions and work through the difficulties they encounter. Berenstain Bear stories typically end with a conflict's resolution, which yields a moral or lesson with universal pertinence. A number of books in this series are also available as English/Spanish bilingual texts.

Stan and Jan Berenstain have also launched a PBS television series based on their books, and a child-friendly Web site (http://www.beren stainbears.com), which features interactive and educational activities.

Title: *The Cat in the Hat; One Fish, Two Fish, Red Fish, Blue Fish; I Can Read With My Eyes Shut;* and other books of Dr. Seuss "Beginner Books" series
Author: Dr. Seuss
Copyright: Random House (1957–Present)
Grade Levels: Preschool–Grade 2
Summary: Even though the Beginner Books series features first-grade vocabulary and simple sentence structures, students whose native language is not English may be confused by Dr. Seuss's nonsense words and occasional flouting of grammar rules (for example, *One Fish, Two Fish* features a moose-like beast called a "gack"; also, the narrator of *Hunches in Bunches* turns to non-standard grammar in phrases like "I sat me down" and "as soon as I got sat"). Such instances of playful language appear in virtually all of Seuss's works, but teachers can help avert potential confusion by pointing out which words are invented, and by preparing students to be on the lookout for nonsense words whenever they read Dr. Seuss's books.

Title: *The Boxcar Children* (series)
Author: Gertrude Chandler Warner
Copyright: Albert Whitman & Company (1942–2005)
Grade Levels: 2–6
Summary: The Alden children, Henry, Jessie, Violet, and Benny are runaway orphans who find an abandoned boxcar and begin living there together. Without any adult supervision or help, they must live as a family, find food, take care of each other, and keep their circumstances secret from the rest of the world. The 100 books in this series follow the Boxcar children through their wide variety of adventures and challenges. Despite their unusual living circumstances and often far-fetched exploits, the Boxcar children's lives also reflect universal themes about growing up, taking responsibility, and valuing family ties.

Title: *Bridge to Terabithia*
Author: Katherine Paterson
Copyright: HarperCollins (1977)
Grade Levels: 4–8
Summary: Jess starts fifth grade with a dream to be the fastest runner in his class. He is proudest of his running because he fears that his other more artistic interests are too "girly" in his father's eyes. In the tradition-

ally all-boy recess races, however, it is a tomboyish girl named Leslie who wins, startling everyone, and angering some of the boys. After his initial disappointment subsides, Jess actually becomes close friends with Leslie, who happens to be his neighbor. Together, Jess and Leslie let their imaginations run wild, and invent a magical land called Terabithia. But the friendship goes deeper than play, because they also talk seriously and confide in one another: Leslie helps Jess fight back his insecurities and become more confident, while Jess is one of the few people in the fifth grade who accepts Leslie in spite of her strange clothes and boyish ways. The story ends on the somber note of Leslie's sudden and shocking death. Jess's grief is tempered by his gratitude for the strength and courage Leslie gave him. In attention to the themes of death and loss, this book also deals with the issues of conformity, peer pressure, restricting gender stereotypes, and the struggle to gain self-acceptance. This book uses southern American English. These variations of English can be difficult for second language learners if they are not familiar with them.

Title: *The Giver*
Author: Lois Lowry
Copyright: Houghton Mifflin (1993)
Grade Levels: 6–12
Summary: This novel describes a utopian society in which there is no pain, pleasure, violence, emotion, or color; the government selects a profession for each citizen, and creates all families by pairing up a man and a woman, and then supplying them with two children, conceived by the community's "Birthmothers." In this world of Sameness and sensory deprivation, a boy named Jonas is selected to become the society's next "Receiver of Memory": this means that he will be solely responsible for keeping all memories of the past. This appointment sets Jonas apart from everyone else, insofar as it exposes him to a larger reality and experiences to which everyone else is immune. As Jonas begins to know emotions, color, and both pleasant and unpleasant sensations, he realizes how impoverished and deprived life is in his utopian society. He resolves to run away, knowing full well that there will be untold suffering beyond the borders of his community. This book deals with very mature social and political themes; it contains echoes of socialist ideologies, and poses pressing moral questions about the existence of good and evil in the world. As it is in part a work of science fiction, *The Giver*'s invented terminology and fictitious ideas could cause confusion for bilingual students. Teachers can prevent this by explicitly identifying which words and ideas are purely fiction.

Title: *Roll of Thunder, Hear My Cry*
Author: Mildred Taylor
Copyright: Phyllis Fogelman (1976)
Grade Levels: 6–12
Summary: In rural Mississippi during the Great Depression, the Logans, an African-American family, must contend with the racial injustice, prejudice and violence in the world around them. When the white owners of a general store try to burn two African American men alive, the Logans rally their community to boycott the store as a nonviolent repudiation and fearless affirmation of racial dignity and strength. Unfortunately, not all families take part in the boycott, and racist violence and lynchings persist in their community. Taylor's frank and straightforward storytelling submits an arresting and realistic portrait of the racist legacy of the American South. This book could also be used in conjunction with a social studies or history unit.

Title: *Hatchet*
Author: Gary Paulsen
Copyright: Houghton Mifflin (1995)
Grade Levels: 5–12
Summary: Brian, a thirteen year old boy from New York City, is flying up to Canada to visit his father, whom his mother has recently divorced. Brian is flying alone with the pilot who, all of a sudden, goes into cardiac arrest. Brian must take the plane's controls, and miraculously survives his crash landing in the wilderness. The pilot has died, and Brian is badly hurt. He has no way to call for help, no matches for a fire, and hardly any food to eat. He does have a hatchet, and a powerful will to survive—despite the brutally inclement weather, his skirmishes with wild animals, and his personal bouts of despondency and feelings of hopelessness.

This book deals with the upheaval caused by divorce and feelings of desperation, coupled with the possibilities of finding one's inner strength and of learning self-reliance in a frightening situation. Paulsen's title hero is not infallible, and comes across as only more resonantly courageous for his weaknesses.

Title: *Island of the Blue Dolphins*
Author: Scott O'Dell
Copyright: Dell (1960)
Grade Levels: 4–12
Summary: On a small island off the coast of California, Karana lives in an indigenous community and is the daughter of its chief. Her tribe also

permits hunters and fisherman to live and work on the island in return for a portion of their profits. When the hunters breach this contract, however, violence and hostility ravage the island. Karana's tribe opts to flee the bloodshed and begin a new life elsewhere. As their boat pulls away from the harbor, however, Karana is not on board: she is still on the island, frantically searching for her brother, who went back to recover a forgotten spear. The two siblings are left behind together, until the boy is killed by wild dogs, thus leaving Karana all alone. In the wreckage of her village, she must somehow learn to survive and stay strong. She finds food, makes a home in a cave, and befriends a wild dog. All the while, she must hide from the hunters, and keep faith that her tribe will be back for her rescue.

O'Dell's book deals with themes of social injustice, economic exploitation, and linguistic and cultural barriers, and also presents a female protagonist who demonstrates stereotypically male virtues, such as courage, physical strength, self-reliance, and a venturesome spirit. This novel is based on a true story.

Title: *The Catcher in the Rye*
Author: J. D. Salinger
Copyright: Little, Brown & Company (1945)
Grade Levels: 8–12
Summary: Holden Caulfield, a sensitive and introspective sixteen year old, flunks out of the fourth boarding school he has attended, and journeys home to New York City a few days before his family expects him for Christmas vacation. Not wanting to surprise his parents with the bad news, Holden wanders the city on his own, consorts with old friends and strangers, and secretly meets up with Phoebe, his beloved little sister. Holden's story takes place in the 1950s, but its portrait of troubled adolescence has an aura of timelessness: never easy, the transition from childhood to adulthood is only made only more trying for Holden because of his inordinate nostalgia for the simplicity and purity of youth.

Holden's frank, confessional style and narrative tone of ennui and melancholy might be unfamiliar to students of certain cultural backgrounds. The book's slang (e.g., "crumb-bum"), occasional profanity, and dated language and cultural references (e.g., Gary Cooper) might also be worth addressing in classrooms with bilingual students. At the same time, students often find that *The Catcher in the Rye*'s conversational tone actually makes it an easier read than other novels at the secondary level.

Title: *Of Mice and Men*
Author: John Steinbeck
Copyright: Viking (1937)
Grade Levels: 8–12
Summary: George and Lennie are migrant workers in California, and also longtime friends. Lennie has a mental disability, and George knows he would have an easier time finding work without him, but he would never abandon his friend. They do find work thanks to George's smooth talking, and in reality Lennie is a very able ranch hand, mostly because of his strength and large stature. But Lennie is also sensitive and childlike, and especially loves to hold small, soft animals, not always realizing how fragile they are in comparison with his brute strength. Lennie accidentally kills a mouse and a puppy, and finally breaks the neck of the ranch owner's daughter-in-law, after she asks him to stroke her hair. Knowing no excuse will exonerate Lennie for this terrible accident, George opts to kill him himself, out of love, because George cannot bear to see anyone else harm or humiliate Lennie.

Teachers of bilingual students may want to address how and where the book's slang and working class dialects (e.g., "I dunno" and "nice fella") depart from Standard English.

Title: *Beloved*
Author: Toni Morrison
Copyright: Plume/Signet Classic (1987)
Grade Levels: 9–12
Summary: Sethe, a former slave, lives in Ohio with her eighteen-year old daughter, Denver, having fled the Kentucky plantation where she was brutally beaten and raped. Sethe was pregnant with Denver at the time of the assault, and journeyed north with her three older children, all of whom arrived safely at the house of Sethe's mother-in-law in Cincinnati. Weeks later, however, the white master who had battered Sethe comes up to Ohio in search of his runaway slaves, and, in a moment of utter desperation, Sethe tries to kill her children, preferring that they die rather than suffer the brutality of slavery. Of her three small children, only the daughter actually dies, whose name is never revealed. This daughter, however, comes to haunt the family's Cincinnati home—or at least she seems to. Referred to simply as "Beloved," the girl's ghost is both a comforting presence and a frightening reminder of a "story not to pass on."

Teachers may wish to address the book's occasional figurative language and insinuation of a supernatural presence, which bilingual students may have a harder time grasping, depending on their cultural and linguistic backgrounds.

Appendix D

Books to Supplement Content Area Instruction for ELL Students

The books listed are narratives that complement content area themes. A number of these narratives include stories of different cultures. The reading level refers to the students' English proficiency. If the level is too advanced for some students, teachers can scaffold the reading by reading it aloud while the students follow the text or students can read in partners. These represent a few examples; teachers should find others for the various topics they cover.

HISTORY AND SOCIAL SCIENCE UNITS

The following books are suggestions to supplement traditional History and Social Science instructions; the list is arranged chronologically, and predominantly features books relating to U.S. history, which can be used to help fill in gaps for recent immigrant students who come to the United States with a limited knowledge of the country's past.

Title: *Johnny Tremain*
Author: Esther Forbes
Copyright: Houghton Mifflin (1973); original date of publication: 1943
Reading Level: Advanced English
Summary: Johnny Tremain is the fourteen-year old apprentice of a Boston silversmith, and is already a very skilled craftsman. Unfortunately, he is also arrogant and patronizing to the other apprentices, and this prompts one of them to play a prank on him which results in a terrible accident.

Johnny's hand is burned and disfigured, making him unable to continue working as a silversmith. Sullen and distraught, Johnny searches for other work, and finally becomes a dispatch rider for the Committee of Public Safety. He crosses paths with famous revolutionary patriots, including Paul Revere, John Hancock, and Samuel Adams, and takes part in the Boston Tea Party. Johnny ultimately becomes much less selfish and more altruistic, devoting himself to a cause much greater than himself: the American Revolution. His final triumph comes when a doctor manages to repair his hand enough so that he can fire a musket and fight in the war for America's independence.

Title: *Daughter of Madrugada*
Author: Frances M. Wood
Copyright: Delacorte (2002)
Reading Level: Intermediate English
Summary: Thirteen-year-old Cesa, the only daughter in a wealthy Mexican family, is growing up in the 1840s on a beautiful ranch in what is today northern California. Her easy, affluent life begins to change as American settlers flood into the region, settling the land ceded to the United States in the 1848 Treaty of Guadalupe Hidalgo. Cesa's family is distrustful of the American settlers. They feel resentment about their invasion and the subordination of their own language and culture. They also feel pressure to learn the English language. Ultimately Cesa's family is forced to leave their beloved ranch, and begin life again south of the United States' borders.

Title: *Across Five Aprils*
Author: Irene Hunt
Copyright: Bentley Books (1986)
Reading Level: Advanced English
Summary: Jethro Creighton is a nine year old boy living in southern Illinois when the Civil War breaks out. His three older brothers, cousin, and teacher join in the fighting, and he initially entertains an idealistic notion of the honor and bravery of being a soldier. Soon enough, however, Jethro recognizes how acutely the war divides and disrupts his family and community: this is especially palpable when one of his brothers joins on the Confederate side, leading to not only turmoil in Jethro's family, but also animosity and even violence from other townspeople. While everyone anxiously awaits news from the front lines and letters from loved ones, images of war also come home, as violent uprisings and the return of wounded soldiers. The war drags on, and Jethro grows up in a world where heroes and loved ones can die; he learns to accept the irrationalities of war, and the impossibility of a simple resolution.

Title: *My Bondage and My Freedom*
Author: Frederick Douglass
Copyright: Miller, Orton & Mulligan (1855); Modern Library Paperback (2003)
Reading Level: Advanced English
Summary: Published in 1881, this is Douglass's extensive autobiographical work, collected in two parts: "Life as a Slave" and "Life as a Freeman." Despite the inhumanities of his enslavement, Douglass learns to read and write, and escapes to the North, where he begins a new life—not without racial discrimination, but with untold opportunities no slave could ever dream of. Douglass is introduced to the Abolitionists, establishes his own newspaper, *The North Star*, and becomes a preeminent leader and compelling spokesman for racial equality and the Abolitionist movement.

Title: *Grandma Essie's Covered Wagon*
Author: David Williams
Copyright: Knopf (1993)
Reading Level: Beginning English, with Illustrations
Summary: Grandma Essie recounts her family's journey by covered wagon from their Missouri home to the frontiers of Kansas and Oklahoma. Her story is set in 1890s, and it renders a vivid portrait of the pioneering dreams and rustic way of life of the Americans who settled the farmlands and shantytowns of the plains states and southwest.

Title: *Dust for Dinner*
Author: Anne Turner
Copyright: HarperCollins (1995)
Reading Level: Beginning English, with Illustrations
Summary: Jake and his family live on a farm in the plains states until the dust storms and draught of the 1930s dry out and destroy their land. They are forced to sell their house and move west to California, to start their lives from scratch. The family radio keeps everyone in good spirits, and when they reach California, they celebrate and embrace their new home.

Title: *Daniel Half-Human and the Good Nazi*
Author: David Chotjewitz; translated from German by Doris Orgel
Copyright: Atheneum (2004)
Reading Level: Advanced English (or German)
Summary: Growing up in Germany in the 1930s, Daniel is the privileged child of affluent parents, and excels both at school and in sports. He can

also be bold and rebellious; he teams up with his best friend, Armin, to paint graffiti swastikas in a neighborhood in Hamburg. The night the boys spend in jail together for this crime only strengthens the bond of their friendship, and both boys become engrossed with the notion of joining the Hitler Youth. But Daniel soon learns that his mother is actually Jewish, a secret she has kept hidden from everyone. While Armin does not disown him outright, their friendship is unavoidably strained. As Daniel struggles to reconcile his own identity, the ideals he had espoused, and growing anti-Semitism in Germany, he resists believing that is own life might be endangered if he stays in his country. Interspersed with the story of Daniel's boyhood is the story of his life as an Allied soldier. Daniel finally does flee Germany, but he can never come to hate his own country and people; instead, he feels great sadness and longing, for the lost nation and culture which he had once known as home.

Title: *Baseball Saved Us*
Author: Ken Mochizuki
Copyright: Lee & Low (1993)
Grade Levels:
Summary: A Japanese American boy describes how he and his family were forced to leave their home and relocate to an internment camp during World War II. Amid the sadness, confusion and outrage, some joy and hope is restored to the inmates of the camp when the boy's father organizes a camp-wide baseball league. Even though the young boy is small and not the best athlete, he practices and improves, and even hits a game-winning home run. When everyone is finally released from the camp, the boy finds that his non-Japanese classmates at school avoid him and treat him coldly; and yet again, by playing baseball, the boy finds the courage to interact and even become friends with his peers, despite the climate of pervasive prejudice.

Title: *Flowers from Mariko*
Authors: Rick Noguchi & Deneen Jenks
Copyright: Lee & Low Books (2001)
Reading Level: Beginning English, With Illustrations
Summary: After three years of living in a bleak Japanese internment camp, Mariko and her family can finally return to Los Angeles, where she was born, and where her father had owned a gardening business. The family now faces the challenge of rebuilding their lives from nothing, and integrating back into a society where racial prejudice and injustice still loom large. Mariko tends her own small garden, and encourages her father to keep faith that he will find gardening work once again.

MATHEMATICS UNITS

These books are stories that address the following math themes: (1) Number Sense and Operations, (2) Patterns, Relations, and Algebra, (3) Geometry, (4) Measurement, and (5) Data Analysis, Statistics, and Probability. These books cover a range of grade and ability levels, and contain activities, experiments, stories, and interesting facts that could supplement traditional mathematics instruction and enhance conceptual learning for bilingual students and all students.

Number Sense and Operations

Title: *Math Appeal: Mind Stretching Math Riddles*
Author: Greg Tang
Copyright: Scholastic (2003)
Reading Level: Beginning English with Illustrations
Summary: Intended for children ages 7–10, *Math Appeal* draws on art and language to promote creative thinking and problem-solving skills. Its riddle-poems and colorful illustrations get students adding, subtracting, and counting, and discovering more efficient problem solving strategies through the recognition of patterns and symmetry. This book lends itself especially well to partner work or independent work.

Title: *The Big Buck Adventure*
Author: Shelley Gill and Deborah Tobola
Copyright: Charlesbridge (2000)
Reading Level: Beginning English with Illustrations
Summary: When a little girl receives her dollar allowance, she goes to a candy shop, a toy store, a deli, and a pet shop, and asks each shopkeeper what she can buy with her money. She considers buying ten gummy bears at ten cents each, or three goldfish at 33 cents each; she is sad to learn that the stuffed bunny in the toy store costs more than she has to pay. Later, when the girl's father returns to take her back home, she tells him that her piggy bank is the best place for her money.

This book offers a real-world context for the application of arithmetic concepts, and also introduces rudimentary ideas of multiplication.

Title: *Anno's Magic Seeds*
Author: Mitsumasa Anno
Copyright: Philomel Books (1995)
Reading Level: Intermediate English with Illustrations
Summary: Jack receives two magic seeds from a wizard, who instructs him to eat one and plant the other. The seed Jack eats is enough nourishment to

sustain him for a whole year, whereas the seed he plants grows into a sprout with two flowers by spring, and two fruits by summer. The fruits supplies one seed each, allowing Jack to begin the cycle again: he eats one seed and plants the other. After a few years of this routine, however, Jack has a new idea. He plants *both* seeds, which grow into two plants, with each one having two flowers, two fruits, and two seeds. Because Jack only needs one seed to eat, he now has *three* seeds to plant. And so soon Jack has three sprouts, and six flowers, six fruits, and six seeds. As the story unfolds, the concept of exponential growth becomes more clear, and from time to time, the book asks the reader to count or calculate how many seeds grow, and how many seeds are planted during a specific year in sequence. Even though readers could find the right answers by counting the seeds in the book's illustrations, the progression of the story helps readers develop pattern recognition strategies, and thus, building blocks of higher math skills.

Patterns, Relations, and Algebra

Title: *Math and Science in Nature*
Author: Robert Gardner and Edward Shore
Copyright: Franklin Watts (1994)
Reading Level: Advanced English
Summary: From its first pages, this book rouses its readers' curiosity by asking questions about patterns, ratios, and relationships that exist in the natural world. It explains how scientists have discovered mathematical relationships that underlie the spacing of planets from the sun, or the pitch progression in a musical scale. The book proceeds to outline dozens of experiments that readers can try to explore the mathematical ideas behind electricity, heat, air density, refracted light, the solar system, and physics involved in sports. The book also describes in impressive detail how readers can collect, sort and analyze data, by putting it in charts and plotting it on graphs. An independent reader could work through and conduct the experiments, but math and science teachers may also find that the book's activities work well in a classroom setting. Students are likely to benefit most from having adult supervision and guidance while they conduct the experiments.

Title: *Real World Algebra: Understanding the Power of Mathematics*
Author: Edward Zaccaro
Copyright: Hickory Grove Press (2001)
Reading Level: Intermediate English, with practice problems in equation form and some illustrations
Summary: The author of this book, Edward Zaccaro, declares that "algebra is the most powerful problem-solving tool ever invented." His hope

in this book is to help students to use and appreciate algebra's power—which will requires first that they learn to translate words and real-life scenarios into the language of algebra. To this end, the first chapter familiarizes readers with the process of translating from word-language to algebra-language. Then, subsequent chapters present essential algebraic concepts and some of their real-world applications. Each chapter is very clear and well organized, featuring diagrams, practice problems, cartoon characters, and other illustrations that both clarify and enliven the material being presented.

Geometry and Spatial Sense

Title: *Shape Up! Fun with Triangles and Other Polygons*
Author: David A. Adler
Copyright: Holiday House (1998)
Reading Level: Beginning English with Illustrations
Summary: This book introduces readers to the names of different-sided polygons and some of their defining attributes. It encourages hands-on shape exploration by outlining multiple discovery-based activities that use cheese slices, bread slices, and pretzel sticks, and also a few activities that use more traditional materials such as pencils, paper, and scissors. Readers learn about scalene, isosceles and equilateral triangles, and obtuse, acute, and right angles. They also learn to differentiate among trapezoids, squares, rectangles, parallelograms, and rhombi. Teachers might decide to try some of the book's activities with a whole class, or perhaps in small groups. Because the activities are visually-based and are taught primarily through demonstrations, they may be especially well-suited for bilingual students.

Title: *What's Your Angle, Pythagoras?*
Author: Julie Ellis
Copyright: Charlesbridge (2004)
Reading Level: Intermediate English with Illustrations
Summary: As a young boy growing up in Greece, Pythagoras is fascinated to explore the right angles in the world around him. Through his own experimentation with rope, square tiles, and runged ladders, Pythagoras discovers 3-4-5 and 5-12-13 triangles, and extends his reasoning to develop the famous Pythagorean Theorem. Pythagoras proudly shares his discoveries with his community, and explains how people can use his findings in the context of their daily lives. The book's diagrams and illustrations are especially clear and helpful in demonstrating the math concepts behind them.

Title: *Sir Cumference and the Sword in the Cone: A Math Adventure*
Author: Cindy Neuschwander
Copyright: Charlesbridge (2003)
Reading Level: Intermediate English with Illustrations
Summary: King Arthur must find a new heir to his throne, and five knights are in competition for the illustrious honor. To be fair, King Arthur creates a puzzle of wits and geometrical reasoning, and declares that the knight who solves it first will be named the rightful heir to his throne. King Arthur explains the he has hidden his sword in a shape that is "three times tall as its base is wide," and that the sum of that shape's faces and points, when subtracted by its number of edges, is NOT equal to 2. The parchment paper copy of the king's puzzle also includes drawing of various flattened shapes that could be the shape in which the sword is hidden. One of the knights, Vertex, works with his young friend, Radius, to construct the flattened images into three-dimensional shapes, and then make a chart of each shape's number of faces, number of sides, and number of edges. They conclude that the special shape must be a *cone*, and then they search all over the castle until they find the cone in which the sword is hidden. Vertex explains his geometric reasoning to the king, who then declares him the worthy heir to the throne.

This book does a superb job of interposing geometry concepts within a literary work; its mystery/quest motif presents geometry in a fun and exciting way, and can help teachers implement new and exciting ideas for their own geometry lessons.

Measurement

Title: *How Tall, How Short, How Far Away*
Author: David A. Adler
Copyright: Holiday House (1999)
Reading Level: Beginning English with Illustrations
Summary: This colorful, child-friendly book begins by introducing different units and methods of measurement that people have been using since ancient times. Next, it outlines hands-on measurement activities that readers can try. The book sheds light on the inevitable inaccuracies resulting from subjective units of measurement—i.e., palm width (palm), finger width (digit), or the length from one's elbow to one's middle finger (cubit); readers recognize why their own "palm" or "cubit" measurements will not be the same as their friends', their parents', or their teachers'. The book differentiates between the metric system and the customary foot-pound system, and asks readers to think critically about which units would be most appropriate for measuring specific lengths—for instance, an odometer

measures the distance a car drives in *miles,* whereas a ruler would be more appropriate for measuring a celery stick in *inches.* The book's hands-on, exploratory approach presents the fundamental ideas of measurement in a fun and engaging way, and with clear real-world application.

Data Analysis, Statistics, and Probability

Title: *Anno's Hat Tricks*
Author: Akihiro Nozaki and Mitsumasa Anno
Copyright: Philomel Books (1985)
Reading Level: Intermediate English with Illustrations
Summary: A magician/hatter tells the reader that he will perform a series of hat tricks, which will require the reader's help, and also the help of his friends, Tom and Hannah. The hatter calls the reader "Shadowchild," and the book's illustrations feature a gray outline that is intended to be the reader's shadow. The hat tricks relate to probability and reasoning: the hatter places either a red or a white hat on the heads of Tom, Hannah, and "Shadowchild," and then asks whether they can guess the color of their own hat, based on what hats they see each other wearing, and how many hats of each color the hatter had originally. Each hat trick is slightly different, and readers gradually begin to recognize that they can *sometimes* be 100% sure of their own hat color, but other times there will be different probability ratios of their hat being either red or white. While the book does get into more advanced probability concepts or the mathematical formulas to calculate them, it does give readers a helpful introduction to thinking about probability, combinations, and ratios.

Featuring Multiple Learning Strands

Title: *The I Hate Mathematics! Book*
Author: Marilyn Burns
Copyright: Little, Brown & Company (1975)
Reading Level: Advanced English with Illustrations
Summary: From its title alone, this book aims to reach out to students who feel that mathematics is too hard, too boring, or simply not "cool." It presents riddles and cartoons, and proposes interactive activities using household items that intend to get readers thinking mathematically, but without even realizing that they are. The book covers addition, subtraction, multiplication, division, geometry, symmetry, and shapes, among other concepts. By favoring tricks, games, and other activities to traditional mathematics problems, *The I Hate Mathematics Book* makes math fun, playful, and relevant to real life.

SCIENCE UNITS

Science teachers can enhance content area instruction with literature books that pertain to a lesson's specific concepts or larger themes. Bilingual students in particular may have an easier time grasping new scientific ideas when they are exposed to concrete illustrations in fictional stories or real-world contexts. The following books could be used to introduce or to accompany a traditional unit in Earth and Space Science class or Life Science and Biology.

For Earth and Space Science Units

Title: *Stone Wall Secrets*
Author: Kristine and Robert Thorson
Copyright: Tilbury House (1998)
Reading Level: Intermediate English with Illustrations
Summary: A young boy named Adam helps his grandfather rebuild the old stone walls on their family's New England farm. While they work, Adam's grandfather teaches him about the "secrets" contained in the stones, about glaciers, volcanoes, and the wind and weather patterns which contributed to the evolution of the landscape. In addition to earth science, the book deals with the importance of connections between generations, mixed race adoption, and how families also evolve over time.

Title: *Stone Wall Secrets Teacher's Guide*
Author: Ruth Deike
Copyright: Tilbury House (1998)
Summary: This is a very comprehensive teacher's guide containing extensive historical and scientific information, geological time lines, detailed lesson plans for in-class experiments, and a lengthy list of references and further resources. Authors indicate that activities are appropriate for grades 3–7, but it could also be used in high school.

Title: *The Paddock*
Author: Lilith Norman and Robert Roennfeldt
Copyright: Knopf (1993)
Reading Level: Beginning English with Illustrations
Summary: "Paddock" is an Australian word that refers to any patch of land; and this story describes how one paddock, which could be anywhere, evolves from the pre-dinosaur days to the current era of modern civilization. The authors describe volcanoes, rivers, plant life, animal life, primitive peoples, and the onset of industrialization, always in celebra-

tion of nature's cycles and the beauty of the earth. The book offers a rich introduction to ecology and earth science vocabulary.

Title: *Where the Forest Meets the Sea*
Author: Jeannie Baker
Copyright: Greenwillow Books (1987)
Reading Level: Beginning English with Illustrations
Summary: A boy and his father take a boat to a remote tropical rain forest in Australia, where they hike through the rocks and fertile ground, staring up at the canopy of greenery. The father tells the boy about crocodiles and kangaroos that used to live there, and the boy wonders what the landscape looked like a million years ago. The book ends with the question: "But will the forest still be here when we come back?" With little technical language and few sentences per page, this book is most appropriate for young children.

Title: *The Boy Who Was Generous with Salt*
Author: Corinne Demas
Copyright: Marshall Cavendish (2002)
Reading Level: Intermediate English with Illustrations
Summary: Set in the 1850s, this book tells the story of Ned, a boy who gets a job working on a fishing boat as a cook, hoping to make more money for his family. Choosing to see his long ocean journey as an adventure, Ned adapts to life on the sea, and learns firsthand about then power and beauty of the ocean habitat. This book could also be used for social studies; its language and vocabulary highlight aspects of 19th century life.

For Life Science and Biology Units

Title: *The Great Kapok Tree: A Story of the Amazon Rain Forest*
Author: Lynne Cherry
Copyright: Harcourt Brace & Company (1990)
Reading Level: Beginning English with Illustrations
Summary: A man goes deep into the Amazon rain forest, intending to chop down a great Kapok tree. After hacking away for some time at the great trunk, he becomes exhausted and falls asleep. Then, all the rain forest's animals gather around him and whisper why he must let the tree live; the animals describe how all they all depend on the tree for their home and sustenance, and how all living things depend on each other. The man then awakes with a change of heart. The book's opening pages feature illustrations and labels of many plants and animals that are native

to the Amazon rain forest; these plants and animals also appear throughout the story itself.

Title: *Antarctica*
Author: Helen Cowcher
Copyright: Farrar, Straus and Giroux (1990)
Reading Level: Beginning English with Illustrations
Summary: This book tells about the lifestyles of emperor penguins, Weddell seals, and Adélie penguins in Antarctica. Readers learn how each species raise their young, live in communities, and peacefully coexist in their frigid habitat. Some technical vocabulary is introduced, but each page features large print and only short segments of text.

Title: *Dory Story*
Author: Jerry Pallota
Copyright: Talewinds (1999)
Reading Level: Beginning English with Illustrations
Summary: A young boy named Danny disobeys his mother's wishes and goes out on a dory alone on the ocean. He is fascinated to watch the plankton, as well as the mackerel, eels, and bluefish. Danny learns about the food chain in the ocean habitat, and watches all the creatures in awe, until his dory capsizes. In the final pages, readers learn that he is actually telling this dory story from the safety of his bathtub. The book features some vocabulary related to sea life, but only a few sentences per page.

Appendix E

Assessment Practices

The following is a brief explanation of some of the recommended assessment practices:

Oral Interviews: Students are asked in a conversational manner to explain what they have learned, understood, or interpreted from a text or lesson. It can also be used to have students explain why they wrote something in a certain way.

Read Alouds: Students read passages from text through which teachers can evaluate fluency and word attack skills.

Retellings: Students recall in descriptive detail and sequentially all the important events of a story. Through retellings, teachers can assess vocabulary development, sequencing of a story, identification of main idea, details, characters, setting, plot, and so forth.

Writing Samples: Students submit different samples (original stories, poems, songs, expository essays) of their own written work in various stages of the writing process (i.e., graphic organizers, first draft, revised sample, edited sample, final drafts, etc.). Teachers can then determine what is to be assessed, for example, organization of content, beginning, middle, end of story, use of descriptive words, character development, use of invented spelling, use of conventional spelling, standard grammar usage, correct use of punctuation, knowledge of audience, clear purpose for writing, revisions, and editing.

Experiments/Demonstrations: Students show knowledge and understanding of what has been read by performing an experiment or showing, through active demonstration, that a concept has been mastered. Teachers can assess for completeness of thought, understanding of main idea, attention to details, and vocabulary development.

Projects/Exhibitions: Through projects and exhibitions students are able to demonstrate, in a multidimensional manner, knowledge, understanding, and application of a concept or lesson. This type of evaluation is especially helpful for the emerging literate student, as well as the second-language student, because it does not rely exclusively on written language.

Response Journals: After the reading of a book, or a passage from a book, students write their reactions in a journal. Teacher-initiated prompts eliciting responses to character development, plot details, vocabulary use, author's purpose, or student's personal reaction to the text can be done. Students may also write freely in response to the reading or a discussion.

Learning Logs: Learning logs can be used to evaluate students' understanding of a concept learned. Students write what they have learned about a specific topic or lesson. Teachers can use learning logs to assess what was actually understood by the students, and what aspects of a lesson may need to be reviewed or retaught.

Constructed Responses: Open-ended questions about a lesson or a passage read are given to assess comprehension. Teachers can assess specific concept understanding of content area passages by using constructed responses.

Conferences: Much can be learned and assessed through individual conferences with students. Conferences can be used to evaluate a student's understanding of a text, or strategies a student uses when faced with unknown words or concepts.

References

Alexandrowicz, V. (2002). Effective instruction for second language learners: What tutors must know. *Reading Improvement, 39*(2).

Allen, J. (1999). *Words, words, words: Teaching vocabulary in grades 4–12.* York, ME: Stenhouse Publishers.

Allwright, J. (1986). Don't correct—reformulate! In ELT Documents 129. *Academic Writing. Process and Product.* Modern English Publications. The British Council: 109–116.

Ashton-Warner, S. (1963). *Teacher.* New York: Simon Schuster.

August, D., & Hakuta, K. (1997). *Improving schooling for language-minority children.* Washington, DC: National Academy Press.

Ballard, B., & Clanchy, J. (1991). Assessment by misconception: Cultural influences and intellectual traditions. In L. Hamp-Lyons (Ed.), *Assessing second language writing in academic contexts.* Norwood, NJ: Ablex.

Basham, C. S., & Kwachka, P. E. (1991). Reading the world differently: A cross-cultural approach to writing assessment. In L. Hamp-Lyons (Ed.), *Assessing second language writing in academic contexts* (pp. 37–49). Norwood, NJ: Ablex.

Beck, I., McKeown, M., & Kucan, L. (2002). Bringing words to life: Robust vocabulary instruction. New York: Guilford Press.

Bialystok, E. (2001). *Bilingualism in development: Language, literacy and cognition.* Cambridge: Cambridge University Press.

Birch, B. M. (2002). *English L2 reading: Getting to the bottom.* Mahwah, NJ: Lawrence Erlbaum Associates.

Brisk, M. E. (1985). Using the computer to develop literacy among bilingual students. *Equity and Choice, 1*(7), 25–32.

Brisk, M. E. (2006). *Bilingual Education: From compensatory to quality schooling. Second Edition.* Mahwah, NJ: Lawrence Erlbaum Associates.

Brisk, M. E., Burgos, A., & Hamerla, S. (2004). *Situational context of education: A window into the world of bilingual learners.* Mahwah, NJ: Lawrence Erlbaum Associates.

Brisk, M. E., Dawson, M., Hartgering, M., MacDonald, E., & Zehr, L. (2002). Teaching Bilingual Students in Mainstream Classrooms. In

Beykont, Z (Ed), *The power of culture*. Cambridge, MA: Harvard Education Publishing Group.

Brisk, M. E., Horan, D., & MacDonald, E. (forthcoming). Scaffolding teaching and learning to write: The rhetorical approach. In L. S. Verplaetse & N. Migliacci (Eds.), *Inclusive pedagogy: Research informed practices for linguistically diverse students*. Mahwah, NJ: Lawrence Erlbaum Associates.

Bromley, K., Winters, D., & Schlimmer, K. (1994). Book buddies: Creating enthusiasm for literacy learning. *The Reading Teacher, 47*, 392–400.

Buckley, M. H., & Boyle, O. F. (1981). *Mapping the writing journey*. Berkeley: University of California/Bay Area Writing Project.

Butzkamm, W. (1998). Code-switching in a bilingual history lesson: The mother tongue as a conversational lubricant. *International Journal of Bilingual Education and Bilingualism, 1*(2), 81–98.

Caldwell, J. S., & Ford, M. P. (2002). *Where have all the bluebirds gone?: How to soar with flexible grouping*. Portsmouth, NH: Heinemann.

Cappellini, M. (2005). *Balancing Reading & Language Learning*. Portland, ME: Stenhouse Publishers.

Caplan, R. (1983). Showing, not telling. In M. Myers & J. Grey (Eds.), *Theory and practice in the teaching of composition* (pp. 226–238). Illinois: National Council of Teachers of English.

Carson, J. F., & Leki, I. (Eds.). (1993). *Reading in the composition classroom*. Boston: Heinle & Heinle.

Cary, Stephen (2000). *Working with second language learners: Answers to teachers' top ten questions*. Portsmouth, NH: Heinemann.

Chamot, A. U., & O'Malley, M. O. (1994). *The CALLA handbook: implementing the cognitive academic language learning approach*. Reading, MA: Addison-Wesley.

Clair, N. (1998). Teacher study groups: Persistent questions in a promising approach. *TESOL Quarterly, 32*, 465–492.

Clay, M. M. (1985). *The early detection of reading difficulties. Third edition*. Portsmouth, NH: Heinemann.

Cochran-Smith, M., & Lytle, S. (1993). *Inside/Outside: Teacher research and knowledge*. New York: Teachers College.

Cohen, A. (1983). Reformulating second-language compositions: A potential source of input for the learner. Papaper presented at the TESOL Conference, Toronto, ON. *(ERIC Document Reproduction Service No ED 228 866)*.

Cohen, R. (1983). Self-generated questions as an aid to reading comprehension. *The Reading Teacher, 36*, 770–775.

Conklin, N. F., & Lourie, M. A. (1983). *A host of tongues: Language communities in the United States*. New York: The Free Press.

Connor, U. (2002). New directions in contrastive rhetoric. *TESOL Quarterly, 36,* 493–510.

Connor, U., & Kaplan, R. B. (1987). *Writing Across Languages: Analysis of L2 Text.* Reading, MA: Addison-Wesley.

Cummins, J. (1991). Interdependence of first- and second-language proficiency in bilingual children. In E. Bialystok (Ed.), *Language processing in bilingual children* (pp. 70–89). New York: Cambridge University Press.

Cummins, J., & Sayers, D. (1995). *Brave new schools: Challenging cultural illiteracy.* New York: St. Martin's Press.

D'Angelo Bromley, K. (1989). Buddy journals make the reading-writing connection. *The Reading Teacher, 43,* 122–129.

Daiute, C. (1985). *Writing and computers.* Reading, MA: Addison-Wesley.

Dale, T. C., & Cuevas, G. J. (1992). Integrating mathematics and language learning. In P. A. Richard-Amato & M. A. Snow (Eds.), *The multicultural classroom: Readings for content-area teachers* (pp. 330–348). White Plains, NY: Longman.

Davey, B., & McBride, S. (1986). Effects of question-generation training on reading comprehension. *Journal of Educational Psychology, 78*(4), 256–262.

de Alvarado, C. S. (1984). From topic to final paper: A rhetorical approach. *TESOL Newsletter, 2,* 9–10.

Derwing, T. M., & Rossiter, M. J. (2003). The effects of pronunciation instruction on the accuracy, fluency, and complexity of L2 accented speech. *Applied Language Learning, 13,* 1–17.

Dickinson, D. K., McCabe, A., Clark-Chiarelli, N., & Wolf, A. (2004). Cross-language transfer of phonological awareness in low-income Spanish and English bilingual preschool children. *Applied Psycholinguistics, 25,* 323–347.

Dien, T. T. (1998). Language and literacy in Vietnamese American communities. In B. Perez (Ed.), *Sociocultural contexts of language and literacy* (pp. 123–161). Mahwah, NJ: Lawrence Erlbaum Associates.

Dixon, C., & Nessel, D. (1983). *Language Experience Approach to Reading and Writing.* New York: Alemany Press.

Duranti, A., & Ochs, E. (1995). *Syncretic literacy: Multiculturalism in Samoan American Families.* Santa Cruz, CA: The National Center for Research on Cultural Diversity and Second Language Learning.

Echevarria, J., Vogt, M., & Short, D. J. (2004). *Making content comprehensible for English learners: The SIOP model, Second Edition.* Boston: Pearson Education.

Einhorn, K. (2002). Welcoming Second-Language Learners. *Instructor.*

Faltis, C. J., & Hudelson, S. J. (1998). *Bilingual Education in elementary and secondary school communities.* Boston: Allyn & Bacon.

Faltis, C. J., & Hudelson, S. J. (1998). *Bilingual Education in elementary and secondary school communities*. Boston: Allyn & Bacon.

Farr, B. P., & Trumbull, E. (1997). *Assessment alternatives for diverse classrooms*. Norwood, MA: Christopher-Gordon.

Flood, J., & Lapp, D. (1988). Conceptual mapping for understanding information texts. *The Reading Teacher, 41*(8), 780–783.

Forcier, R. C. (1996). *The computer as a productivity tool in education*. Englewood Cliffs, NJ: Merrill.

Freeman, D. (1998). *Doing teacher research: From inquiry to understanding*. Boston: Heinle & Heinle.

Freeman, Y. S., & Freeman, D. E. (1989). Whole Language Approaches to Writing with Secondary Students of English as a Second Language. In D. M. Johnson & D. H. Roen (Eds.), *Richness in writing: Empowering ESL students* (pp. 177–192). New York: Longman.

Freeman, Y. S., & Freeman, D. E. (1998). *ESL/EFL teaching: Principles for success*. Portsmouth, NH: Heinemann.

Freeman. D. E., & Freeman, Y. S. (2000). *Teaching reading in multilingual classrooms*. Portsmouth, NH: Heinemann.

Friedman, A., Zibit, M., & Coote, M. (2004). Telementoring as a collaborative agent for change. *The Journal of Technology, Learning, and Assessment, 3*(1), 2–41.

Garcia, G. E., Jimenez, R. T., & Pearson, P. D. (1998). Metacognition, childhood bilingualism, and reading. In D. J. Hacher, J. Dunlosky, & A. C. Graesser (Eds.), *Metacognition in educational theory and practice* (pp. 193–219). Mahwah, NJ: Lawrence Erlbaum Associates.

Gee, J. P. (1989). What is literacy? *Journal of Education, 171*, 18–25.

Genesee, F., & Hamayan, E. V. (1994). Classroom-based assessment. In F. Genesee (Ed.), *Educating second language children* (pp. 212–239). Cambridge: Cambridge University Press.

Genesee, F., Paradis, J., & Crago, M. B. (2004). *Dual language development and disorders: A handbook on bilingualism & second language learning*. Baltimore: Paul Brookes.

Gersten, R., Baker, S., & Keating, T. (1998). El Paso programs for English language learners: A longitudinal follow-up study. *READ Perspectives, 5*(1), 4–28.

Gibbons, P. (2002). *Scaffolding language, Scaffolding learning: Teaching second language learners in the mainstream classroom*. Portsmouth, NH: Heinemann.

Gillespie, C. (1990). Questions about student-generated questions. *Journal of Reading, 34*, 250–257.

Goldenberg, C., Reese, L., & Gallimore, R. (1992). Effects of literacy materials from school on Latino children's home experiences and early reading achievement. *American Journal of Education, 100*(4), 497–536.

Gravelle, M. (2000). *Planning for bilingual learners: An inclusive curriculum.* Stafordshire, UK: Trentham Books.

Griffith, P. L., & Olson, M. W. (1992). Phonemic awareness helps beginning readers break the code. *The Reading Teacher, 45,* 516–523.

Grosjean, F. (1982). *Life with two languages.* Cambridge, MA: Harvard University Press.

Grosjean, F. (1989). Neurolinguists, beware! The bilingual is not two monolinguals in one person. *Brain and Language, 36,* 3–15.

Hadaway, N. L. (1992). Letters to literacy: Spurring second language development across the curriculum. *Childhood Education, 69*(1), 24–28.

Heath, S. B. (1983). *Way with words: Language, life and work in communities and classrooms.* Cambridge: Cambridge University Press.

Heath, S. B. (1986). Sociocultural contexts of language development. In Bilingual Education Office (Ed.), *Beyond language: social and cultural factors in schooling language minority students* (pp. 143–186). Los Angeles: Evaluation, Dissemination and Assessment Center.

Henry, R. (1984). Reader-generated questions: A tool for improving reading comprehension. *TESOL Newsletter, June,* 4–5.

Herrell, A., & Jordan, M. (2004). *Fifty strategies for teaching English Language Learners, Second Edition.* Upper Saddle River, NJ: Pearson, Merrill, Prentice Hall.

Hinkel, E. (2002). *Second language writers' text.* Mahwah, NJ: Lawrence Erlbaum Associates.

Holdaway, D. (1979). *The foundations of literacy.* Portsmouth, NH: Heinemann.

Holdaway, D. (1982). *Theory into Practice, 21*(4), 293–300.

Holdaway, D. (1984). Developmental teaching of literacy. In D. Holdaway (Ed.), *Stability and Change in Literacy Learning* (pp. 33–47). Exeter, NH: Heinemann.

Hollins, E. R. (1995). Revealing the deep meaning of culture in school learning: Framing a new paradigm for teacher preparation. *Action in Teacher Education, 17*(7), 70–79.

Homza, A. (1996). Using graphic organizers to develop bilingual literacy processes. *NABE News, 15*(December), 15–20.

Hudelson, S. (1984). "Kan yu ret an rayt en ingles": Children become literate in English as a second language. *TESOL Quarterly, 18,* 221–238.

Hulstijn, J. H., & Matter, J. F. (1991). *Reading in Two Languages* (Vol. 8). Amsterdam: Free University Press.

Isom, D. M. (1995). Telecommunications at Paul Robeson High School: Making Global Connections from the Inner City. *Language Association Bulletin, 46*(4), 7–23.

Jacobs, G., & Small, J. (2003). Combining dictogloss and cooperative learning to promote language learning. *The Reading Matrix, 3,* 1. Retrieved

July 22, 2005 from http://www.readingmatrix.com/articles/jacobs_small.

Jimenez, R. T., Garcia, G. E., & Pearson, P. D. (1995). Three children, two languages, and strategic reading: Case studies in bilingual/monolingual reading. *American Educational Research Journal, 32,* 67–97.

Johnson, D. M., & Roen, D. H. (Eds.). (1989). *Richness in Writing: Empowering ESL Students.* New York: Longman.

Juel, C. (1991). Cross-age tutoring between student athletes and at-risk children. *The Reading Teacher, 45,* 178–186.

Kagan, S. (1992). *Cooperative Learning.* San Juan Capistrano, CA: Resources for Teachers, Inc.

Kinginger, C. (2000). Learning the pragmatics of solidarity in the networked foreign language classroom. In J. K. Hall & L. S. Verplaetse (Eds.), *Second and foreign language learning through classroom interaction* (pp. 23–46). Mahwah, NJ: Lawrence Erlbaum Associates.

Kreeft Peyton, J. (1990). Dialogue journal writing: Effective student-teacher communication. In A. M. Padilla, H. H. Fairchild & C. M. Valadez (Eds.), *Bilingual Education. Issues and Strategies* (pp. 184–194). Newbury Park, CA: SAGE Publications.

Kucer, S. B. (2001). *Dimensions of literacy: A conceptual base for teaching reading and writing in school settings.* Mahwah, NJ: Lawrence Erlbaum Associates.

Labbo, L. D., & Teale, W. H. (1990). Cross-age reading: A strategy for helping poor readers. *The Reading Teacher, 43,* 362–369.

Lapkin, S., Swain, M. K., & Smith, M. (2002). Reformulation and the learning French pronominal verbs in a Canadian French immersion context. *The Modern Language Journal, 86,* 485–507.

Leong, C. K. (1978). Learning to read in English and Chinese: Some psycholinguistic and cognitive considerations. In D. Feitelson (Ed.), *Cross-cultural perspectives on reading and reading research* (pp. 157–173). Newark, DE: International Reading Association.

LeVine, J. E. (2002). Writing letters to support literacy. *The Reading Teacher, 56*(3), 232–239.

Li, D. & Nes, S. L. (2003). Using paired reading to enhance the fluency skills of less-skilled readers. *Reading improvement, 38,* 50–61.

Lightbown, P. M., & Spada, N. (2003). *How languages are learned. Seventh Edition.* Oxford: Oxford University Press.

Lombardo, M. E. (1979). *The construction and validation of the listening and reading components of the English as a Second Language Assessment Battery.* Unpublished doctoral dissertation: Boston University.

Long, T. W., & Gove, M. K. (2003). How engagement strategies and literature circles promote critical response in a fourth-grade, urban classroom. *The Reading Teacher, 57,* 350–361.

Lucas, T., & Katz, A. (1994). Reframing the debate; The roles of native languages in English-only programs for language minority students. *TESOL Quarterly, 28,* 537–561.

Lyon, J. (1996). *Becoming bilingual: Language acquisition in a bilingual community.* Clevedon, England: Multilingual Matters.

Mackey, W. (1968). The description of bilingualism. In J. A. Fishman (Ed.), *Readings in the sociology of language* (pp. 554–584). The Hague: Mouton.

Marzano, R. J., Pickering, D., & McTighe, J. (1993). *Assessing Student Outcomes.* Aurora, CO: McREL Institute.

McCarty, T. L., & Watahomigie, L. J. (1988). Language and literacy in American Indian and Alaska Native communities. In B. Perez (Ed.), *Sociocultural contexts of langauge and literacy* (pp. 69–98). Mahwah, NJ: Lawrence Erlbaum Associates.

McCauley, J. K., & McCauley, D. S. (1992). Using choral reading to promote language learning for ESL students. *The reading teacher, 45,* 526–533.

McLaughlin, B. (1984). *Second language acquisition in childhood* (Vol. 1 & 2). Hillsdale, NJ: Lawrence Erlbaum Associates.

Menyuk, P., & Brisk, M. E. (2005). *Language and Education: Children with varying language experience.* New York: Palgrave-MacMillan.

Michaels, S., & Foster, M. (1985). Peer-peer learning: Evidence from a student-run sharing time. In A. Jagger & M. T. Smith-Burke (Eds.), *Observing the language learners* (pp. 143–158). Newark, Delaware: International Reading Association.

Moll, L.C., Amanti, C., Neff, D., & González, N. (1992). Funds of knowledge for teaching: Using a qualitative approach to connect homes and classrooms. *Theory into Practice, 31*(2), 132–141.

Montague, N. (1995). The process oriented approach to teaching writing to second language learners. *New York State Association for Bilingual Education Journal, 10*(Summer), 13–24.

Mooney, M. (1994). Shared reading: Making it work for you and your children. *Teaching K–8* (November–December), 70–72.

Myers, M. (1983). Drawing as prewriting in the teaching of composition. In M. Myers & J. Grey (Eds.), *Theory and practice in the teaching of composition* (pp. 75–85). Urbana, IL: National Council of Teachers of English.

Myers, M. (1985). *The teacher-researcher: How to study writing in the classroom.* Urbana, Illinois: National Council of Teachers of English.

Nagy, W. E. (1988). *Teaching vocabulary to improve reading comprehension.* Urbana, IL: ERIC Clearinghouse on Reading and Communication Skills, NCTE and IRA.

Nagy, W. E., & Scott, J. A. (2000). Vocabulary process. In M. L. Kamil, P. B. Mosenthal, P. D. Pearson, & R. Barr (Eds.), *Handbook of reading research, Volume III* (pp. 269–284). Mahwah, NJ: Lawrence Erlbaum Associates.

Nation, I. S. P. (2005). Teaching and learning vocabulary. In E. Hinkel, (Ed.), *Handbook of research in second language teaching and learning.* (pp. 581–595). Mahwah, NJ: Lawrence Erlbaum Associates.

O'Malley, J. M., & Valdez Pierce, L. (1996). *Authentic assessment for English langauge learners: Practical approaches for the K–12 classroom.* Reading, MA: Addison-Wesley.

Paratore, J. R., Homza, A., Krol-Sinclair, B., Lewis-Barrow, T., Melzi, G., Stergis, R., et al. (1995). Shifting boundaries in home and school responsibilities: The construction of home-based literacy portfolios by immigrant parents and their children. *Research in the Teaching of English, 29,* 367–389.

Pardon, D. J. (1992). *Jigsawing with Wordless Picture Books.* Paper presented at the Annual Meeting of the West Regional Conferences of the International Reading Association, Portland, OR.

Peregoy, S. F., & Boyle, O. F. (2005). *Reading, Writing and Learning in ESL: A Resource Book for K–12 Teachers. Fourth Edition.* Boston: Pearson.

Perez, B. (Ed.). (1998). *Sociocultural contexts of language and literacy.* Mahwah, NJ: Lawrence Erlbaum Associates.

Perez, B. (Ed.). (1998). *Sociocultural contexts of language and literacy.* Mahwah, NJ: Lawrence Erlbaum Associates.

Perez, B., & Torres-Guzman, M. E. (2002). *Learning in Two Worlds: An Integrated Spanish/English Biliteracy Approach. Third Edition.* Boston: Allyn & Bacon.

Peterson, R., & Eeds, M. (1990). *Grand conversations: Literate groups in action.* New York: Scholastic.

Prinz, P. (1998). *The influence of strategic teaching on reading in a second language.* Unpublished doctoral dissertation, Boston University.

Proctor, C. P., Carlo, M., August, D., & Snow, C. (2005). Native Spanish-speaking children reading in English: Toward a model of comprehension. *Journal of Educational Psychology, 97.2,* 246–256.

Radencich, M., & McKay, L. J. (Eds.). (1995). *Flexible groupings for literacy in the elementary grades.* Needham, MA: Allyn & Bacon.

Readance, J. E., Bean, T. W., & Baldwin, R. S. (1981). *Content area reading: An integrated approach.* Dubuque, IA: Kendall-Hunt.

Reyes, M. d. L. L. (1992). Challenging venerable assumptions. *Harvard Educational Review, 62*(4), 427–446.

Reyes, M. L. (1991). A process approach to literacy using dialogue journals and literature logs with second language learners. *Research in the Teaching of English, 25,* 291–313.

Reynolds, K. M. (2000). *ESL learners' and tutors' expectations of conversational participation, roles and responsibility.* ERIC ED 447 696 Report-Reseach (143).

Rigg, P. (1989). Language experience approach: Reading naturally. In P. Rigg & V. G. Allen (Eds.), *When they don't all speak English: Integrating the ESL student into the regular classroom* (pp. 65–76). Urbana, IL: National Council of Teachers of English.

Romaine, S. (1995). *Bilingualism* (Second ed.). Cambridge, MA: Blackwell.

Rosenshine, B., Meister, C., & Chapman, S. (1996). Teaching students to generate questions: A review of the intervention studies. *Review of Educational Research, 66*(2), 181–221.

Saravia-Shore, M., & Arvizu, S. (Eds.). (1992). *Cross-cultural literacy: Ethnographies of communication in multiethnic classrooms.* New York: Garland.

Savignon, S. (1983). *Communicative competence: Theory and classroom practice.* Reading, MA: Addison-Wesley.

Saville-Troike, M. (1984). What really matters in second language learning for academic achievement? *TESOL Quarterly, 18,* 199–219.

Schleppegrell, M. J. (2004). *The language of schooling: A functional linguistic perspective.* Mahwah, NJ: Lawrence Erlbaum Associates.

Schleppegrell, M. J., Achugar, M., & Oteiza, T. (2004). The grammar of history: Enhancing content-based instruction through a functional focus on language. *TESOL Quarterly, 38,* 67–93.

Schwarzer, D., Haywood, A., & Lorenzen, C. (2003). Fostering multiliteracy in a linguistically diverse classroom. *Language Arts, 80*(6).

Staton, J. (1998). *Dialogue journal communication: classroom, linguistic, social and cognitive views.* Norwood, NJ: Ablex.

Stefanakis, E. H. (1998). *Whose judgment counts: Assessing bilingual children K–3.* Portsmouth, NH: Heinemann.

Suárez-Orozco, C., & Suárez-Orozco, M. M. (2001). *Children of immigration.* Cambridge, MA: Harvard University.

Swain, M. K., Brooks, L., & Tocalli-Beller, A. (2002). Peer-peer dialogue as a means of second language learning. *Annual Review of Applied Linguistics, 22,* 171–185.

Swan, M., & Smith, B. (2001). *Learner English: A teacher's guide to interference and other problems.* Cambridge: Cambridge University.

Tan, A., & Nicholson, T. (1997). Flashcards revisited; Training poor readers to read words faster improves their comprehension of text. *Journal of Educational Psychology, 89* (2), 276–288.

Tierney, R., Readance, J. E., & Dishner, E. K. (1995). *Reading strategies and practices.* Boston: Allyn & Bacon.

Torres-Guzman, M. E. (1992). Stories of hope in the midst of despair: Culturally responsive education for Latino students in an alternative high school in New York City. In M. Saravia-Shore & S. Arvizu (Eds.), *Cross-cultural literacy: Ethnographies of communication in multiethnic classrooms* (pp. 477–490). New York: Garland.

Torres-Guzman, M. E., Abbate, J., Minaya-Rowe, L., & Brisk, M. E. (2002). Defining and documenting success for bilingual learners: A collective case study. *Bilingual Research Journal, 26*(1), 23–44.

Trelease, J. (1982). *The reading aloud handbook.* New York: Penguin Books.

Urzua, C. (1995). *Cross-Age Tutoring:* ERIC Digest.

Vygtosky, L. S. (1978). *Mind in society: The development of higher psychological processes.* Cambridge, MA: Harvard University Press.

Wajnryb, R. (1990). *Grammar dictation.* Hong Kong: Oxford University Press.

Williams, C., & Hufnagel, K. (2005). The impact of word study instruction on kindergarten children's journal writing. *Research in the Teaching of English, 39,* 233–270.

Wixon, V., & Wixon, P. (1983). Using talk-write in the classroom. In M. Myers & J. Gray (Eds.), *Theory and practice in the teaching of composition: Processing, distancing and modeling* (pp. 129–135). Urbana, IL: National Council of Teachers of English.

Zamel, V. (1985). Responding to student writing. *TESOL Quarterly, 19,* 195–202.

Zoellner, R. (1985). Talk-write: A behavioral pedagogy for composition. In M. Myers & J. Gray (Eds.), *Theory and practice in the teaching of composition: Processing, distancing and modeling* (pp. 122–128). Urbana, IL: National Council of Teachers of English.

Students' Book References

Aardema, V. (1975). *Why mosquitoes buzz in people's ears: A West African tale.* New York: Penguin USA.

Aardema, V. (1979). *Who's in rabbit's house?* New York: Penguin USA.

Ada, A. F. (1997). *Querido Pedrín.* New York: First Aladdin Paperbacks/Libros Colibrí.

Ada, A. F. (1994). *Dear Peter Rabbit.* New York: Aladdin.

Ada, A. F. (1998). *Yours truly; Goldilocks.* New York: Atheneum.

Ahlberg, J., and Ahlberg, A. (1986). *The jolly postman: Or other people's letters.* London: Little.

Armstrong, J. (2001). *Dear Mr. President: Theodore Roosevelt: Letters from a young coal miner.* Delray Beach, FL: Winslow Press.

Anderson, H. C. (1990). *The ugly duckling.* New York: Putnam Publishing Group.

Angelou, M. (1994). *The completed collected poems of Maya Angelou.* New York: Random House.

Bang, M. (1987). *Paper crane.* New York: William Morrow & Co., Inc.

Bantock, Nick (1991). *Griffin & Sabine: An extraordinary correspondence.* San Francisco: Chronicle

Beisbier, B. (1995). *Sounds great: Intermediate pronunciation and speaking (Book 2).* Boston: Heinle and Heinle.

Blocksma, M. (1992). *All my toys are on the floor.* Danbury, CT: Grolier Inc.

Brashares, A. (2005). *Keep in touch: Letters, notes and more from the sisterhood of the traveling pants.* New York: Delacorte Press.

Brown, M. W. (1991). *Goodnight moon:* Harper & Row.

Carrillo, G. (1982). *Legend of Food Mountain.* Emeryville, CA: Children's Bk. Pr.

Cleary, B. (1983). *Dear Mr. Henshaw.* New York: Morrow.

Daily Math Practice. (1999). *Grade three.* Monterrey, CA: Evan-Moor.

De Paola, T. (1991). *The Legend of the indian paintbrush.* New York: Putnam Publishing Group.

Dooley, N. (1991). *Everybody cooks rice.* Minneapolis: Carolrhoda.

Dorris, M (1989). *Guests.* New York: Hyperion.

Flack, M. (1971). *Ask Mr. Bear*: Collier Books.

Gantos, J. (1988). *Rotten Ralph's trick or treat*. Boston: Houghton Mifflin Co.

Garcia, J., Gelo, D., Greenow, L., Kratch, J., & White, D. (1997). *The world and its people*. Parsippany, NJ: Silver Burdett Ginn.

Giff, P. R. (1989). *Love, from the 5th grade celebrity*. New York: Bantam Doubleday Dell Publishing.

Graham, C. (1978). *Jazz chants: Rhythms of American English for students of English as a second language*. New York: Oxford University Press.

Gomi, T. (1984). *Coco can't wait*. New York: William Morrow. (Spanish version *Coco ya no espera más*, translated by Aída E. Marcuse).

Grifalconi, A. (1986). *The village of the round & square houses*. New York: Little, Brown, & Co.

Hayes, Joe (NA). *The weeping woman/La Llorona, a Hispanic legend told in Spanish and English*. El Paso, Texas: Cinco Punto Press.

Hinton, S. E. (1968). *The outsiders*. New York: Bantam Doubleday Dell.

Holly, H. (1999). *Toot & Puddle*. New York: Scholastic.

Jaffe, N. (1993). *Sing, Little Sack! ¡Canta, Saquito! A Folktale from Puerto Rico*. New York: Bantam Books.

Jin, S. (1990). *My first American friend*. Austin, TX: Raintree Steck-Vaughn.

Joslin, S. (1962). *Dear Dragon . . . and other useful letter forms for young ladies and gentlemen engaged in everyday correspondence*. New York: Harcourt, Brace, & World, Inc.

Kraus, R. (1987). *Milton the early riser*. Old Tappan, NJ: Simon & Schuster Children's.

Lobel, A. (1979). *Frog and Toad are friends*. New York: Harper & Row.

Marshall, E. (1994). *Three by the sea*. New York: Penguin USA.

Martin, B. J. (1989). *Chicka Chicka Boom*. New York: Simon & Schuster.

McCloskey, R. (1976). *Make way for ducklings*. New York: Penguin USA.

McGovern, A. (1992). *Too much noise*: Scholastic Book Services.

McKissack, P., & McKissack, I. (1985). *The little red hen*. Chicago: Children's Press.

O'Neill, M., & Wallner, J. (1989). *Hailstones & halibut Bones*: Scholastic Book Services.

Pinkney, A. D. (2001). *Abraham Lincoln: Letters from a young slave girl*. Delray Beach, FL: Winslow Press.

Rylant, C. (1982). *When I was young in the mountains*. New York: Penguin USA.

San Souci, R. D. (1987). *The legend of Scarface*. New York: Bantam Doubleday Dell.

Sendak, M. (1986). *Chicken soup with rice*. New York: Scholastic Inc.

Seuss, D. (1990). *Oh the places you'll go*. New York: Random House.

Shulevitz, U. (2003). *One monday morning*: Charles Scribener's Sons.

Silverstein, S. (1987). *The giving tree.* New York: Harper and Row Publishers.

Spurr, E. (1996). *The long, long letter.* New York: Hyperion.

Steptoe, J. (1987). *Mufaro's beautiful daughters: An African tale.* New York: William Morrow & Co., Inc.

Stewart, S. (1997). *The gardener.* New York: Scholastic.

Tang, G. (2003). *Math appeal.* New York: Scholastic.

Taylor, C. (1992). The house that crack built. San Francisco: Chronicle Books.

Torres, B. L. (1990). *The Luminous Pearl.* New York: Orchard Books.

Walker, A. (1982). *The color purple.* New York: Washington Square Press.

Williams, T. (1987). *The glass menagerie.* New York: New American Library.

Williamson, T. (1991). *Ricitos de oro y los tres ositos.* Santiago de Chile: Editorial André Bello.

Winthrop, E. (2001). *Dear Mr. President: Franklin Delano Roosevelt: Letters from a mill town girl.* Delray Beach, FL.: Winslow Press.

Author Index

A

Aardema, V., 253
Abbate, J., 252
Achugar, M., 155, 251
Ada, A. F., 253
Ahlberg, A., 253
Ahlberg, J., 253
Alexandrowicz, V., 177, 243
Allen, J., 41, 243
Allwright, J., 179, 243
Amanti, C., 30, 249
Anderson, H. C., 253
Angelou, M., 253
Armstrong, J., 253
Arvizu, S., 3, 251
Ashton-Warner, S., 87, 243
August, D., 3, 131, 243, 250

B

Baker, S., 44, 246
Baldwin, R. S., 122, 250
Ballard, B., 154, 243
Bang, M., 253
Bantock, N., 253
Basham, C. S., 33, 243
Bean, T. W., 122, 250
Beck, I., 136, 243
Beisbier, B., 253
Bialystok, E., 4, 243
Birch, B. M., 9, 40, 82, 132, 243
Blocksma, M., 253
Boyle, O. F., 93, 96, 98, 145, 160, 244, 250
Brashares, A., 253

Brisk, M. E., 4, 11, 13, 67, 71, 82, 89, 155, 156, 158, 159, 169, 189, 243, 244, 249, 252, xiv
Bromley, K., 108, 244
Brooks, L., 177, 251
Brown, M. W., 253
Buckley, M. H., 160, 244
Burgos, A., 11, 82, 158, 171, 243
Butzkamm, W., 21, 244

C

Caldwell, J. S., 38, 244
Caplan, R., 149, 244
Cappellini, M., 191, 244
Carlo, M., 131, 250
Carrillo, G., 253
Carson, J. F., 67, 244
Cary, S., 43, 132, 244
Chamot, A. U., 155, 244
Chapman, S., 102, 251
Clair, N., 205, 244
Clanchy, J., 154, 243
Clark-Chiarelli, N., 114, 245
Clay, M. M., 88, 244
Cleary, B., 253
Cochran-Smith, M., 200, 244
Cohen, A., 179, 244
Cohen, R., 102, 244
Conklin, N. F., 33, 244
Connor, U., 6, 33, 156, 245
Coote, M., 71, 246
Crago, M. B., 130, 133, 246
Cuevas, G. J., 155, 245
Cummins, J., 5, 42, 71, 245, xiv

D

Daiute, C., 3, 71, 245
Dale, T. C., 155, 245
D'Angelo Bromley, K., 63, 245
Davey, B., 102, 245
Dawson, M., 89, 243
de Alvarado, C. S., 67, 245
De Paola, T., 253
Derwing, T. M., 131, 245
Dickinson, D. K., 114, 245
Dien, T. T., 32, 245
Dishner, E. K., 122, 251
Dixon, C., 145, 245
Donahue, Van Tassell, Patterson, xii
Dooley, N., 253
Dorris, M., 253
Duranti, A., 12, 245

E

Echevarria, J., 44, 245
Eeds, M., 96, 101, 250
Einhorn, K., 43, 44, 245

F

Faltis, C. J., 3, 246
Farr, B. P., 193, 246
Flack, M., 254
Flood, J., 160, 246
Forcier, R. C., 71, 246
Ford, M. P., 38, 244
Foster, M., 117, 249
Freeman, D., 200, 204, 246, xii
Freeman, D. E., 23, 63, 108, 137, 246
Freeman, Y. S., 23, 63, 108, 137, 246
Friedman, A., 71, 246

G

Gallimore, R., 3, 246
Gantos, J., 254
Garcia, G. E., 5, 246, 248, xiv
Garcia, J., 10, 254
Gee, J. P., 2, 246, x

Gelo, D., 10, 254
Genesee, F., 130, 133, 191, 246
Gersten, R., 44, 246
Gibbons, P., 137, 155, 246
Giff, P. R., 254
Gillespie, C., 53, 246
Goldenberg, C., 3, 246
Gomi, T., 254
González, N., 30, 249
Gove, K. G. M., 97, 248
Graham, C., 254
Gravelle, M., 23, 247
Greenow, L., 10, 254
Grifalconi, A., 254
Griffith, P. L., 87, 247
Grosjean, F., 4, 247

H

Hadaway, N. L., 57, 247
Hakuta, K., 3, 243
Hakuta and D'Andrea, xiv
Hamayan, E. V., 191, 246
Hamerla, S., 11, 82, 158, 170, 243
Hartgering, M., 89, 243
Hayes, J., 254
Haynes, 200
Haywood, A., 251
Heath, S. B., 12, 32, 247
Henry, R., 102, 247
Herrell, A., 132, 247
Hinkel, E., 6, 133, 154, 156, 247
Hinton, S. E., 254
Holdaway, D., 85, 93, 247
Hollins, E. R., 29, 247
Holly, H., 254
Homza, A., 160, 200, 247, 250
Horan, D., 67, 159, 244
Hudelson, S., 25, 247
Hudelson, S. J., 3, 246
Hufnagel, K., 87, 252
Hulstijn, J. H., 9, 247

I

Isom, D. M., 42, 247

J

Jacobs, G., 137, 247
Jaffe, N., 254
Jimenez, R. T., 5, 246, 248, xiv
Jin, S., 254
Johnson, D. M., 67, 248
Jordan, M., 132, 247
Joslin, S., 254
Juel, C., 108, 248

K

Kagan, S., 163, 248
Kaplan, R. B., 6, 33, 245
Katz, A., 21, 249
Keating, T., 44, 246
Kinginger, C., 71, 248
Kratch, J., 10, 254
Kraus, R., 254
Kreeft Peyton, J., 63, 248
Krol-Sinclair, B., 200, 250
Kucan, L., 136, 243
Kucer, S. B., 50, 248
Kwachka, P. E., 33, 243

L

Labbo, L. D., 108, 248
Lapkin, S., 179, 248
Lapp, D., 160, 246
Leki, I., 67, 244
Leong, C. K., 12, 248
LeVine, J. E., 57, 248
Lewis-Barrow, T., 200, 250
Li, D., 137, 248
Lightbown, P. M., 13, 248
Lobel, A., 254
Lombardo, M. E., 21, 248
Long, T. W., 97, 248
Lorenzen, C., 251
Lourie, M. A., 33, 244
Lucas, T., 21, 249
Lyon, J., 4, 13, 249
Lytle, S., 200, 244

M

MacDonald, E., 67, 89, 159, 243, 244
Mackey, W., 13, 249
Marshall, E., 254
Martin, B. J., 254
Marzano, R. J., 193, 249
Matter, J. F., 9, 247
McBride, S., 102, 245
McCabe, A., 114, 245
McCarty, T. L., 28, 30, 33, 249
McCauley, D. S., 93, 249
McCauley, J. K., 93, 249
McCloskey, R., 254
McGovern, A., 254
McKay, L. J., 38, 250
McKeown, M., 136, 243
McKissack, I., 254
McKissack, P., 254
McLaughlin, B., 4, 249
McTighe, J., 193, 249
Meister, C., 102, 251
Melzi, G., 200, 250
Menyuk, P., 155, 156, 249
Michaels, S., 117, 249
Minaya-Rowe, L., 252
Moll, L. C., 30, 249
Montague, N., 63, 249
Mooney, M., 93, 249
Myers, M., 53, 249, xii

N

Nagy, W. E., 41, 131, 249, 250
Nation, I. S. P., 131, 250
Neff, D., 30, 249
Nes, S. L., 137, 248
Nessel, D., 145, 245
Nicholson, T., 131, 251
Nieto, 27

O

Ochs, E., 12, 245
Olson, M. W. 87, 247
O'Malley, J. M., 191, 250
O'Malley, M. O., 155, 244

O'Neill, M., 254
Oteiza, T., 155, 251

P

Paradis, J., 130, 133, 246
Paratore, J. R., 200, 250
Pardon, D. J., 163, 250
Paul, x
Pearson, P. D., 5, 246, 248, xiv
Peregoy, S. F., 93, 96, 98, 145, 160, 250
Perez, B., 4, 6, 18, 32, 82, 160, 250, x
Peterson, R., 96, 101, 250
Pickering, D., 193, 249
Pinkney, A. D., 254
Prinz, P., 35, 250
Proctor, C. P., 131, 250

R

Radencich, M., 38, 250
Readance, J. E., 122, 250, 251
Reese, L., 3, 246
Reyes, M. d. L. L., 63, 177, 250
Reyes, M. L., 250
Reynolds, K. M., 177, 251
Rigg, P., 145, 251
Roen, D. H., 67, 248
Romaine, S., 4, 7, 251
Rosenshine, B., 102, 251
Rossiter, M. J., 131, 245
Rylant, C., 254

S

San Souci, R. D., 254
Saravia-Shore, M., 3, 251
Savignon, S., 117, 251
Saville Troike, M., 140, 251
Sayers, D., 42, 71, 245
Schleppegrell, M. J., 50, 155, 251
Schlimmer, K., 108, 244
Schwarzer, D., 43, 251
Scott, J. A., 250
Sendak, M., 254

Seuss, D., 254
Short, D. J., 44, 245
Shulevitz, U., 254
Silverstein, S., 255
Sizer, 47
Small, J., 137, 247
Smith, B., 18, 131, 251
Smith, M., 179, 248
Snow, Burns, Griffin, x
Snow, C., 131, 250
Spada, N., 13, 248
Spurr, E., 255
Staton, J., 63, 251
Stefanakis, E. H., 189, 251
Steptoe, J., 255
Stergis, R., 200, 250
Stewart, S., 255
Suárez-Orozco, C., 17, 251
Suárez-Orozco, M. M., 17, 251
Swain, M. K., 177, 179, 248, 251
Swan, M., 18, 131, 251

T

Tan, A., 131, 251
Tang, G., 255
Taylor, C., 255
Teale, W. H., 108, 248
Tierney, R., 122, 251
Tocalli-Beller, A., 177, 251
Torres, B. L., 255
Torres-Guzman, M. E., 4, 140, 160, 250, 251, 252
Trelease, J., 186, 252
Trumbull, E., 193, 246

U

Urzua, C., 108, 252

V

Valdez Pierce, L., 191, 250
Vogt, M., 44, 245
Vygotsky, L. S., 50, 53, 252

W

Wajnryb, R., 137, 252
Walker, A., 255
Wallner, J., 254
Watahomigie, L. J., 28, 30, 33, 249
White, D., 10, 254
Williams, C., 87, 252
Williams, T., 255
Williamson, T., 255
Winters, D., 108, 244
Winthrop, E., 255

Wixon, P., 125, 252
Wixon, V., 125, 252
Wolf, A., 114, 245

Z

Zamel, V., 79, 252
Zehr, L., 89, 243
Zibit, M., 71, 246
Zoellner, R., 125, 252

Subject Index

A

Abraham Lincoln: Letters from a young slave girl, 57
Abuelita, 207
Academic discourse, 27, 130, 154–159
Academic writing, 155–156
  scaffolding, 158–159
Acoustic similarity, 40, 132
Acronyms, 40
Across Five Aprils, 230
Additive perspective, 27
African American, book about growing up, 219
Age
  Cross-Age Project, 23, 86, 107–113
  literacy and, 1, 13
Algebra, 234–235
Ali, Muhammad, 221–222
All My Toys Are on the Floor, 112
Alphabetic principle, 87
Alphabets, display of, 23
America Celebrates!, 221
American culture, books about, 221–222
American multiculturalism, 31
American Sign Language (ASL) students, 9
  Talk-Write Approach and, 126–129
American texts, 31, 155–156
Analysis, of teacher research, 205–206
Analytic genres, 27
Anecdotal records, 197–199
Anno's Hat Tricks, 237
Anno's Magic Seeds, 233–234
Antarctica, 240
Anticipation Guide, 19, 46, 86, 116–117, 122–125, 159

assessment and, 192
  in practice, 123–125
  procedure, 122–123
  purpose of, 122
Arabic writing, 156
Artwork, cross-cultural, 31
Asian texts, 156
Ask Mr. Bear, 93
ASL. *See* American Sign Language students
Assessment, 189–200
  assessment practices, 191–194
  home-school connection and, 200
  observations and anecdotal records, 197–199
  practices, 241–242
  Reader-Generated Questions as tool for, 194–196
  records, 193–194
  traditional methods, 193
Assimilation, books about pressure to, 218
Audience, defining, 67, 73
Audio recordings, for assessment, 193

B

Background, student, 16–20
  Anticipation Guide activity and eliciting, 123
  protocol to gather, 213–215
  teacher research and knowledge of, 202
  tutors and knowledge of, 175–177
  using Dialogue Journals to reveal, 64–66

Background knowledge
  assessment and, 191
  content area texts and, 141–145
Baseball Saved Us, 20, 82, 232
Be-auxiliary, 133
Be-copula, 133
Bed to bed stories, 26
Beloved, 228
Berenstain Bears series, *The*, 223–224
Biculturalism, 4–6
  ambivalence regarding, 16–17
Big Buck Adventure, The, 233
Bilingualism, literacy and, 1–14
Bilingual programs, 21
  teaching reading in, 83
Bilingual students
  acquisition and application of literacy
    skills among, 4–5
  assessment of, 190–191
  controlling level of difficulty and, 33–34
  environmental literacy and, 11–12
  expectations for, 33–42
  identification with cultures, 16
  interaction between languages and, 7–8,
    21–23
  learning about background of. *See*
    Background
  new English language learners, 42–45
  prior knowledge of, 6
  providing support for, 34–42
  relationship with tutors, 174–177
  working effectively with, 15–47
Biliteracy, 4–6
Biology, 239–240
Biracial/bicultural identities, books about,
  217–218
Body language, 134
Books
  about American culture, 221–222
  about biracial/bicultural identities,
    217–218
  about incarcerated parents, 219
  about mixed race adoption, 218–219
  about overcoming hardships of
    immigration, 216–217
  about pressure to assimilate, 218
  cross-cultural/multicultural, 30–31,
    216–222
  for English language learners, 84
  as models for writing, 49

  for new English language learners, 43
  related to specific heritage, 219–220
  to supplement content area instruction,
    229–240
  taught in American English and
    language arts classes, 223–228
Boxcar Children series, *The*, 224
Boy Who Was Generous with Salt, The, 239
Brainstorming, 53, 72
Bridge to Terabithia, 224–225
Brown Bear, Brown Bear, 93
Burgos, Angela, 98–102
Business letter, 61

C

Captions, 53, 107
Casulli, Judy, 160–163
Catcher in the Rye, The, 227
Cat in the Hat, The, 224
Champion: The Story of Muhammad Ali,
  221–222
Charts, 134
Checklists, assessment, 193, 197
Chicken Soup with Rice, 163
Chinese
  language characteristics of, 12
  using Shared Reading activity and,
    94–96
  Word Card activity and word-symbol
    connection in, 89–91
Choral reading, 92
Clark, Caroline, 143
Classroom, bilingual, 158
  allowing for extra time in, 40
  culture in, 27
  languages in, 20–24
  new English language learners and,
    42–45
Clipping, 40
Coaching, Shared Reading activity and, 92
Codeswitching, 7–8, 62
Cognates, 132–133
Collaboration
  culturally relevant instruction and, 30
  in teacher research, 205
College students, as tutors, 174–175
Color Purple, The, 57
Comic strips, 23

Community, role in literacy development, 45–46
Comparison and contrast, 150
Comprehension, speech, 131
Computers
Process Writing and, 70–81
use of to promote literacy, 41–42
Concepts, bilingualism and, 10
Conferences
assessment, 191, 192, 242
writing, 20, 80
Conjunctions, 133
Connectors, 133, 156
rhetorical, 154
Constructed responses, 191, 192, 242
Content areas
books to supplement, 229–240
Dialogue Journals and, 52
teaching literacy in, 153–159
using Graphic Organizers, 159–163
using Jigsaw, 163–170
using Situational Context Lessons, 170–173
vocabulary development and, 41
Content knowledge/learning, 9–10
culture and, 8–9
teaching language and literacy to support, 26–27
Context
literacy development and, 11–13
teaching vocabulary from, 136–137
Context clues, 40–41, 195
Conversational language, 154
Cooperative learning, 104, 109–113, 157, 163–170
assessment and, 192
Corrective feedback, 37
Cross-Age Project, 23, 86, 107–113
assessment and, 192
Dialogue Journals and, 52
in practice, 108–113
procedure, 108–109
purpose of, 107–108
reading instruction and, 84, 85
Cross-cultural materials, 30–31, 216–222
Cultural groups, 16
Culture
assessment and, 191
bilingual students' identification with, 16–17

in classroom, 27
content knowledge and, 8–9
cross-cultural materials, 30–31, 216–222
culturally relevant instruction, 29–30
defined, 27
influence on literacy, 1–2, 5–6
knowledge and, 153–154
teachers as cultural brokers, 31–33
text organization and, 6, 156
as tool for learning, 28–29
word meaning and, 6, 32–33

D

Dadigan, Meredith, 171–173
Daniel Half-Human and the Good Nazi, 231–232
Darlington, Katherine, 64–66
Data analysis, 237
Data collection, 203–204
Daughter of Madrugada, 230
David Goes to School, 132
Deaf children, language acquisition by, 4. *See also* American Sign Language students
Dear Dragon, 57
Dear Mr. Henshaw, 57
Dear Mr. President, 57
Dear Peter Rabbit, 57
Decoding, 2, 4, 18, 56, 87, 92, 148, 149
Definitions, in academic writing, 154
Demonstrations, 191, 192, 193, 241
Determiners, 134
Dialogue Journals, 41, 51–52, 62–66
assessment and, 192
materials, 63
in practice, 64–66
procedure, 63–64
purpose of, 62–63
Dictionaries, picture, 49
Dictogloss, 37, 86, 135–136, 137–140, 159
assessment and, 192
in practice, 138–140
procedure, 138
purpose of, 137–138
Discipline, use of native language and, 21
Dissemination of teacher research, 205–206
District-mandated approaches to literacy, 46–47

Dory Story, 240
Double-entry journals, 97
Dr. Seuss, 224
Draft, writing, 68, 73
Drake, Susan, 54–56, 197–199
Drawing as Prewriting, 19, 22, 25, 34, 37, 41, 50, 52–56, 72
    assessment and, 192
    in practice, 54–56
    procedure, 53–54
    purpose of, 52–53
Dust for Dinner, 231

E

Earth science, 238–239
Editing, 74
Elementary grades
    using Anticipation Guide in, 123–125
    using cooperative learning in, 164–170
    using Cross-Age project in, 109–113
    using Dictogloss in, 138–140
    using Drawing as Prewriting in, 54–56
    using Graphic Organizers in, 160–163
    using Literature Response in, 98–102
    using Mailbox Game in, 58–62
    using Reader-Generated Questions in, 104–107
    using Reformulation Strategy in, 180–182
    using Rhetorical Approach in, 68–70
    using role-playing in, 143–145
    using Shared Reading in, 94–96
    using Show Not Tell in, 150–152
    using Student-Directed Sharing Time in, 119–122
    using Word Card activity in, 89–91
E-mail, 42
Encoding, 2, 4
English classes, books taught in, 223–228
English language learners, new, 42–45
    suggestions for, 49, 84, 115, 134, 157
Environmental literacy, 11–12
E-reader, 41
Errors
    transfer, 133
    word order, 133
    in writing, 48–50

ESL classroom, 158
ESL services, pull-out, 176
Esperanza Rising, 216–217
Everybody Cooks Rice, 28
Exhibitions, 191, 192, 193, 242
Experiments, 191, 192, 193, 241
Explicit instruction, 35
Expository reading, 86

F

Factual genres, 27
Family
    assessment and, 200
    bilingual learners and, 1–2
    home literacy habits, 12, 200
    role in literacy development, 45
    Word Card activity and, 91
Feedback, corrective, 37
Fiction, 86
Field trips, 113
Finding clues in pictures, word meaning and, 40
Flags, 31
Flexible grouping, 38–39
Flowers from Mariko, 232
Frog and Toad Are Friends, 57

G

Games, language, 36
Gardener, The, 57
Genres
    choosing, 67, 71, 73
    culture and, 33
    types of, 27
Geometry, 235–236
Gestures, use of, 132
Ghost's Hour, Spook's Hour, 110
Giver, The, 225
Giving Tree, The, 98, 99
Glass Menagerie, The, 75
Going Home, 219
Goldilocks and the Three Bears, 57, 206
Goodnight Moon, 93
Grammar, 130, 133
    culture and, 33

Grammatical morphemes, 133–134
Grandma Essie's Covered Wagon, 231
Graphic Organizers, 35, 108, 134, 157,
  159–163
  assessment and, 192
  in practice, 160–163
  procedure, 160
  purpose of, 159–160
  teacher research on, 206–210
Graphs, 134, 157
Great Kapok Tree, The, 239–240
Griffen & Sabine: An extraordinary
  correspondence, 57
Grouping, flexible, 38–39
Growing Up Black, 219
Gunderson, Nicole, 187–188

H

Hailstones and Halibut Bones, 93
Haitian culture, 121–124, 220
Harrington, Margaret M. (Peggy), 123–125,
  138–140, 164–170
Hatchet, 226
Hersi, Afra Ahmed, 178, 180–182
Hispanic Americans, book about, 219
History texts
  developing vocabulary to comprehend,
    141–143
  using Jigsaw activity and, 164–170
History units, books to supplement, 229–232
Holidays, American, 220
Home literacy, 12, 200
Homework, 39, 59
Homonyms, 40
Homophones, 40
House That Crack Built, The, 173
How Tall, How Short, How Far Away, 236–237

I

I Can Read with My Eyes Shut, 224
I Hate Mathematics! Book, The, 237
I Love Saturdays Y Domingos, 217–218
Immigrant children
  impact of violence on, 171–173
  language acquisition by, 4

Immigration
  books about overcoming hardships of,
    216–217
  stories of, 31
Incarcerated parents, book about, 219
Independent reading, encouraging, 85
Individualized instruction. *See*
  Tutors/tutoring
Individual reading aloud, 186
Institutional context, literacy and, 2
Instruction
  culturally relevant, 29–30
  explicit, 35
  individual. *See* Tutors/tutoring
  small group, 180–185
Internet
  motivation to read and write and, 41
  sharing writing via, 70–71
Interviews, 20, 191, 192, 240
Intonation, 131
Invented spelling, 18, 48–49
Irregular past tense, 134
Island of the Blue Dolphin, 226–227

J

Jacobs, Anthony, 183–185
Jacques, Mary, 68–70
Jalapeño Bagels, 217
Japanese text, 156
Jazz Chants, 131, 222
Jigsaw activity, 24, 39, 86, 115, 157–158,
  163–170
  assessment and, 192
  in practice, 164–170
  procedure, 164
  purpose of, 163
Jin Woo, 218–219
Johnny Tremain, 229–230
Join In: Multiethnic Short Stories by Outstanding
  Writers for Young Adults, 220
Jolly Postman, The, 57
Journal exchanges, 108, 109
Journals
  double-entry, 97
  in Response to Literature activity, 96–97,
    101–102
  See also Dialogue Journals

K

Kanel, Alice, 119–122
*Keep in Touch: Letters, Notes and More
    from the Sisterhood of the Traveling
    Pants*, 57
Knowledge
    content, 9–10
    culture and, 153–154
    of language, 9–10
    of literacy, 9–10
    needed for literacy, 8–11
    prior, 6, 28–29, 153–154
KWL approach, 34, 35

L

Language
    proficiency and use of, 4, 24
Language arts classes, books taught in,
    223–228
Language characteristics, 12
Language Experience Approach (LEA), 86,
    137, 145–149
    assessment and, 192
    follow-up activities, 146
    in practice, 147–149
    procedure, 145–146
    purpose of, 145
Language(s)
    academic, 130, 154–159
    conversational, 154
    development of, 25–27
    Dictogloss activity and, 137–140
    interaction between, 7–8
    knowing, 9–10
    Language Experience Approach and,
        145–149
    learning and attitudes toward, 18
    school, 131–132
    Show Not Tell and, 149–152
    teaching, 130–137
    Vocabulary Connections and, 140–145
    See also Native language; Oral discourse;
        Second language
Languages in classroom
    choice of, 7, 20, 71, 83
    functional use of, 23–24
    for literacy instruction, 21–23

for Process Writing, 71
for reading instruction, 83
LEA. *See* Language Experience Approach
Learning
    as active process, 29–30
    cooperative, 104, 109–113, 157, 163–170,
        192
    cultural background as tool for, 28–29
    language attitudes and, 18
    using native language to promote, 23
Learning logs, 191, 192, 242
Legend of Scarface, The, 98, 100
Legend of the Food Mountain, The, 98, 100
Legend of the Indian Paintbrush, The, 98, 100,
    101
Lesson planning, assessment and, 189–190
Letter recognition, 2
Letter writing, 50, 56–62, 128–129, 168–170
Leung, Musetta, 89–91
Life sciences, 239–240
Listening comprehension, 115
Literacy
    acquisition and application of among
        bilinguals, 4–5
    age of onset, 1
    assessment of. *See* Assessment
    bilingualism and, 1–14
    context and process and, 2
    defining, 2–3
    development of, 2–4, 11–13, 26
    embedding strategies into district-
        mandated approaches to, 46–47
    environmental, 11–12
    function of in American context, 32
    homes and communities as partners in,
        45–46
    individualized attention and, 174
    influence of culture on, 5–6, 32
    influence of family on, 12
    knowledge of, 9–10
    oral language learning and, 114–115
    as psycholinguistic process, 2
    as social practice, 3
    to support content learning, 26–27
    teaching in content areas, 153–159
    teaching second language in context of, 26
    types of knowledge needed for, 8–11
    using native language to promote, 23
    vocabulary and acquisition of, 136
Literacy teachers, preparing, 210–211

Literature
based on letters, 57
content knowledge acquisition and, 27
Response to Literature activity and, 96–102
Literature/learning logs, 98, 242
Little Monster's Neighborhood, 112
Little Red Hen, The, 191, 199
Logs
home literacy activity, 200
learning, 98, 242
Long, Long Letter, The, 57
Lost in Translation, 219–220
Love, from the 5th grade celebrity, 57
Lucy's Family Tree, 218
Luminous Pearl, The, 98

M

Magic Shell, The, 28
Mahoney, Andrew, 177
Mailbox Game, 24, 50, 56–62
assessment and, 192
materials, 57
in practice, 58–62
procedure, 58
purpose of, 56–57
Main idea-supporting details, 159
Make Way for Ducklings, 113
Mama Rocks, Papa Sings, 220
Maps, 134, 157
Materials
cross-cultural, 30–31, 216–222
for new English language learners, 43
Math and Science in Nature, 234
Math Appeal, 27
Math Appeal: Mind Stretching Math Riddles, 233
Mathematical word problems, 155
Mathematics units, books to supplement, 155, 233–237
Measurement, books about, 236–237
Medina, Antolin, 141–145
Milton the Early Riser, 147, 149
Miscue analysis, 191
Miscues, in writing, 48–50
Mixed race adoption, books about, 218–219
Modeling, 35–36
reading instruction and, 85, 92, 95, 110–111
Moneda de Oro, La, 123

Monolingual programs, 21
Morse, Elizabeth (Beth) E., 150–152
Mufaro's Beautiful Daughters, 98, 100
Multiculturalism, exposing students to
American, 31
Multicultural learning, 218–220
Multicultural themes, books with, 30–31, 216–222
Multilingual posters, 43
Music, cross-cultural, 31
My Bondage and My Freedom, 231
My First American, 28

N

Name Jar, The, 218
Native language
assessment and, 190–191
thinking in, 22
use of in classroom, 21
using to promote literacy and learning, 7–8, 23
writing development in, 48
Nelson, Ivelisse, 206–210
Note-taking, 157
Number sense and operations, books about, 233–234

O

Observations, 197–199
O'Connell, Ciara, 143–145
Of Beetles and Angels, 217
Of Mice and Men, 228
Oh the Places You'll Go, 93
One Fish, Two Fish, Red Fish, Blue Fish, 224
One Monday Morning, 93
Oral discourse
Anticipation Guide and, 124–127
development of, 25, 114–117
Dialogue Journals and, 62
Student-Directed Sharing Time and Group Discussions and, 116, 117–122
Talk-Write Approach and, 125–129
vs. written, 49–50
Oral interviews, 191, 192, 241
Orilla a Orilla, 42
Outsiders, The, 127

P

Paddock, The, 238–239
Paper Crane, 28, 94
Paraphrasing, 132
Past tense, 134
Patterns, mathematical, 234–235
Personal genres, 27
Personal stories, writing, 49
Personal variables
  literacy development and, 11, 13
  teaching effectively and, 16–18
  See also Background, student
Persuasive argument/writing, 150, 156
Phonemic awareness, 87
Phonological awareness, 114
Phonology, 130
Photographs, 31, 106
Picture Book of Jackie Robinson, A, 222
Picture dictionaries, 49
Pictures, 106, 130, 134
  writing through, 54–56
Pidgin Signed English (PSE), 126–127
Plagiarism, culture and, 33
Planning, for teacher research, 201–203
Plurals, 134
Poems, 36, 92, 93
Point-of-view pieces, 97
Polish immigrants, book about, 219–220
Portfolios, 191, 204
Possessive constructions, 133, 134
Poster sessions, 205–206, 209
Practice, 36–37
  theory, research and, 210–211
Prepositions, 134
Prereading activities, 19
Prewriting, Semantic Organizers and, 160.
  See also Drawing as Prewriting
Primary discourses, 2
Printed text, cultural attitudes toward, 32
Prior knowledge, 6, 28–29
  content areas and, 153–154
Privacy, journals and, 63
Probability, 235
Process Writing, 36, 52, 70–81, 150
  assessment and, 191, 192, 193
  conferences, 20
  in practice, 75–81
  procedure, 71–75
  purpose of, 70–71

Proficiency
  cultural attitudes toward, 32
  language use and, 4, 24
Projection, 131
Projects, assessment, 191, 192, 193, 242
Pronouns, 133
Pronunciation, 130, 131
PSE. *See* Pidgin Signed English
Publishing student writing, 68, 74, 94–96
Pull-out ESL services, 175
Purpose, defining writing, 67

Q

Querido Pedrín, 57

R

Read Aloud Intervention, 25, 41, 85, 115,
    136, 143, 177–178, 185–188, 190
  assessment and, 192
  as assessment tool, 241
  individual *vs.* whole class reading
    aloud, 186
  in practice, 187–188
  procedure, 186–187
  purpose of, 185–186
Read-aloud modeling, 110–111
Reader-Generated Questions, 36, 46, 85–86,
    102–107, 115, 159, 175, 188
  assessment and, 192
  as assessment tool, 194–196
  follow-up, 103–104
  in practice, 104–107
  procedure, 102–103
  purpose of, 102
Reading
  assessing skills, 195
  choral, 92
  Cross-Age Project and, 107–113
  cultural attitudes toward, 32
  emotional engagement with, 82–83
  expository, 86
  finding appropriate materials for, 17
  Graphic Organizers and preparation for,
    206–210
  prior knowledge and motivation for,
    28–29

Reader-Generated Questions and, 102–107
Response to Literature and, 96–102
scaffolding, 85
Shared Reading and, 92–96
as sociocultural endeavor, 82
teacher as partner in, 37–38
teaching, 82–86, 147–149
vocabulary and, 86–91, 114
Word Cards and, 86–91
Reading aloud, 44
in English, 45
with expression, 37–38
Reading comprehension
Anticipation Guide activity and, 123
explicit instruction and, 35
Graphic Organizers and, 157
promoting, 46
Read Aloud Intervention and, 185–188
Reader-Generated Questions activity
and, 102
Shared Reading and, 86
vocabulary knowledge and, 131, 136
Real World Algebra, 234–235
Redding, Reginald, 128–129
Reformulation Strategy, 37, 135–136,
177–178, 179–185
assessment and, 192
in practice at elementary level, 180–182
in practice at secondary level, 183–185
procedure, 179–180
purpose of, 179
Rehearsing, 36–37
Relations, mathematical, 234–235
Repetition, 36–37
Research, 72, 158–159
theory, practice and, 210–211
use of Situational Context Lessons
activity and, 172–173
See also Teacher research
Response journals, as assessment tools, 191,
192, 242
Response to Literature, 96–102
assessment and, 192
double-entry journals, 97
journals, 86, 96–97, 101–102
literature/learning logs, 98
point-of-view pieces, 97
in practice, 98–102
procedure, 96–98
purpose of, 96

Retellings, 191, 192, 241
Revision, 125
Process Writing and, 70, 73–74
Rhetorical Approach and, 68
Rhetorical Approach, 46, 66–70, 158–159
assessment and, 192
in practice, 68–70
procedure, 67–68
purpose of, 66–67
Rhetorical connectors, 154
Rhythm, pronunciation and, 131
Riggs, Renate Weber, 104–107, 194
Rivka's First Thanksgiving, 221
Robinson, Jackie, 222
Role playing, vocabulary development and,
143–145
Rolling Stone magazine, 127
Roll of Thunder, Hear My Cry, 226
Rotten Ralph's Trick or Treat, 162
Rubric, developing writing sample, 183
Running records, 193

S

Scaffolding
independent reading, 85
writing, 92
School language, 131–132
Science texts, Reader-Generated Questions
activity and, 104–107
Science units, books to supplement, 238–240
Secondary discourses, 2
Secondary level
use of Reformulation Strategy in,
183–185
using Dialogue Journals in, 64–66
using Process Writing with Computer
in, 75–81
using Talk-Write Approach in, 126–129
using Vocabulary Connections in,
141–143
Second language
assessment and, 190–191
holistic approach to, 25
teaching in context of literacy
instruction, 26
teaching to support content learning,
26–27
writing development in, 48

Second-language programs, 21
Semantic mapping, 36, 39, 41, 72, 106,
  159–163, 178
  assessment and, 192
Sense matrices, 159
Sentence comprehension, 2
Sentence starters, 115
Sentence stress, 131
Sentence strips, 84, 147, 148
Sequencing, 150
*Shape Up! Fun with Triangles and Other
  Polygons*, 235
Shared Reading, 25, 85, 86, 159
  assessment and, 192
  materials, 93
  in practice, 94–96
  procedure, 93
  production of big book, 94
  purpose of, 92–93
Sharing Time, 159
Show Not Tell, 137, 149–152
  assessment and, 192
  procedure, 149–150
  purpose of, 149
Sing, Little Sack, 7
*Sir Cumference and the Sword in the Cone:
  A Math Adventure*, 236
Situational Context Lessons, 19–20, 86, 158,
  170–173
  assessment and, 192
  in practice, 171–173
  procedure, 171
  purpose of, 170
Skidmore, Charles, 75–81
Skovholt, Mary Eileen, 109–113
Small group instruction, 180–185
Small Talk: More Jazz Chants, 222
Social science units, books to supplement,
  229–232
Social studies texts, prior knowledge
  necessary for understanding, 10–11
Sojourners, language acquisition by, 4
Songs, 36, 92, 93
Sound, vocabulary comprehension and,
  132
Sounding out words, spelling and, 38
Sound-letter correspondence, 87
Sounds Great, 131
Sound-symbol connection, 86–87
Sound system, acquisition of, 130–131

Space science, books about, 238–239
Spanish, language characteristics of, 12
Spatial sense, 235–236
Speaking proficiency, 115
Special education resource room, teaching
  reading in, 147–149
Speech rate, 131
Spelling
  errors in, 79
  invented, 18, 48–49
  sounding out words and, 38
  vocabulary comprehension and, 132
  word study and, 85, 87
Sports, books about American, 221–222
Statistics, 237
Stone Wall Secrets, 238
Stone Wall Secrets Teacher's Guide, 238
Storyboard, 49
Story maps, 159
Story writing, 149–152
Strategies to help students reach
  curriculum goals, 34–42
Student-Directed Sharing Time and Group
  Discussions, 24, 116, 117–122
  assessment and, 192
  in practice, 119–122
  procedure, 117–118
  purpose of, 117
Student teachers, 176
Study design, 202
Subordinate clauses, 154
Synonyms, 134
Syntactic class, 132

T

Talk-Write Approach, 117, 125–129, 159
  assessment and, 192
  in practice, 126–129
  procedure, 125–126
  purpose of, 125
Teacher research, 200–210
  in action, 206–210
  analysis, reflection, dissemination,
    204–206
  benefits of, 201
  implementation and data collection,
    203–204
  planning and preparation, 201–203

Teachers
    as cultural brokers, 31–33
    new English language learners and,
        42–45
    as partners in reading and writing
        process, 37–38
    preparing literacy, 210–211
    relation with family in literacy
        development, 45
    responses to bilingual students' writing,
        75–81
    role in Process Writing, 76, 77, 79
    student, 178
Teaching
    language, 26–27, 130–137
    literacy in content areas, 153–159
    reading, 82–86, 147–149
    writing, 48
Tenses, 134
Tests, 193
Text organization
    academic writing, 155
    culture and, 6
Text(s)
    Anglo-American, 31, 155–156
    Asian, 156
    content area, 141–145
    cultural attitudes toward, 32, 156
    cultural knowledge and interpreting, 18
    history, 141–143, 164–170
    science, 104–107
    social studies, 10–11
*Theodore Roosevelt: Letters from a young coal
    miner*, 57
Theory, practice, research and, 210–211
Thinking, native language and, 22
Third person, errors in use of, 134
Three by the Sea, 111
Tilton, Melissa, 58–62
Time, allowing for extra classroom, 40
Too Much Noise, 93
Toot & Puddle, 57
Topics, choosing in writing, 67, 69, 71–72
Transfer errors, 133
Transition, facilitating, 36
Tutors/tutoring
    oral discourse and, 115
    purpose of, 177
    relationships with bilingual students,
        174–178

sources of, 174–175
student teachers as, 178
support for bilingual students and, 34
vocabulary development and, 143–145

U

Ugly Duckling, The, 111

V

Venn diagrams, 134, 159
Video recordings, for assessment, 193
Village of the Round and Square Houses, The, 98
Violence, impact on immigrant students,
    171–173
Visiting Day, 219
Visual aids, 157
Vocabulary
    academic language, 154–155
    acquisition of, 130, 131–132, 136–137
    content learning and, 27
    development of, 40–41
    introducing, 84
    reading and, 114
    shared reading and, 92–93
    textual understanding and, 10–11
    See also Vocabulary Connections; Word
        Cards
Vocabulary Connections, 33, 39, 41, 136,
    140–145, 159
    assessment and, 192
    in practice, 141–145
    procedure, 140–141
    purpose of, 140

W

Weeping Woman, The/La Llorona, 98, 100
What Are You?, 217
What's Your Angle, Pythagoras?, 235
When I Was Young in the Mountains, 54
Where the Forest Meets the Sea, 239
Whitten, Laurie, 147–149
Who Belongs Here?, 216
Whole class reading aloud, 186
Who's in Rabbit's House, 110

"wh" (who, what, when, where, why)
   framework, 152
Why Mosquitoes Buzz in People's Ears, 98, 99,
   100, 101
Woman Work, 93
Word Cards, 25, 34, 37, 39, 41, 50, 56, 85,
   86–91
   assessment and, 192
   in practice, 89–91
   procedure, 87–89
   purpose of, 86–87
Word connotations, culture and, 6
Word order errors, 133
Word problems, 155
Word processor, motivation for writing
   and, 41
Words
   in cultural context, 32–33
   finding meaning of, 40
   multiple meanings of, 132
   recognition of, 2
   sounding out, 38
Word stress, 131
Word-symbol connection, 89
Writer's Workshop model, 46
Writing
   academic, 155–156, 158–159
   assessing skills in, 195–196
   in Cross-Age Projects, 112
   cultural attitudes toward, 32
   development of, 25
   Dialogue Journals and, 51–52, 62–66
   dictation and, 38

Drawing as Prewriting and, 19, 22, 25,
   34, 37, 41, 50, 52–56, 72
   fear of, 52
   gauging language needs and, 26
   Graphic Organizers and, 157
   handling errors in, 48–50
   knowledge of language and, 10
   letter writing, 50, 56–62, 128–129, 168–170
   Mailbox Game and, 50, 56–62
   vs. oral language, 49–50
   paired, 23
   planning for, 72–73
   prior knowledge and, 28–29
   Reformulation Strategy and, 177–178,
   179–185
   Rhetorical Approach and, 66–70
   scaffolding, 92
   story writing, 149–152
   Talk-Write Approach and, 125
   teacher as partner in, 38
   teacher responses to, 75–81
   teaching, 48
   through pictures, 54–56
   See also Process writing
Writing samples, 191, 192, 193, 241
Writing systems, display of, 23

       Y

Yeh, Peggy, 94–96
Young, Brigham, 92
Yours Truly, 57

About the Authors

María Estela Brisk is a professor at the Lynch School of Education, Boston College. Her research and teacher-training interests include bilingual education, bilingual language and literacy acquisition, methods of teaching literacy, and preparation of mainstream teachers to work with bilingual learners. She is the author of the books: *Bilingual Education: From Compensatory to Quality Schooling, Second Edition* (2006); *Situational Context of Education: A Window into the World of Bilingual Learners* (2004); and with P. Menyuk, P. (2005), *Language Development and Education: Children with Varying Language Experiences.*

For nearly 30 years, she has taught methods courses to advanced undergraduates and graduate students and school-based professional development workshops. Participants not only employ approaches included in this handbook in the classroom, they also analyze and report the results.

Margaret M. Harrington is an elementary school teacher with 28 years experience working with bilingual students. She earned a doctorate in education at Boston University. She has taught students from second through sixth grade in various types of bilingual programs. She is currently teaching in a fourth-grade transitional bilingual education classroom in Providence, Rhode Island. For 2 years, she worked in Honduras as a teacher trainer for the Peace Corps instructing teachers on ways to integrate environmental education into their curriculum. Her interests are language and literacy development of bilinguals.